The Latin American Narcotics Trade and U.S. National Security

Recent Titles in
Contributions in Political Science

The Latin American Narcotics Trade and U.S. National Security

Edited by
Donald J. Mabry

Foreword by
Janos Radvanyi

Contributions in Political Science, Number 240

Greenwood Press
New York • Westport, Connecticut • London

Library of Congress Cataloging-in-Publication Data

The Latin American narcotics trade and U.S. national security / edited
by Donald J. Mabry ; foreword by Janos Radvanyi.
   p.   cm.—(Contributions in political science, ISSN 0147-1066
; no. 240)
   Bibliography: p.
   Includes index.
   ISBN 0-313-26786-3 (lib. bdg. : alk. paper)
   1. Narcotics, Control of—United States. 2. Drug traffic—Latin
America. 3. United States—National security. I. Mabry, Donald
J. II. Series.
HV5825.L37 1989
363.4′5′0973—dc19   89-12030

British Library Cataloguing in Publication Data is available.

Library of Congress Catalog Card Number: 89-12030
ISBN: 0-313-26786-3
ISSN: 0147-1066

First published in 1989

Greenwood Press, Inc.
88 Post Road West, Westport, Connecticut 06881

Printed in the United States of America

The paper used in this book complies with the
Permanent Paper Standard issued by the National
Information Standards Organization (Z39.48-1984).

10 9 8 7 6 5 4 3 2

To the Children of the World

Contents

PART IV. THE VIEW FROM MEXICO

PART V. POLICY OPTIONS

Foreword

Anthologies are often accompanied by a statement of defense for their existence. Yet, in the case of the present volume it is surely redundant to justify the relevancy of a study of the impact of illegal drug trafficking on American national security--one of the most important concerns of our society today. This intricate web of international issues was analyzed in depth during this past year by the best scholars in the field under the expert leadership of Professor Donald Mabry, a Senior Fellow of the Center for International Security and Strategic Studies, Mississippi State University.

These studies are the fruit of long debate on the importance of narcotics diplomacy within the context of U.S.-Latin American relations. Since Mexico is both a source country and an important link in the trans-shipment route for South American narcotics, and therefore a focal point in the trafficking flow, special attention was given to the views of the Mexican members of the study group. Moreover, the complexity of the issues examined also required that the potential role of the U.S. military in the war on illegal drugs be addressed fully. Ultimately, through their endeavor the group has not only provided a historical perspective on U.S. narcotics policies towards Latin America but also offered a workable solution to the difficult multi-faceted problem of illegal drug trafficking.

Professor Mabry and his team advance immediate clues and longer range perspectives. They quite rightly emphasize the point that the narcotic trade is not only an American national security issue but a grave hemispheric security problem. The solution must come in wide range hemispheric cooperation, including the elimination of the U.S. illegal drug market.

The Center for International Security and Strategic Studies is honored to sponsor this study and extends special thanks to His Excellency Cesar Atala, Ambassador of Peru; the Honorable Mike Moore, Attorney General of the State of Mississippi; Louisa O. Dixon, Public Safety Commissioner of the State of Mississippi; Lt. General Stephen Olmstead, Deputy Assistant Secretary (Drug Policy and Enforcement), Office of the Secretary of

Defense; Representative Larkin Smith (R-MS); and John Martsh, Office of International Programs, U.S. Drug Enforcement Administration for their invaluable assistance. We are also indebted to the Blue Lightning Task Force in Gulfport, Mississippi, for the briefing on their drug interdiction operations. For the continuous encouragement, we express our deep gratitude to Miss Martha T. Muse, Chairman and President of the Tinker Foundation, and we thank the Tinker Foundation for its generous support without which this study would not have been possible.

It is hoped that this volume will contribute to national efforts to create a drug-free America and the safeguarding of American international security interests threatened by illegal narcotics trafficking.

Janos Radvanyi,
Director, Center for International Security
and Strategic Studies, Mississippi State University

I
Background

1

Narcotics and National Security
Donald J. Mabry

The flow of illegal narcotics from Latin America is a serious national security issue for the United States. This may be a surprising statement for those accustomed to thinking of national security as defense, weapons, alliances, and the military, but, as noted national security analysts Amos A. Jordan and William J. Taylor, Jr., explain, national security now includes "protection...of vital economic and political interests, the loss of which could threaten fundamental values and the vitality of the state."[1] In examining the effects of the drug trade on Latin American source countries such as Peru and Bolivia, or transit countries such as Colombia, it is obvious that the violence and corruption accompanying the drug business are destabilizing these nations and are thus a national security threat to them. Inasmuch as they are allies of the United States, their instability is a threat to the U.S. alliance system, a bulwark of its national security policy. Less obvious to many Americans, however, is the impact of the drug trade inside the United States. The domestic drug trade has a destabilizing effect on the U.S. as well. President Ronald Reagan recognized this fact on April 8, 1986, when he signed a National Security directive designating the international drug trade as a national security issue.[2] The reasons why the Latin American narcotics trade adversely affects the national security both of the United States and of Latin American nations is the subject of this volume.

Within the United States, the consumption of over $100 billion of illicit narcotics by an estimated 84 million people means lower worker productivity, more frequent accidents with consequent loss of life and property, and the diversion of economic resources into non-productive purposes. As an illicit activity, it enhances the power of criminals and criminal organizations, shifting power away from legitimate authority. Beyond the growing problem of the violence (both public and private) associated with the illicit drug trade inside the U.S., dependence on psychotropic drugs weakens rational decision making, a fundamental value of the democratic process. Even if one limits the definition of national security to military matters, illicit drug use is a threat to national security;

young people habituated to psychotropics do not make reliable soldiers, important since the U.S. must maintain a large standing army and be prepared to expand it rapidly in time of major war.

The U.S. has long considered Latin America vital to its national security. As part of its overall national security strategy, the U.S. depends upon the assurance of stable and friendly nations to the south so that it can focus its main efforts in Europe and Asia.[3] To achieve this goal, U.S. policy seeks "the creation of a stable political environment that promotes the evolution of democratic governments and addresses the problems and sources of social unrest in the region."[4] The illicit narcotics trade promotes political instability, as several authors in this volume convincingly demonstrate. Put another way, to the extent that the drug trade promotes political or economic instability in Latin America, that trade threatens the security of the United States.

U.S. policy makers fear that there is an actual or potential relationship between terrorists or guerrillas (called "narcoterrorists"), on the one hand, and drug production and trafficking on the other hand. Assertions have been made that the drug trade must be stopped because it has been one means by which guerrilla or terrorist groups have obtained funds with which to finance their subversive activities.[5] If, in fact, such groups as Sendero Luminoso, the Maoist-style guerrilla-terrorist group in Peru, or groups such as the Revolutionary Armed Force of Colombia (FARC), the 19th of April Movement (M-19), the National Liberation Army (ELN), and the Popular Liberation Army (EPL) in Colombia, all dedicated to establishing authoritarian socialist regimes, are profiting from the drug trade, then that trade represents an immediate threat to the national security of those nations and, because of the Rio Pact, to the national security of the United States. One of the principal difficulties faced by such guerrilla groups is obtaining sufficient funds with which to finance their operations. Such funds do not have to be large, as evidenced by the small amount of money Fidel Castro obtained to finance his Rebel Army before he forced out Batista in 1959.[6] Drug trafficking, therefore, presents an excellent opportunity for such groups to develop large sources of income. Since the principal drug market is the United States, the world's leading capitalist power and the defender of the regimes which the guerrillas seek to overthrow, engaging in drug trafficking has the elegance of using capitalist means and appetites to destroy capitalism.

Some observers and analysts argue, in fact, that anti-U.S. nations such as Cuba and Nicaragua in Latin America and the Soviet Bloc in Europe are actively supporting drug trafficking as part of their efforts to displace U.S. influence in Latin America with their own.[7] In the early 1980s, the fear that the drug trade was providing a new means for anti-U.S. terrorists and guerrillas to finance their activities and to destabilize Latin American nations gained considerable currency in some U.S. political circles. If this scenario is true, then it would certainly make Latin American governments more amenable to U.S. narcotics policy since they would see the drug trade as a threat to themselves instead of just being a source of export income.

Further complicating the issue of narcoterrorism have been the assertions that the Contras have also engaged in drug trafficking to finance their efforts to overthrow the Nicaraguan government when the U.S. Congress refused to provide sufficient funds and that highly-placed persons in the U.S. government knew that the Contras were doing this.[8] The Contras are, of course, also terrorists-guerrillas; President Ronald Reagan implicitly (but no doubt inadvertently) acknowledged this fact when he compared the Contras to those who fought the British in the 1770s to establish U.S. independence. Terrorists and guerrillas do not have to be left-wing in their politics.[9]

Thus, the entire issue of narcoterrorism is confused. Part of the difficulty is that narcotics are greatly feared and mention of their use produces a powerful, and usually negative, emotional reaction. Determining the reality of the situation is difficult for, as Diego Asencio, former ambassador to Colombia and Brazil, has put it:

> The case of political and terrorist involvement in narcotics trafficking often takes on the aspect of a *tu quoque*, ie., "You're one too" defense. With every charge that Havana is undermining American youth through drug sales, there is a charge that the Contras are doing the same. Whenever an arms smuggler on the left turns out to have had significant narcotics smuggling experience one is identified on the right.[10]

Evidence does exist that terrorist groups have been involved in drug trafficking. In Colombia, there are several examples. FARC has served as protectors of drug traffickers in exchange for money and arms. M-19, the urban terrorist group which, in 1980, held hostage a group of diplomats, including Asencio,[11] and, in 1985, which murdered half of the Colombian Supreme Court has been involved in drug smuggling. In Peru, Sendero Luminoso has worked closely with drug traffickers in the Upper Huallaga Valley.

Both the Cuban and Nicaraguan governments have been implicated in drug smuggling. According to Major Florentino Aspillaga Lombard, until his defection to the U.S. in 1988, an officer of the Cuban intelligence service, as early as 1978 Cuba became a transit base for illicit narcotics shipments to the U.S. and the smugglers were protected by Cuban troops.[12] Similar charges have been levied against Nicaraguan officials, including the mysterious Federico Vaughn, reputedly a close associate of Interior Minister Tomás Borge; in July, 1984, a Miami federal grand jury indicted Vaughn and others on cocaine smuggling charges.[13]

The difficulty in assessing the importance of such charges are twofold. That some Cuban or Nicaraguan officials have engaged in drug smuggling does not mean that those actions represent the policy of their governments. That is, even in such states, high government officials can engage in independent action. The other problem is that past U.S. officials have made similar, but erroneous, charges against Communist regimes, including those of Cuba and China.[14] It is difficult to assess the validity and importance of the charges in light of the fact that the U.S. government has consistently sought to blame non-U.S. persons for the drug trade. This is a major point of Douglas Kinder's chapter in which he not only traces prior U.S.

narcotics policy but also demonstrates the work of the nation's previous "drug czar," Harry J. Anslinger. Whether newly-appointed William Bennett will act as did Anslinger remains to be seen.

Peru, the largest single producer of coca recognizes the threat that drug trafficking represents. In the words of César Atala, Peruvian ambassador to the United States: "we are in total and absolute agreement with the United States government in the effect and the necessity to eradicate this vice and the necessity and the obligation to fight this scourge which affects not only Americans, not only Latin Americans, but the whole world."[15] Peru, as Atala pointed out, suffers the ills of drug trafficking more than most countries because it is poor, weak, indebted to international banks, unable to export sufficient quantities of its principal products, and besieged by narcoterrorists.

Since the early 1970s, the United States has taken a variety of steps to interdict the illegal importation of psychotropics such as cocaine, heroin, and marijuana from Latin America. Most of these efforts have focused on the destruction of psychotropic crops at their source, specifically in Bolivia, Colombia, Mexico, and Peru, thus making the anti-narcotics campaign an important issue in Inter-American affairs. Source country governments have been cajoled into launching their own anti-narcotics campaigns as well as into allowing United States government officials to operate in their national territory. In the case of Operation Blast Furnace in Bolivia, U.S. military personnel assisted Bolivian officials in their search and destroy operations.

Source country governments have responded to American pressure by diverting local resources to the anti-narcotics campaign as well as using funds, materiel, and civilian and military personnel supplied by the United States. As a bordering nation, which is both a producer and a conduit of narcotics, Mexico has been a principal focal point of the anti-narcotics effort and Mexican officials cooperate with U.S. narcotics agents. Cooperation with the United States on this issue by these nations diverts scarce resources needed for economic development and risks political backlash from the peasant growers, who depend upon this income for survival, rich and powerful traffickers, and nationalists. Although source country governments universally condemn the use of these narcotics, they are also sensitive to assertions that they are allowing the United States to interfere in their internal affairs, a longterm issue in U.S.-Latin American relations.

Complaints about U.S. actions in the anti-narcotics battle surface frequently in U.S.-Latin American affairs. At the October, 1986, Regional Meeting of Justice Ministers and Attorneys General held in Puerto Vallarta, Mexico, the delegates from the 12 Latin American nations attending demanded that the problem be recognized as international in scope and addressed with international solutions. In particular, they called for a hemispheric solution to the problem rather than one imposed by the United States.[16] Earlier in the year, charges by U.S. Senators that Mexico was failing to do its part in the anti-narcotics campaign and that Mexican government officials were connected to the illegal drug trade became a major and bitter issue between the two nations. In 1988, the Colombian Supreme Court ruled key provisions of the U.S.-Colombian extradition treaty unconstitutional in response to nationalistic protests. Pressures not to cooperate with U.S. anti-narcotics policy are mounting in Latin America.

The existence of widespread narcotics cultivation and trafficking in Latin American countries, inevitably accompanied by corruption of government officials, weakens the reliability of such countries as allies. Thus, the United States considers the illegal flow of psychotropics from Latin America a serious enough threat to U.S. national security to warrant trying to eliminate the illegal narcotics supply at the source even at the risk of angering allies.

One controversial weapon in the United States diplomatic arsenal is the certification process. The certification process has been criticized   by foreign governments and by scholars alike. The certification process has both an international and a domestic aspect. Within the United States, its purpose is to give Congress an oversight role on the execution of international narcotics diplomacy and, as such, indicates Congressional distrust of the Executive branch. The process allows people in Congress to demonstrate their "toughness" on the drug trade. On the international level, it is clearly a use of U.S. economic power to accomplish a foreign policy goal; the U.S. is trying to establish a quid pro quo, i.e. to obtain U.S. resources, nations in which narcotics are produced or through which they are transshipped or in which drug money is laundered must cooperate with the U.S. on its drug policy.

Some nationalists in the affected nations object to the certification process, however. Some believe that the process means that the U.S. is passing a moral judgment on their nations. A common assertion is that the policy is interference in their internal affairs. Some object to what they see as hypocrisy in the application of the policy, pointing out that the U.S. certifies nations which do not cooperate with U.S. policy and that the U.S. does not threaten its own drug-producing states in the same manner. Others simply object to the use of U.S. power. These arguments are presented by several authors in this volume.

By early 1989, the national security threat to the United States and to Mexico was becoming more imminent as evidence began surfacing that Colombian drug traffickers were purchasing Mexican land near the U.S.-Mexican border. Commensurate with this land acquisition has been a large influx of Colombians into this region, indicating that it is to be a staging base for better penetration of the U.S. market. Further, Colombian traffickers are going into partnership with Mexican heroin traffickers. The Colombians are more violent than other trafficking groups and their presence threatens to raise the level of violence along both sides of the border. To counter this threat, both the U.S. and Mexico may have to station troops along the border, an action which would disrupt the border economy.

Given the serious and complex problems of U.S.-Latin American relations, the fundamental question is whether this antinarcotics campaign is a legitimate and productive foreign policy and national security issue. Should the United States, in order to reduce consumption of illegal narcotics, expend energy and resources to convince source country governments in Latin America to reduce production and exportation? Or is the U.S. risking resolution of more pressing inter-American problems such as the debt crisis, the fragility of democratic institutions, conflict in Central America, and migration to the United States? Is the illegal narcotics trade a sufficient threat to national security to warrant using the U.S. military as drug enforcement agents?

Narcotics use and diplomacy have a long history in the United States, a fact too often forgotten in the current flurry of attention in the media and the halls of government. Douglas Clark Kinder, a historian from Ohio University, draws on his extensive research on narcotics diplomacy to explain the origins of U.S. efforts to control narcotics within the United States and abroad from the first decades of the twentieth century until 1965. Throughout the history of narcotics diplomacy, the U.S. adopted a nativistic approach, blaming "foreigners" for the narcotics epidemic, and pursued an unsuccessful diplomatic strategy. Richard Craig of Kent State University brings the story up to date in his chapter on U.S.-Mexican narcotics diplomacy. Mexico was, until very recently, the focal point of U.S. narcotics policy towards Latin America.

Bruce Bagley of the University of Miami and Rensselaer Lee, a private consultant who has published extensively on the narcotics issue, examine the dimensions of the narcotics business inside Latin America and of international trafficking. Their studies include not only South America, where they did the bulk of their research, but also Central America and Mexico.

Raphael Perl clarifies the role of Congress in making international narcotics policy, and Don Mabry explains the role of the U.S. military in the antidrug crusade. Perl is especially well suited to write on his subject; as the narcotics expert for the Congressional Research Service of the Library of Congress, he works daily with congresspersons and experts on the issue. The chapter by Mabry examines the implications of using the military to combat the drug trade and the potentially serious effects on military readiness, nationalistic reactions in Latin America, and the evolution of domestic politics within the United States.

Because Mexico is the major focus of U.S. narcotics diplomacy, two prominent Mexican scholars look at the issue from a Latin American perspective. Samuel I. del Villar, Mexico's leading expert on the issue and a former advisor to President Miguel de la Madrid, eloquently argues Mexican objections to U.S. narcotics policy and suggests different approaches to the problem. José Luis Reyna, an eminent Mexican political sociologist, examines the narcotics trade and U.S. diplomacy as destabilizing influences on Latin America and the United States. The Latin American narcotics trade is put into the context of U.S.-Latin American foreign policy and national security concerns. Gregory Treverton of the Council on Foreign Relations delineates the relative importance of narcotics diplomacy within the context of U.S.-Latin American diplomacy. In the concluding chapter Don Mabry and Raphael Perl summarize the volume's major findings and offer policy options.

The selective bibliography is more than a compilation of the sources cited in the chapters. Additional reports, articles, and books were listed to aid future researchers and others concerned with this issue. Both the drug trade and the policy debate over it will be with us for a long time; no bibliography can be more than a snapshot.

2

Nativism, Cultural Conflict, Drug Control: United States and Latin American Antinarcotics Diplomacy through 1965

Douglas Clark Kinder

Although drug control attracted less public attention as a foreign policy issue twenty-three years ago, by 1965, U.S. officials had already unsuccessfully attempted to stem the flow of Latin American narcotics into this country for nearly six decades. Such an unsuccessful record occurred largely because the United States antidrug program ignored the distinct economic, political, and social conditions south of the border.[1] Further complicating Washington's task in the hemisphere, achieving a popular consensus against drugs at home required three-fourths of a century of reform agitation. Indigenous narcotics restriction--given the country's large and expanding addict population--would also entail vigilant law enforcement and effective national legislation. U.S. authorities had long held, however, that thorough countrywide drug control depended primarily upon international antinarcotics diplomacy. Desiring to confine opium, coca, and cannabis cultivation in producing nations to amounts necessary for legitimate global scientific and medical purposes, Washington's antidrug advocates conducted both a bilateral and multilateral foreign policy towards Latin America. Every U.S. effort, naturally enough, appeared to Latin American governments as the intrusion of an aggressive alien society, or, if acceptable to them, seemed to the Indians and mestizos residing for generations in narcotics-growing areas as the continuation of earlier Spanish, creole, or national government encroachments upon their life style.[2]

Aggravating the cultural conflict generated by Washington's activities, U.S. narcotics restrictionists translated nativistic rhetoric and policies into a strident antidrug campaign. A small group of social reformers, physicians, pharmacists, diplomats, and muckraking journalists launched this antidrug movement in the late nineteenth century to reduce the country's widespread addiction. Though none of this group agreed on the precise level of substance abuse (there were no accurate estimates of the habitue population), they perceived addiction as a serious and growing problem that could only be corrected by purging habit-forming products from the nation. The advocates of control had little success until they encouraged an antidrug hysteria with fear-provoking accounts of ethnic minorities misusing narcotics.[3]

Specifically, drug reformers ignored the domestic causes of addiction and argued that other countries and certain undesirable ethnic groups within the United States engendered drug abuse. Antinarcotics activists asserted that European nations such as Great Britain, France, and the Netherlands promoted opiate exportation from their colonies to raise revenue. They claimed, too, that underdeveloped states around the world--China, Persia, Turkey, Peru, Bolivia, and Mexico, for example--could not or would not eradicate the overcultivation of opium and other narcotics, that foreign drug imports increased more rapidly than legitimate needs warranted, and, consequently, that exporting nations weakened the United States. California spokespersons voiced apprehension over the smoking of opium in West Coast Chinese communities, while white southerners expressed concern that the sexual passions of blacks might be unleashed by the use of cocaine and alcohol. Southwesterners occasionally exhibited alarm at Mexican-American violence supposedly linked to marijuana use. Antidrug reformers, like temperance leaders, suggested that narcotics addiction and alcoholism among ethnic groups contributed to America's poverty, crime, and disease.[4]

By contending that the drug problem was "foreign"--both in use as well as source--the advocates of limitation tapped deep nativistic undercurrents in the nation's tradition and justified punitive legislation. Through identifying racial minorities and other countries with drug abuse, therefore, restrictionists obtained a series of laws collectively prohibiting nonmedical narcotics consumption in the United States and entrusting drug limitation to the federal government. These antidrug proponents also persuaded Congress to create a separate national narcotics law enforcement agency, the Federal Bureau of Narcotics (FBN), in 1930.[5]

Directed by Harry J. Anslinger, the most successful champion of harsh antinarcotics statutes, the FBN for the next thirty-two years administered countrywide narcotics restrictions, regulated legitimate drug traffic, and participated in all facets of narcotics control diplomacy. The FBN convinced state and federal legislators to enact additional antidrug measures and mobilized the public to support narcotics limitation activities. While supervising the Bureau, moreover, Anslinger updated the earlier drug restrictionists' allegations associating foreign narcotics abusers and sources with complex and disturbing domestic problems to explain the necessity for maintaining and expanding strict antinarcotics legislation. He coerced several Latin American governments to implement punitive antidrug laws and improve enforcement, threatened to stop medicinal narcotics shipments from the United States to compel specific actions by others, and dispatched agents on clandestine missions in that area, sometimes without the approval of indigenous authorities.[6]

Anslinger and the earlier advocates of narcotics restriction claimed that other nations and internal minorities had spawned addiction in this country. In reality, physicians had long overprescribed powerful, habit-forming drugs, and the general public had routinely bought unregulated opiates, cocaine, cannabis, and narcotic-laced proprietary medicines. Throughout the nineteenth century, the medical profession failed to comprehend many serious diseases and dispensed narcotics--primarily opium and morphine--to arrest perplexing symptoms, to aid natural healing, and to relieve discomfort. Compounding the nation's exposure to drugs, untrained practitioners, druggists, general stores, and mail order houses sold opium, morphine, heroin, cocaine, cannabis, and patent medicine virtually without restriction; most home medical handbooks included recipes for opiate- and alcohol-laden products. Narcotics use was so widespread that opium importation rose more rapidly than the country's population rate between the 1840s and the 1870s, while proprietary medicine consumption increased seven times faster than the population during the nineteenth century. Not surprisingly, some entrepreneurs of that period attempted to cultivate and refine cheap opium in the United States.[7]

Although nineteenth-century medical practitioners achieved considerable advances in preventing communicable diseases and in using experimental science, they never understood addiction and relied on dangerous and habit-forming substances. Despite his warning to the medical community against excessive use, even Oliver Wendell Holmes, the well-known American physician, author, and medical professor, perceived opium as "God's own medicine."[8] Nevertheless, after the 1840s new generations of physicians hoped to ease discomfort through scientific healing, an attitude encouraging many to prescribe recently discovered and incompletely tested drugs that medical journals erroneously recommended for a variety of ailments. Morphine, the nation's universal pain reliever in the nineteenth century, was hypodermically injected after the Civil War to combat sciatica, cholera, asthma, sunstroke, seasickness, hernia, and persistent headaches. Cocaine gained acceptance between 1870 and 1900 for its power to ease sinusitis, hay fever, and drug addiction. Cannabis in a water and alcohol solution became a standard treatment in the late nineteenth century for insomnia, convulsions, venereal infections, chorea, and strychnine poisoning. Heroin originated in 1876 a cough suppressant and as a remedy for congestion, asthma, bronchitis, catarrh, and morphine dependence. By the turn of the century, the medical community's inadequate information and excessive narcotics distribution had created a large, socially diverse addict population that was predominately white, middle class, and female.[9]

The medical profession aside, the public had nearly unlimited access to habit-forming drugs. People generally perceived self-medication as a legitimate practice in the 1800s because the United States lacked physicians and the medical community was mistrusted. Virtually anyone could acquire narcotics from general merchants, druggists, and mail order companies. Retailers satisfied a huge demand for powerful drugs and paraphernalia: gum, powdered, and smoking opium; laudanum (opium mixed with alcohol and water); paregoric (opium in a camphorated solution of alcohol and water); morphine powder, tablets, and liquid; hypodermic kits; cocaine ointments and tablets; tincture of cannabis; and heroin tablets. Supplementing their appetite for drugs, North Americans bought opiate- and cocaine-laced proprietary elixirs, tonics, and syrups; cocaine-laden wines; and candy, food, and drinks containing cannabis. Narcotics were so prevalent in nineteenth-century United States, in fact, that Coca-Cola contained cocaine (until 1903) and the Parke-Davis Company marketed coca leaf cigarettes.[10]

In spite of the nation's largely unregulated narcotics practices, addiction generated little concern until the 1870s. Medical practitioners frequently realized that chronic opiate users needed increasing dosages of the drug to achieve the same results, but contemporary articles in professional journals, popular newspapers, and magazines insisted that heavy drug consumers enjoyed long and normal lives. Even after the Civil War, physicians misinterpreted the impact of narcotics on the human body, and many of them refused to believe that drugs were habit-forming. Before the 1870s narcotics abuse, unlike alcoholism, was seldom linked with irresponsibility, lust, or violence and the general public perceived drugs as acceptable inebriants, ignoring America's 250 thousand to one million habitues. Indeed, the country's elite often abused opiates instead of liquor.[11]

Even though North Americans viewed narcotics primarily as legitimate healing agents, pain relievers, and intoxicants, a small disorganized group of drug restrictionists soon began to identify addiction with ethnic minorities and criminal behavior. Motivated by fear of foreign narcotics, a few progressive professionals formed an antidrug movement. The reformers--paternalists believing in the nation's moral superiority and moral progress--wanted to protect racial minorities and "old stock" society from the drug evil. According to these activists, narcotics seductively led foreigners and native-born citizens too closely associated with immigrants to immorality, criminality, and death. The only way to save them was to purge habit-forming substances from the country. Prodded by new medical discoveries, a tiny coalition of young physicians and pharmacists argued that excessive exposure to drugs caused mental and physical decay. They supported state pharmacy laws limiting narcotics distribution. In the American Foreign Service, social reformers and medical experts, oversimplifying cultural differences, contended that drug addiction plagued all nations and that the United States should lead an international campaign against narcotics abuse and trafficking. As these antinarcotics advocates attacked drug abuse, muckraking American newspapers and magazines published highly sensational reports of ethnic groups committing acts of passion and vendetta while abusing narcotics. Whatever their individual orientation, most drug restrictionists held or employed strong nativistic feelings. Refusing to recognize that native-born citizens could abuse drugs without foreign instigation, they feared that immigrant narcotics consumption would undermine cherished values, and endorsed strict antidrug laws directed against minorities.[12]

This fledgling antinarcotics movement evolved from a few adverse accounts of drug abuse and smuggling in the early and middle nineteenth century. Medical authorities, social reformers, and the press, for instance, sporadically asserted that narcotics were poisonous during prolonged use and that alcoholics, prostitutes, and the mentally ill were typical recreational drug consumers. They also occasionally claimed that narcotics trafficking occurred in all of the country's major ports and cities, that the abuse of habit-forming substances was a part of urban corruption and decadence, and that drug abuse was growing rapidly in the United States. Additionally, while "old stock" society embraced rationality, responsibility, productivity, and progress, some narcotics detractors expressed concern about extensive upper-class drug consumption--especially among white women and southern white males--and about the peril of substance abuse to the competitive work ethic. But, after 1840, intermittent drug criticism focused almost exclusively on foreign narcotics smugglers and habitues. In particular, social reformers and journalists contended in popular newspapers and magazines that the major drug traffickers were English, Chinese, and Near Eastern, and that the nation's most significant narcotics abusers, because of their alleged genetic inferiority and cultural backwardness, were Chinese. By 1875, these occasional antidrug reports associated Chinese-American opiate consumption with the poverty, crime, and unsanitary conditions of Chinatowns. Nativists and social activists played upon this linkage to achieve a San Francisco city ordinance forbidding the Chinese practice of opium smoking. Based on infrequent and negative accounts of narcotics peddling and abuse and on strident anti-Chinese passions, the infant, disorganized drug restriction campaign persuaded eleven western states to enact similar antiopium legislation between 1877 and 1900.[13]

Besides aiming antinarcotics laws at West Coast Chinese, drug limitation advocates charged southern blacks with immoderate cocaine use. Though some North American factory and mine owners in the early twentieth century supposedly extracted more labor from their employees by supplying them with cocaine, most white southerners of that period feared that liquor and cocaine abuse among blacks might encourage rebellion against white society. Initially, southern whites believed that liquor consumption would increase racial violence, and several of the region's states adopted prohibition statutes. Within these "dry" states, poor blacks then allegedly substituted cola drinks--or some source of cocaine--for liquor, and whites began to identify "black crimes" with cocaine abuse. During the height of racial segregation and lynching early in the 1900s, white newspaper reporters and police officers argued that cocaine use gave blacks superhuman strength, improved their marksmanship, and made them difficult to kill. Armed with these assertions, most southern cities and states passed strict anticocaine ordinances, and many southern police departments changed from .32 caliber to .38 caliber revolvers to insure the control of black cocaine abusers.[14]

After 1910, southwestern drug restrictionists began to link Mexican-American violence with marijuana smoking--just as Chinese immigrants were associated with opium smoking and as blacks were identified with recreational cocaine consumption. Marijuana became known to some in the early twentieth century as a narcotic abused by the "underworld" in Gulf Coast port cities, but the public generally associated it with Mexicans in the southwestern United States. Among these Hispanics, marijuana smoking was part of the poor's life style and a folk remedy. Most Anglo-Americans knew or cared little about the drug's effects until around 1915, when several southwestern officials and journalists advocated regional antimarijuana legislation, claiming that the drug made Mexican-Americans "lust for blood" and "insensible to pain." As a consequence, eighteen western states approved marijuana restrictions founded on racial prejudice and fear of the narcotic.[15]

While xenophobia sustained drug limitation in the West, South, and Southwest, small professional groups and muckraking reporters from mass circulation newspapers and magazines promoted, through more genteel rhetoric, uniform state (and eventually national) controls on the sale and administration of habit-forming substances, but they, too, linked ethnic groups with narcotics abuse. By 1901, the American Medical Association (AMA)--representing primarily urban M.D.s from the East--and the American Pharmaceutical Association (APhA)--representing highly-trained and licensed drug preparers and dispensers--realized that narcotics ordinances should be coordinated with the emerging professional standards of medicine and pharmacy. Because patent medicines, besides offering inadequate medical treatment, contributed to the country's addiction problem, provided ethnic minorities with drugs, and competed with physicians and pharmacists, both the AMA and the APhA discouraged proprietary substances and supported the regulation of narcotics-laden trademarked preparations. Specifically, the APhA wanted drug legislation to favor pharmacists over retail druggists and other merchants selling patent medicines. In fact, it adopted a model state law in 1903 solely licensing medical practitioners and pharmacists to dispense narcotics. After some compromises permitted drug trade organizations to endorse the proposed statute, in 1906 Congress promulgated a pharmacy act similar to the model law for the District of Columbia.[16]

In addition to protecting pharmacists' interests, the 1906 District of Columbia Pharmacy Act furnished a format for future drug restrictions. Although the measure allowed physicians to distribute habit-forming substances to their patients, narcotics could only be administered when "necessary for the cure" of addiction or when treating a "disease, injury, or deformity." In order to dispense drugs, medical practitioners were required to write prescriptions, and both physicians and pharmacists were compelled to keep prescription records for three years. To gain the proprietary medicine manufacturers' acceptance, nevertheless, the pharmacy law tolerated limited amounts of narcotics in trademarked preparations available in drug and general stores and through the mail.[17]

Seeking stronger antinarcotic controls, journalists from a number of newspapers and magazines (including the *Nation, Good Housekeeping,* and *Harper's Monthly Magazine*) simultaneously disclosed that many proprietary medicines without ingredient labels contained drugs often used by immigrants. The muckraking reporters claimed that elixirs, syrups, and tonics advertised as pain relievers, digestive remedies, infant pacifiers, teething soothers, and miracles cures frequently included substantial amounts of morphine, heroin, cocaine, and cannabis. Besides revealing the ingredients in popular preparations, the journalists maintained that patent medicines caused addiction and death.[18]

Many of these writers, along with other antidrug advocates, also urged the legislative branch to establish countrywide regulation for trademarked products. The combined efforts of social reformers, the AMA, the APhA, and the press kindled the first national concern with narcotics, but most congresspersons asserted that a federal statute controlling patent medicines would exceed the government's constitutional interstate commerce power. The drug industry's lobbyists, moreover, dissuaded senators and representatives from formulating a measure governing proprietary substances. By enacting the Pure Food and Drug Act of 1906, nonetheless, Congress forced the manufacturers of trademarked preparations to list all contents, including narcotics, on each product transported across state boundaries.[19]

Despite widespread agitation over patent medicines with dangerous ingredients, legislative attention soon shifted to the Chinese habit of smoking opium. While the Pure Food and Drug Act apparently reduced proprietary medicine sales, and domestic antinarcotics activists sought stronger laws to eradicate these substances, other prominent North Americans attempted to end drug trafficking in the Far East. Indeed, non-medical opiates had been excluded from the Philippines while William Howard Taft served as the governor-general there and as Secretary of War (the cabinet officer with responsibility for that area) between 1901 and 1908. But because numerous foreign spheres of influence on the Asian mainland complicated narcotics law enforcement, drug restriction was virtually impossible in China. When Taft began his presidency in 1909, one of his acquaintances in the Philippines, Episcopal Bishop Charles H. Brent, urged the chief executive to promote the elimination of narcotics trading in China, which had an addict population comprising an estimated 25 percent of its adult male inhabitants.[20]

The Taft administration, responding to Brent's initiative, summoned representatives of thirteen countries to an antiopium conference in Shanghai in 1909. Embarrassed that the United States had no federal narcotics limitation statute, the nation's delegates requested the State Department to seek rapid passage of such a law. Domestic drug reformers suggested that Congress amend the Pure Food and Drug Act to remove drug-laden patent medicines from interstate commerce. To their consternation, however, the State Department recommended a new, less controversial national antiopium bill. Congress quickly approved and Taft signed the proposed act, forbidding the importation of smoking opium. This Opium Exclusion Act, ironically, struck at a practice symbolically associated with the country's Chinese populace.[22]

Though few accomplishments other than the smoking opium prohibition can be credited to the international gathering in China, social reformers and medical experts in the State Department used it to justify a drug restriction foreign policy. Designated as a mere fact-finding "commission" immediately before it convened, the Shanghai meeting achieved only weak proposals to control opiates, monitor opium shipments, and reevaluate narcotics regulations. U.S. delegates to the commission nevertheless convinced many congresspersons and much of the public that drug limitation in other countries would eliminate the indigenous narcotics problem, that this nation should establish statutes to provide an example for the rest of the world, and that the nonbinding Shanghai agreements warranted more antidrug legislation in the United States.[22]

In fact, shortly after the international opium restriction conference adjourned, its chief coordinator and a member of Washington's mission to the meeting, Hamilton Wright, lobbied both for additional domestic narcotics control laws and multinational antidrug gatherings. Since earlier attempts to compose a federal regulation for patent medicines or narcotics grounded on constitutional interstate commerce powers had failed in Congress, Wright suggested a measure combining the District of Columbia Pharmacy Act and the legislative branch's revenue authority. In the spring of 1910, he persuaded Representative David Foster of Vermont, chair of the Foreign Affairs Committee, to sponsor his model legislation in the House of Representatives. While presenting the Shanghai commission's findings to congresspersons, furthermore, Wright argued that Chinese immigrants encouraged opium smoking among North Americans and that black cocaine users often raped white women. Yet, drug trade associations, desiring simpler record-keeping requirements and exemptions for trademarked substances, opposed the proposal, and the House of Representatives defeated it.[23]

Undaunted by the Foster bill's rejection, Wright sought and attained the U.S. government's participation in a series of international antinarcotics conferences at The Hague. Washington's delegations to the meetings which usually included Wright, pursued treaty status for the Shanghai opium limitation recommendations, promoted global control of cocaine and marijuana as well as opiates, and urged all countries to confine narcotics production to legitimate medical and scientific needs. Wright expended much effort; the Hague conference of 1911-12 fashioned the earlier commission's proposals into a formal diplomatic agreement, the Hague Opium Convention of 1912, and the cooperating nations, at Great Britain's request, discussed morphine, cocaine, and marijuana restriction.[24]

The antidrug meetings accomplished little, however. The 1911-12 conferees, because of international rivalries over drug-generated revenue, failed to conclude a treaty regulating narcotics other than opium. The document merely promised "to use their best endeavors" to suppress trafficking; it did not define acceptable drug usage, and refused to endorse the limitation of opium at its source. Few of the participating countries ratified the document. The United States attended two later meetings (The Hague conferences of 1913 and 1914) that reduced the number of consenting nations necessary to implement the convention. By the Paris Peace Conference's adjournment in 1919, only Britain, the United States, and sixteen other countries had adopted the opium restriction treaty, but Wright and the State Department founded the nation's drug control diplomacy through 1931 upon The Hague agreement.[25]

Meanwhile, Wright compromised with drug trade organizations in this country and renewed his campaign for a domestic antinarcotics law. Suspecting that a drug-regulating statute would soon be implemented, the APhA and many of the U.S. drug trade groups pledged to cooperate with Wright in formulating a federal narcotics limitation measure. Representative Francis Burton Harrison of New York, moreover, offered to introduce a drug-taxing bill in the House of Representatives. Equipped with these commitments and the Senate ratification of the 1912 International Opium Convention, Wright and the State and Treasury Departments prepared a bill in 1913 that the APhA, drug trade organizations, the AMA, and the Internal Revenue Bureau (IRB)--the major enforcer of the proposed law--supported. Representative Harrison then sponsored the legislation, and both houses of Congress and the chief executive approved the Harrison Narcotics Act in 1914.[26]

Though somewhat weaker than the 1910 Wright proposal (the Foster bill), the Harrison law followed a similar record-keeping and revenue scheme. The statute, controlling opiates and cocaine alone (marijuana would not be restricted by the federal government until 1937), compelled all dealers in these narcotics to report transactions on standard order forms to be preserved for inspection. Furthermore, they had to register with the IRB and pay an occupational tax. To pacify medical and pharmaceutical interests, the Harrison Act exempted physicians "in attendance" on patients from recording drug distributions, required medical practitioners and retail druggists to pay only a one dollar per year occupational fee, excluded the trademarked preparation industry from revealing its distribution, sales, and narcotics procurements, and permitted proprietary substances to contain small amounts of opiates and cocaine.[27]

Concern about "un-American" drug abusers during and after World War I caused the Harrison law to evolve from rather limited powers to a non-medical narcotics proscription. The measure authorized physicians to dispense habit-forming substances for medical purposes; hence, practitioners could distribute opiates and cocaine to their addicted patients, a practice that "maintained" narcotics habitues. In March 1915, the Treasury Department's IRB announced regulations obliging pharmacists to determine both the validity and legitimacy of physicians' prescriptions. At the same time, Justice Department prosecutors argued that an unregistered person possessing restricted narcotics without a medical practitioner's approval violated the 1914 legislation.[28]

The *United States v. Jin Fuey Moy*, 241 U.S. 401 (1916), Supreme Court decision nevertheless held that only failure to provide adequate records or pay the one dollar annual tax constituted an infraction of the law. In 1919, however, the identification of drug abuse with anarchists, radicals, and undesirable aliens, and the fear that liquor prohibition would encourage more recreational narcotics consumption induced the high court to reverse its earlier contention. *United States v. Doremus*, 249 U.S. 86 (1919), and *Webb et al. v. United States*, 249 U.S. 96 (1919) claimed that the Harrison Act forbade drug maintenance and possession of opiates and cocaine by unlicensed individuals without an M.D.'s written order. In that year, Congress, disturbed about "un-American" narcotics abuse, adopted Representative Henry T. Rainey's proposed amendments to the Harrison law. These revisions allowed the IRB to exact reports from patent medicine manufacturers about their operations, to assess an excise on controlled drugs by weight, and to consider possession of untaxed opiates and cocaine not prescribed by a medical practitioner as a violation of the statute.[29]

As the Harrison Act grew into the centerpiece of federal antinarcotics legislation, both the nation's habitues and the narcotics limitation movement underwent important changes, but internal minorities and other countries were still blamed for the domestic drug problem. Unrestrained access to dangerous drugs in the nineteenth and early twentieth centuries had produced a large, socioeconomically and ethnically diverse addict population, yet, the typical pre-1914 was a middle-aged, middle class, white female from the South. Paralleling late nineteenth- and early twentieth-century progressive reform campaigns to eradicate alcohol abuse and prostitution and to improve the lives of women, children, and the poor, a small ad hoc group of social activists responded to the nation's widespread narcotics consumption by launching a drug restriction crusade. Since this antinarcotics movement, like the Prohibition campaign, claimed that substance abuse contributed to poverty, crime, and disease, drug reformers received low-key and sporadic support from the Anti-Saloon League and the Women's Christian Temperance Union.[30]

Although motivated by a progressive impulse to purify American society--indeed all societies--these antidrug advocates also believed or uncritically argued that foreign narcotics users and sources generated drug abuse in the United States. Specifically, they promoted order, efficiency, and medical and pharmaceutical professionalism while ignoring the indigenous causes of North American drug addiction. Narcotics control activities portrayed, and many perceived, opiate and cocaine abuse as an activity alien to native-born U.S. citizens, contending, therefore, that outsiders must have introduced and encouraged recreational drug consumption in this country. Largely because of its allegations that domestic ethnic minorities and global narcotics overcultivation created the nation's addiction problems, the drug limitation movement made narcotics appear more evil, sinister, and powerful. It built a popular antidrug consensus, whereas alcohol prohibitionists never developed a large following and achieved a series of state ordinances, the Opium Exclusion Act, and the Harrison law, which collectively banned non-medical narcotics usage.[31]

But effective drug control, even with the stronger 1914 antinarcotics measure, required vigilant law enforcement, additional federal legislation, and a national narcotics foreign policy; such a program exceeded the capabilities of a tiny decentralized reform group. U.S. drug restriction activities after 1914 became a function of the government bureaucracy and the Congress. Since the Harrison Act reduced the availability of opiates and cocaine to the general public (even as medical and social commentators viewed addiction throughout the 1900s as a serious and growing problem), post-1914 habitues were more likely to be young, lower class, urban, white males who chose escapist life styles. Nonetheless, new bureaucratic or organizational antinarcotics advocates increasingly asserted--as earlier drug limitation proponents had--that foreign narcotics abusers, traffickers, and producers engendered the country's recreational consumption.[32]

Accordingly, federal drug control officials, despite some internal dissension, treated Harrison law violators as social lepers. While contending that the 1914 antidrug legislation proscribed addiction maintenance and unauthorized opiate and cocaine possession, the IRB, prodded by the Public Health Service's promotion of therapeutic narcotics restriction, explored alternative remedies for the nation's drug problem between 1914 and 1919. Because strict Harrison Act enforcement, though arduous, had not eliminated opiate and cocaine abuse, the IRB also sanctioned the operation of forty-four drug maintenance clinics in 1919 as well--just before the Supreme Court and Congress fortified the national antinarcotics statute. The IRB's experiment nevertheless proved less adequate than attempting to forbid drug abuse, and the agency closed its clinics in July 1920 as the Public Health Service recanted its support for "curing" habitues.[33]

Armed with the *Doremus* and *Webb et al.* rulings and the Rainey amendments, the IRB by mid-1920 sought to incarcerate all narcotics addicts and peddlers. Congress encouraged this effort by establishing the Prohibition Unit within the IRB during 1919 and by doubling the antidrug appropriation. In 1922, it enacted the Narcotic Drug Import and Export Act (which expanded the 1909 Opium Exclusion Act to regulate the importation of coca leaves and all varieties of opium) in spite of the AMA's opposition (based upon the belief that the legislation would expand government supervision of physicians and inflate the cost of medicinal narcotics). In 1927, the legislative branch created the independent Prohibition Bureau to administer the Harrison law as well as alcohol proscription more efficiently. Throughout the 1920s, the Narcotics Division of the Prohibition Unit (the Prohibition Bureau after 1927) enforced a non-medical narcotics ban. Under the direction of Levi G. Nutt, a registered pharmacist and longtime civil servant, it arrested an average of nine to ten thousand habitues per annum, ignoring a Supreme Court decision, *Linder v. United States*, 268 U.S. 5 (1925), which arguably weakened the two 1919 rulings. The Narcotics Division confined so many opiate and cocaine addicts and peddlers that at the end of Fiscal Year (FY) 1928 almost one-third of all federal prisoners were drug law violators. Indicating the acceptance of the division's policies in the national government, Lawrence Kolb of the Public Health Service argued that habitues were psychopaths by choice.[34]

Kolb's contention was even more significant. Given the Public Health Service's abandonment of therapeutic narcotics limitation, his statement signified that the U.S. bureaucracy--a steadfast defender of the country's revered cultural values--had adopted the nativistic attitudes of the drug control movement. Federal officials, in addition to indiscriminately employing xenophobic rhetoric associating narcotics abuse with racial minorities, often viewed all addicts and traffickers, whatever their ethnicity, as "foreign" because they engaged in amoral, asocial, irresponsible, and, consequently, criminal behavior. Since various regions of the world supplied illicit drugs to the nation's habitues, U.S. authorities also believed that global overcultivation of opium and coca threatened the country's security. As a result, drug restriction bureaucrats conducted a general antinarcotics diplomacy; Latin America, however, received special attention. It was the nation's closest major drug source, a smuggling center and an area in which Washington exerted political and economic influence. Between the 1920s and the mid-1960s, U.S. officials learned, to their dismay, that Latin

Americans could use nativism equally well to maintain narcotics production and trafficking.[35]

Latin America's numerous, distinct cultures had long deemed drug cultivation and use legitimate practices. In so doing, they approximated the popular U.S. attitude before the twentieth century but shared little of U.S. reformers' subsequent interest in narcotics limitation. Indeed, Indian and mestizo communities frequently perceived drug production, consumption, and trading as expressions of self-assertion and cultural independence. Besides ingesting intoxicants to conform with religious customs and to cope with physical and psychological hardships imposed by native leaders or Spanish colonists, they passively resisted alien intrusions on their way of life by abusing narcotics. The establishment of independent Latin American countries after the 1810s merely amplified the aboriginal and mixed-blooded people's nativistic drug activities. Constituting an impoverished and politically powerless group existing outside the dominant national societies, rural Indians and mestizos--Latin America's majority population until the mid-twentieth century--often responded to deprivation and acculturation with lucrative and time-honored narcotics pursuits.[36]

While such behavior sporadically caused anxiety among individual journalists and officials in a few countries by the 1920s, a complex set of factors precluded meaningful drug control. Chronic economic and political instability, for instance, compelled Latin American leaders to expend much effort securing and retaining authority, acquiring approval from influential coteries (commonly the exploiters of aboriginal and mixed-blooded people), stimulating business investments and trade, and promoting orderly national administrations. These endeavors, though only partially successful, depleted meager resources necessary to alleviate the dislocation and disaffection of rural Indians and mestizos and, in turn, to restrict narcotics cultivation, use, and trafficking. Governments tolerated and occasionally abetted drug enterprises; narcotics profited alienated communities, appeared generally harmless over the years to the ruling elite, and raised revenue for Latin American oligarchies. Despite antinarcotics maneuvering by the United States and isolated, indigenous recognition that drugs engendered detrimental effects, little actually changed south of the border even after 1920. Latin American administrations usually disliked Washington's meddlesomeness, and the large, destitute, non-urban population distrusted both.[37]

But specific objects of suspicion or reasons for subjugation scarcely mattered to rural Indians and mestizos. Significant numbers had countered virtually all encroachments on their cultures and drug activities, which later extended to people of other socioeconomic and racial backgrounds. For perhaps two millennia before the founding of the Inca empire, natives of the area now comprising Colombia, Bolivia, and Peru chewed coca to ease hunger, quench thirst, and lessen fatigue. Thus, coca chewing, or *el coqueo*, mitigated difficulties, such as famine, otherwise beyond the Indians' mastery. Although Inca authorities attempted to limit the narcotic's consumption to particular social and occupational groups, the dispatches of Francisco Pizarro's secretary in the sixteenth century depicted most natives as coca users. Andean Indians, largely ignoring decrees of King Philip II of Spain designed to curb coca ingestion, practiced *el coqueo* throughout the colonial period to abate miserable living conditions and to rebel passively against their subjection. Meanwhile, royal officials in Peru violated the crown's directives and encouraged coca production for domestic use to reap expected profits. By the late 1700s, Spanish soldiers also discerned a value in the narcotic, chewing it to withstand the rigors of field operations. Besides the continued corporal and nativistic motivations for *el coqueo* following the inauguration of independent South American nations, other forces induced more intensive cultivation of the drug. During the late nineteenth and early twentieth centuries, global demand for cocaine--a crystalline alkaloid obtained from the raw narcotic--further expanded coca plant growing, and Peru became the world's leading coca leaf exporter. Because the raw drug could generate much revenue, no South American country implemented anticoca laws by 1920.[38]

An equivalent situation existed in Mexico, except that aboriginal and mixed-blooded people there produced, consumed, and traded a variety of intoxicants. For example, the psychological burden of debt peonage and human sacrifice at the zenith of the Aztec empire fostered the use of pulque, an alcoholic drink. While the Spanish conquest of central Mexico eliminated obvious elements of the natives' religion, European subjugators aggravated existing socioeconomic dislocation. Indians and mestizos reacted to dispossession of land, expansion of peonage, and loss of traditional culture by ingesting pulque and peyote (the buttonlike tops of a small, spineless cactus and the source of a psychedelic drug). After more than two hundred years, even the nomadic Yaqui Indians in the region of the present states of Sonora and Sinaloa came under Spanish influence. Yet, they continued to resist outside authority until the twentieth century in part by cultivating and trafficking opium and marijuana. Since Mexican independence left essentially the same Indian and mestizo poverty and disaffection intact, various drug enterprises remained as well. The 1910 Mexican Revolution created economic growth, industrialization, a larger middle class, and expanded political power, but rural Indians and mestizos remained too poorly organized to efficiently use these gains for many years. After the revolution's achievements were institutionalized, a modern version of earlier oligarchic rule emerged. Not surprisingly, narcotics pursuits continued.[39]

Given these traditions, Latin Americans often did not understand or accept U.S. attacks on their societies. Narcotics were not a problem within their countries. They did not encourage people in the U.S. or elsewhere to use drugs; users made their own decisions on such matters. If the U.S. government was concerned about narcotics use in the United States, that was an internal matter of the United States. Of course, given the immense power of the U.S., Latin American countries could not ignore what they considered to be hysteria over drugs.

By suggesting that the drug problem was foreign in both use as well as source earlier narcotics restrictionists tapped deep nativistic undercurrents in the American tradition and justified punitive legislation. As the Cold War took shape, Anslinger at first argued that a cohesive Italian-American "Mafia" conspiracy with international ties controlled illicit narcotics traffic in the United States. Later, during the Korean conflict, Anslinger claimed that Communist China was "dumping" narcotics on the free world for economic and political purposes. By 1953 Anslinger explained that, although the Chinese Communists were making the major profits, the "Mafia" was distributing narcotics manufactured in mainland China.[40]

In the early 1960s, after the break with Castro's Cuba, Anslinger charged that Castroite agents were smuggling cocaine into America to gain foreign currency, and that Communist China was using Cuba as an advance base for its narcotics trafficking network. At first Anslinger revealed that Castroite agents were selling monthly, in New York, cocaine worth $2 million. Soon, however, the commissioner alleged that small boats brought cocaine from Cuba to Florida, where the narcotics were shipped to New York, in order "to spread havoc in our largest city" and to discredit Cuban refugees by fostering addiction among them. A year later Anslinger charged that Cuba was distributing Chinese Communist opium in the Western Hemisphere, and that an undercover narcotics agent learned that Chinese agricultural workers were cultivating opium in Cuba.[41]

Anslinger attracted little attention with his anti-Castro accusations because he left the IRB at the end of 1962. He was forced from office both because of the mandatory retirement age and because his presence embarrassed the Kennedy administration. The commission had harassed Anslinger's greatest critic, Alfred Lindesmith, since the 1930s, and after the publication in 1962 of the anti-Anslinger book, *Drug Addiction: Crime or Disease?*, the FBN investigated both Lindesmith and the Indiana University Press. This investigation of an author and publisher who had broken no drug laws outraged members of the Kennedy administration, and the Treasury Department began to monitor Anslinger's actions very closely. In September, 1962, Anslinger officially left his position, but he continued his Communist narcotics trafficking rhetoric from his United Nations post.[42]

Ultimately, Anslinger updated the early-twentieth century drug restrictionists' pattern of linking ethnic and foreign elements with drug trafficking. In doing so, he helped condition the way Americans perceived current narcotics use in the United States. Rather than recognize the reasons so many Americans began using marijuana in the 1960s and cocaine since the late 1970s--reasons that must lie within the nature of American society--drug restrictionists blamed foreigners, in this case Latin Americans.

II

Contemporary U.S. Narcotics Policy

3

Mexican Narcotics Traffic: Binational Security Implications*
Richard B. Craig

Recent years have witnessed the emergence of illicit drug abuse and trafficking as both a national security issue and foreign policy priority. Many consider substance abuse the most serious challenge facing contemporary American society. Others contend the problem is sensationalized and exaggerated with minimal repercussions vis-à-vis alcohol and tobacco consumption. Such debate aside, there can be no doubt that the use of drugs, both licit and illicit, constitutes a first-order problem for politicians, police, diplomats American citizens. An estimated 500 thousand Americans are addicted to heroin. Some 20 million are said to be regular users of marijuana, while approximately 25-30 million have experimented with cocaine or use the drug regularly. The results have been profound.

Drug abuse and trafficking are undeniably America's most serious crime problems. They generate, according to some analysts, annual retail earnings in excess of $100 billion. They spawn everything from death to prime time television series, seriously erode the nation's quality of life, corrupt its institutions, influence its foreign policy, and indirectly threaten its national interests.

The U.S. government's primary response has always been to seek a solution at the foreign source in those countries whose fields and laboratories produce the illicit products so demanded by American users. As a multi-ton producer of heroin and marijuana and an increasingly important conduit for cocaine, Mexico has become a primary target of Washington's international narcotics policy. It is within this context that the binational security implications of illicit Mexican narcotics are examined.

LOOKING BACK

Historically, American interest in illicit Mexican drugs can be traced to the onset of U.S. concern over its own drug abuse problems at the turn of the century.[1] But it was not until the late 1960s, when increasing amounts of Mexican marijuana and a consistent supply of heroin entered the United

States, that the Nixon administration began new initiatives to ease America's drug dilemma by attacking the problem at its foreign source. Turkey became the primary target of Washington's heroin diplomacy, and Mexico came under increasing diplomatic pressure as the principal supplier of marijuana.

Such pressure was epitomized in Operation Intercept in September, 1969. Designed ostensibly to halt the flow of marijuana into the United States in one massive maneuver, Intercept was in fact a classic example of economic blackmail. Its relative merits and demerits have long been debated, but there is no doubt that Intercept constitutes a bench mark in U.S.-Mexican drug diplomacy and a critical juncture in Mexico's antidrug program.[2]

Under Intercept's successor, Operation Cooperation, Mexico accelerated its eradication and interdiction efforts, particularly in the opium-growing northeastern states, for, with Turkey's decision in the early 1970s to control opium production, Mexico soon became the principal source of heroin in the United States and consequently the primary object of Washington's narcotics diplomacy.[3] But when accelerated manual eradication efforts by the military proved inadequate, the Mexicans made a critical decision: with U.S. assistance they would launch an unprecedented aerial herbicide program code named Operation Condor.[4]

No program has so affected the Mexican drug scene and so pleased Washington. Condor initially had it all, including the political advantage of being impersonal or antiseptic. Plants, not people, were its target. And as the Mexicans eradicated field after field of poppy and marijuana, Mexico became Washington's antidrug showcase. Simultaneously. Condor salvaged the country's international image, proved a critical means of reclaiming control of the lawless tristate area of Sinaloa, Durango, and Chihuahua, and in the process enabled the Procuracy to acquire a formidable air wing. Finally, Operation Condor's impact on the American drug scene was most impressive. Mexico's share of the U.S. heroin market shrank dramatically from 85 percent in 1974 to 37 percent in 1984, and its portion of the marijuana market plummeted from an estimated 90 percent in 1974 to roughly 5 percent in 1981.[5]

Given such results, how do we explain the resurgence of Mexican drug traffic in the 1980s? A combination of factors, including the weather, marked the comeback. The year 1984, for example, was unusually wet, which meant more bountiful drug crops and fewer clear days for aerial spraying. Grower/trafficker ingenuity was another cause: fields were made smaller and planted year round in more inaccessible areas. Interagency rivalries and the lack of an independent verification system resulted in crops going unsprayed or being sprayed too late. Colombia's emergence as a major drug producer meant a greater and more profitable role for Mexican *traficantes* as cocaine trans-shippers. Some 40 percent of the cocaine · reaching the United States is today routed through Mexico. Economic deterioration also contributed, meaning fewer dollars for Mexico's campaign and greater desperation on the part of the *campesinos* with literally nothing to lose by their involvement in the drug cycle.

Unprecedented drug-related corruption and terror also proved critical to the trafficking renaissance. In the wake of the scandalous Enrique Camarena affair, the list of tainted officials, many of them direct representatives of Mexico's federal and state governments, appeared endless. Public disclosure of their corruption at the hands of notorious traficantes made a mockery of President Miguel de la Madrid's campaign for "moral renovation," damaged the stature of Mexico's attorney general, spawned widespread cynicism by the public and the press, and seriously undermined the government's credibility. Meanwhile, narcoterror, often inseparable from drug-related corruption, reached unheard-of levels in the mid-1980s. Armed with the most sophisticated weapons, traficantes became the law unto themselves in many rural areas.

The Mexican connection's revival was also abetted by the twin problems of inertia and complacency, clearly evidenced during the final months of President José López Portillo's term. The antidrug *campaña* suffered from neglect and a dearth of leadership during 1981 and 1982. Washington, meanwhile, took Mexico's program for granted and put forth Condor as the model to be emulated.

The final and perhaps decisive factor in reviving Mexican drug production and trafficking was external demand. American consumption of the three major illicit drugs has not decreased appreciably in the 1980s. It has remained constant for heroin, decreased slightly for marijuana, and increased dramatically for cocaine. Inseparable from the pull factor of demand are, of course, huge profits, violence, and corruption, each with its own security implications for the United States and Mexico.

DRUGS AND MEXICAN SECURITY INTERESTS

The impact of *la droga* on Mexico's security interests, while largely indirect, is indeed real. The cultivation and trafficking of illicit narcotics have become crucial ingredients in what Mexicans call *la crisis*. While surely not the primary cause of Mexico's contemporary crisis, drugs have compounded the nation's political, social, and economic problems at domestic and international levels. Mexico has, in fact, been victimized in the 1980s by the "South American effect" of illicit narcotics. Drug-related corruption and violence have besmirched the nation's image; greatly exacerbated public cynicism towards politicians, bureaucrats, police, and judges; threatened national government control at local and regional levels; and abetted the burgeoning problem of domestic substance abuse. In short, *narcotráfico* now poses a verifiable threat to Mexican society and the Mexican political system.

Narcocorruption

Mexicans are virtually inured to corruption. They would actually be suspicious of any totally honest bureaucrat, politician, policeman, or judge. But *narcotráfico* has done what even the most corrupt politicians could not do; it has rendered dysfunctional the cement of Mexican politics and society. And in the process it has transformed the subtle and necessary art of the *mordida* into an outrageous, system-threatening *corrupción desaceptable*. The full extent of *la droga's* corrosive power over national, state, and local officials became painfully clear in the wake of Enrique Camarena's murder in February, 1985.

Scores of commanders and agents from Mexico's prestigious Federal Judicial Police and Federal Security Directorate were directly implicated in drug trafficking; several were literally on the payroll of notorious drug capos. They received thousands of dollars not to spray herbicides on poppy and marijuana plots, to irrigate instead of fumigate, to look the other way when cocaine and heroin cargoes were flown into and out of drug trafficking zones, to escort overland caches to the border, to arrest thousands of *campesinos* while allowing major *traficantes* to operate with impunity or leave the country, and to ignore the blatantly obvious reality of marijuana farming and processing centers employing hundreds of *campesino* laborers.

Federal judges, after reportedly receiving huge payoffs, freed at least three of Mexico's most infamous traffickers "for lack of sufficient evidence." Governors and ex-governors have been implicated directly and indirectly with drug trafficking. An ex-governor of Morelos is wanted by Costa Rica in connection with Caro Quintero's organization. Two ex-governors of Sinaloa have been consistently linked by national and international reports to major drug traffickers. The previous Chihuahua head of state could not possibly have been ignorant of the conspicuous marijuana plantation "El Búfalo" in the mid-1980s. According to the United States Drug Enforcement Administration (DEA), the amount of marijuana under cultivation at this one "ranchito" in late 1984 exceeded Mexico's entire annual share of the U.S. market.

The list of tainted officials suddenly appeared endless, the extent of their venality outrageous. The critical factor was the very public nature of their posts as direct representatives of Mexico's federal and state governments. Public disclosures of their corruptibility at the hands of notorious *traficantes* came at the worst possible time for a beleaguered President Miguel de la Madrid. They made a mockery of his campaign for "moral renovation," seriously undermined the stature of Mexico's attorney general, and spawned unprecedented cynicism by the public and press. In league with post-earthquake scandals, narcocorruption tainted the de la Madrid administration, perhaps irreparably, in the eyes of its citizenry and has seriously undermined the government's credibility.

Narcoterror

A more blatant and direct challenge to Mexico's security interests is drug-related violence. Operation Condor appeared in the late 1970s to have cleansed the nation of its most visible example of narcoterror in the tristate region of Sinaloa, Durango, and Chihuahua, but the campaign eroded, the aerial herbicide program fell into disarray, and the *traficantes* regrouped.

New and more powerful capos emerged. They relocated in Guadalajara, revived the Sinaloa drug scene, multiplied production, and established vertical linkages to South America. Some specialized in marijuana, others in heroin, and still others in cocaine trans-shipment. They moved into the southern and central states, buying off regional officials and *campesinos* when possible, physically eliminating them when necessary. In a country long noted for violence, drug traffickers have added new meaning to the term. Armed with the most sophisticated weapons, traficantes have become a law unto themselves in many rural areas. Their response to dedicated local and state police, federal gents, and soldiers is invariably the same--unmitigated violence. The Mexican drug traffickers do not simply shoot their opponents; they torture, mutilate, and execute them. Whenever possible they set an example; they teach them a lesson; they massacre!

Hundreds of soldiers, federal police agents, and local police have been killed by Mexico's narcomafia. The brutal sagas of Minatitlán, Veracruz; Chichicapán, Oaxaca; and Enrique Camarena are not mere examples of drug-related violence: they are case studies in anti-system narcoterror. Federal and state agents were not just killed *mano a mano* in Veracruz and Oaxaca; that kind of violence the Mexican can understand. They were mutilated and then executed. The American DEA agent and his Mexican pilot were not merely gunned down. Camarena and Zavala were tortured and beaten to death.[6]

In effect, Mexico's *narcotraficantes* have carved out regional fiefdoms and posted "Keep Out" signs. Whether by corruption or intimidation, they exercise de facto power in portions of six states: Sinaloa, Durango, Chihuahua, Guerrero, Veracruz, and Oaxaca. In the process, *los narcos* have demonstrated time and again that the supposedly all-encompassing government in Mexico City does not truly enjoy unlimited reach. They have laid to rest the myth that Mexico's national government, unlike its narco-plagued counterparts in South America, exercises unchallenged control nationwide, and anytime a government does not control its entire national territory it can be said to have a security problem. Such is particularly the case if those forces enjoying enclave status should establish ties with that perennial nonentity, the Mexican guerrilla. Officially, Mexico has not witnessed a rural guerrilla insurgency since the demise of Lucio Cabañas' movement in the early 1970s. However, there are the disquieting phenomena of rural desperation and de facto terrorism, each of which is inseparable from *la droga*.

The greatest failure of the Mexican government over the past quarter century has been rural neglect. In a word, life for today's *campesinos* amounts to bare subsistence. They have only two options for true self-improvement, both unlawful: become illegal migrants or cultivate illicit crops. In choosing either option they are rejecting the system that has so blatantly rejected them in recent years. Official rhetoric aside, *campesinos* become drug cultivators out of necessity; they are seldom forced to do so by unscrupulous traffickers. Once involved in the drug cycle they often acquire modern weapons and face the real likelihood, if caught, of losing their land and being imprisoned. Such individuals become ideal recruits for any kind of antigovernment movement. All they know is that the government treated them "like Indians" before and now treats them like criminals because they have come to live with a modicum of decency. At this stage they personify Che Guevara's guerrilla in germ.

A second unsettling reality is de facto terrorism. Perhaps government spokespersons are correct when they repeat incessantly "there are no guerrillas in Mexico." Perhaps there are no official terrorist groups, but drug traffickers' tactics--their use of violence and terror against the nation's police and soldiers--earn them de facto terrorist status. Today's Mexican traficante is, in fact, more violent in deed than either Lucio's rural "Army of the Poor" or the ill-fated "23rd of September" movement that plagued urban areas in the early 1970s.

Domestic Abuse

Accurate statistics on the number of Mexican drug addicts and abusers are virtually nonexistent. Over the last decade government spokesmen have pegged the figure at anywhere between 10 thousand and 100 thousand. They tend in the process to lump addicts and casual users under the generic heading *drogadicto*.

The use of marijuana by contemporary Mexican young people has long been deemed a serious problem. Refusing to accept the reasoning that no direct connection exists between marijuana smoking and eventual hard drug use, federal narcotics officials and Mexican parents deem such activity a serious first step to ultimate addiction. If this is indeed the case, the Mexican body politic may be facing an important, though indirect, challenge, because there is far more marijuana available today than ever before. It is considerably more potent than in previous years, and it is being smoked by thousands of urban youth.

Substance abuse is now acknowledged to be a very serious domestic problem in Colombia, Bolivia, and Peru. Far more marijuana and coca derivatives are being produced than can be exported with enormous quantities available for internal use at increasingly lower prices. As a result, South American source countries are experiencing alarming increases in the smoking of marijuana and *basuco*, a dangerous combination of marijuana and cocaine paste. The same holds true in the case of Mexican marijuana: while not flooded, the Mexican market is clearly overstocked. Young consumers are increasingly taking advantage of available goods.

With the exception of border cities, the same does not hold true for opium and heroin, and that introduces an anomaly. Mexico is the only significant opium/heroin producer in the Americas. It is also the world's only major source country for these drugs in the world without a serious addiction problem. Such is not the case with inhalants. Accurate figures are not available, but all Mexican experts concur that the use of glues and solvents has reached alarming levels in urban areas throughout Mexico. The problem is, in fact, growing in direct proportion to the nation's massive urbanization. Solvents are priced within the reach of the poorest slum dweller, and, most alarming to Mexican officials, there appears to be no means of curing or rehabilitating the solvent addict. Like his rural counterpart who opts for drug cultivation as a last resort, the ghetto "glue head" sucks on his plastic bag to escape the reality of a life hardly worth living. The political system has failed these forgotten ones, rendering itself ever more vulnerable in an era of acute vulnerability.

MEXICAN DRUGS AND U.S. SECURITY INTERESTS

No one, with the exception of Mexican officials themselves, is more aware of Mexico's current systemic vulnerability than the United States. As regards the role played by *narcotráfico* in this crisis scenario, Washington often appears more concerned than Mexico City. So acute is American preoccupation with the problem that it has often been equated with interventionist paranoia by government spokespersons and Mexican journalists, many of whom sense ulterior motives behind a façade of concern. Their feelings crystallized in the aftermath of the Camarena affair.

Washington's disgust over the kidnapping and murder was made abundantly clear through diplomatic channels, press conferences, news talk shows, and media interviews. What stunned the Mexicans and their governmental officials, however, was not Washington's critique but its decidedly public nature. This in turn touched the hypersensitive nerve of Mexican nationalism and turned a serious, regrettable event into a vitriolic diplomatic incident. All the old ghosts were hauled out and paraded, particularly those of American imperialism and demand for drugs. Is the death of one U.S. drug agent, queried the well-oiled Mexican press machine, the true reason behind your official outburst, or is it perhaps a pent-up response to our *dignidad*, our independent foreign policy, particularly in Central America? More to the point, are you really going to permit one regrettable event to spoil our otherwise amicable relations?[7]

The entire scenario surrounding Enrique Camarena's death is a microcosm of U.S.-Mexican narcopolitics. It also reflects three dimensions of America's security interests in Mexican drug trafficking, each is inseparable from the fundamental question of Mexico as a major source drug country during an era of systemwide crisis.

Narcocorruption

With rare exceptions, corruption has functioned for the health of Mexico's political system. Without it legions of Mexicans, from the mozo who marks one's bag at Nuevo Laredo's customs station to the worker who eventually installs one's telephone, would not earn a living. However, the López Portillo administration, Petrólcos Méxicanos (PEMEX), and *la droga* are notable exceptions to this rule of functionality. Each went far beyond the bounds of propriety, stealing or bribing enough to outrage the normally complacent citizenry. Each turned the Mexican against the government, seriously eroding its stability. One directly affects United States security interests, *narcocorrupción*.

It bears repeating that drug abuse is a monumental problem in the United States. Any habit that seriously impairs citizen health threatens America's security interests. One must also recall, first, that Mexico is perhaps the primary fount of illicit drugs on the U.S. market and, second, that the foundation of America's antidrug campaign is halting cultivation at the foreign source before the finished product enters the trafficking stream. By extension, the unprecedented narcocorruption in Mexico, without which the Mexican connection could not survive, becomes a security issue for Mexico and the United States. The greater the corruption, the greater Mexico's narcotics production. The greater the production, the greater the amount of drugs on the U.S. market and, concomitantly, the greater the corruption of American officials. If one reasons, as does the author, that drugs fuel Mexican corruption, one must likewise acknowledge the obvious: narcotics have undermined the integrity of American police and judicial officials to an unprecedented degree. Americans in all walks of life have belatedly come to appreciate Mexico's dilemma. If illegal activity corrupts, narcodollars corrupt absolutely--in Culiacán and New York City.

Narcoterror

Working from the premise that the unprecedented violence perpetrated by Mexican *traficantes* has become a bona fide threat to ordinary citizens and to Mexican national police and soldiers, one may hypothesize that narcoterror poses a serious challenge to Mexico's embattled political system. Given Mexico's vital importance to this country, narcoterror thus threatens U.S. national interests. Like corruption, drug-sponsored violence undermines Mexico's political stability. An unstable Mexico is, by definition, anathema to U.S. security.

A far more direct threat is clearly visible at the level of individual American citizens. Enrique Camarena was surely not the first official representative of the United States to fall victim to Mexico's narcoterrorists, nor will he be the last. It must not be forgotten that Camarena, like other DEA agents, was warned before he was murdered. He had threatened the interests of one of Mexico's most notorious trafficking organizations; he was instrumental in the multimillion dollar November, 1984 marijuana bust in Chihuahua. Camarena was used to send a blunt message to both Mexico and the United States: anyone challenging the authority of Mexico's narcomafia would be eliminated, their nationality notwithstanding. Similar examples of trafficker gall are becoming alarmingly commonplace in the United States. Witnesses are assassinated *a la Colombiana*: judges are threatened, even murdered. Honest citizens opposing narcogangs are bullied and brutally assaulted. Like Mexico, the United States is increasingly plagued by the "South American effect" of narcoterror.

A more hypothetical U.S. security concern may involve the Mexican military's role in antidrug activities. Of all the actors in Mexico's political drama, none is less understood than the military. Even experts acknowledge this. State Department narcotics analysts, in their fixation with the Procuraduría's airborne herbicide program, pay scant attention to the army's role in *la campaña*. Yet, the Mexican army and its commander, the secretary of defense, are key variables in Mexico's drug equation.

The army's raison d'être is maintaining internal order. Recent modernization and developments in Central America notwithstanding, the Mexican military is neither equipped nor trained as a national defense force. Its role, particularly in the countryside, is pacification. And it is in the *campo* that the army has honed its skills, not against system-threatening guerrillas, but by combatting drug cultivators and traffickers. Today the Mexican army's primary task is to rid Mexico's countryside of its drug curse. Some 25 thousand soldiers are "permanently" assigned to the antidrug effort. While perhaps exaggerated, that figure illustrates the extent of Mexico's drug problem and its importance to the government. It is also a reflection of the increased power of the army and its commander during Mexico's current hour of crisis.

Unlike his immediate predecessors, de la Madrid's Secretary of Defense, General Juan Arévalo Gardoqui, became a pivotal figure in Mexico's highly visible antidrug campaign. It was he, not Attorney General Sergio García Ramírez, who repeatedly bore good news about *la campaña*. It was Arévalo who, with amazing regularity, claimed the destruction of 80 percent of the poppy and marijuana plants in Mexico, always implying that the army accomplished the task. According to official Mexican statistics, for example, the army soldier manually destroyed approximately 38 percent more opium poppy hectares in 1984 and 1985 than did federal judicial police and their helicopter spray ships.

In lauding the military's antidrug record, General Arévalo never failed to praise the honesty of his men and the dedication of the president to the campaign. Miguel de la Madrid, in turn, was ever-effusive in his accolades for the general and his soldiers. This is hardly novel. Mexican presidents and secretaries of defense generally comprise mutual admiration societies. What was unusual under the de la Madrid administration is the focus on the military as the honest, dedicated phalanx of Mexico's *campaña antidroga* at the expense of the Procuraduría and its head, Sergio García Ramírez.

A dedicated and renowned criminologist, the attorney general appeared constantly on the defensive. Racked with drug-related scandals and reeling under vocal public criticism from the United States, García Ramírez saw his position as the legitimate head of Mexico's antidrug effort eroded by Arévalo Gardoqui and the army. The military, always crucial during times of crisis, increased its influence in the Mexican political process through a highly visible and positive image in the campaign against illicit narcotics. Any such change in Mexico's political balance of power at this stage becomes a U.S. security concern. The same holds true for Mexico's dominant political party.

Knowledgeable Mexicanists are virtually unanimous in their belief that U.S. security interests are best served by the continuation in power of the Partido Revolucionario Institucional (PRI). The PRI admittedly has its faults, a conspicuous reality unnecessary to elaborate in this chapter. But at this crucial juncture in Mexican history, it is clearly preferable to either the uncertainties of military rule or the unacceptable anti-American radicalism of a left-wing regime. Any development substantially enhancing the army's visibility and prestige at the expense of civilian authority, including a more prominent role in the program against illicit narcotics, must be carefully monitored by U.S. security analysts. The Mexican procuracy and its federal judicial police, despite their recent problems with corruption, are the most logical choice to lead *la campaña*. This holds true for Mexico, the United States, and the border that divides yet joins.

The Border

International borders are by their very nature hubs of smuggling activities. No frontier more clearly evidences a contraband ambience than the approximately two-thousand-mile artificial barrier between Mexico and the United States. Despite elaborate statutes in both countries, thousands of items and people illegally traverse the border daily. In the words of a Laredo customs agent: "Anything that doesn't cross this border illegally in one direction or the other at one time or another just hasn't been invented."

The impact of illicit drug trafficking is felt acutely along the U.S.-Mexico border area, and they are even more pronounced if one extends the line to include southern Florida. The border has been described as "penetrable almost at will," "completely out of control," a "porous sieve," and a "smuggler's dream." Despite increased personnel, the latest in detection/interdiction technology, and on-again-off-again, search-and-discourage operations, drug smuggling has increased alarmingly. With it have come turf battles among border law enforcement agencies and serious repercussions for border residents, including manifold increases in drug-related violence, corruption, and abuse. Narcotics traffic, more than any other issue, has strained traditionally friendly transboundary relations. All the while, control of day-to-day affairs has slipped from the hands of those who manage them best, the borderites themselves, into those who know the least about the area, federal bureaucrats. Causal relations aside, the deleterious effects of drug trafficking have changed the ambience of many border cities during this decade.

Most Americans are aware of the border's role as an illicit drug conduit. They are, however, essentially ignorant of its position as a springboard for illegal goods *into* Mexico. Hundreds of products, from stereo equipment to apples, are smuggled into Mexico daily from the United States. But only one *contrabandista* specializing in south-bound merchandise is of particular interest to U.S. and Mexican narcotics officials--the arms merchant.

Media accounts notwithstanding, Mexican *traficantes* seldom acquire weapons through barter, guns-for-dope swaps accounting for only a fraction of their supply. Sophisticated automatic weaponry is simply purchased with cash on the flourishing Mexican arms market. Efforts by the military to "depistolize" the countryside make good journalistic copy, but their impact on large clandestine arms caches has been minimal. Drug trafficker arsenals often surpass those of federal agents and army soldiers in both firepower and sophistication. It bears repeating that the foundation of narcoterror is lethal weaponry, most originally purchased or stolen in the United States then smuggled across the border into Mexico. For those who know the border well, it takes little imagination to envisage clandestine shipments of far more sophisticated and lethal cargoes.

Mexican observers are quick to point out that the United States should do more to combat this facet of the arms-drugs cycle by improving security on military bases where some of these weapons are stolen, enacting stricter arms control laws to curtail the legal purchase of guns in general and automatic rifles in particular, and better policing the internal flow of weapons, particularly along the U.S. side of the border, before they enter Mexico. Logic supports the Mexican reasoning. As illicit Mexican drugs must be controlled in the field, so too must illegal arms be controlled in the United States. Once either enters the contraband stream, the chances of it being intercepted are remote at best. More stringent gun control legislation thus appears to be in America's security interests in more ways than one.

The same holds true for more careful scrutiny of the banking industry on the U.S. side of the border. Contrary to most opinions emanating from Washington, large amounts of drug trafficking dollars are reinvested in Mexico. Note for example the impact of narcodollars on the legitimate economies of Guadalajara, Durango, Mazatlán, and Tijuana. The second largest outlet for illicit Mexican drug profits appears to be legitimate real estate and banks on the U.S. side of the border. This is not to claim that San Diego, El Paso, and Laredo banks are awash with Mexican drug money, but it is becoming increasingly clear that millions in narcodollars are being laundered in these institutions. It is equally obvious that the trafficker's Achilles' heel is most exposed during the laundering phase.

In this regard it is imperative that the Justice Department expand and accelerate its recent enforcement of banking regulations along the border. In so doing it will kill two drug birds with one stone. First, it will disrupt the Mexican-U.S. drug laundering nexus in border banks. Second, it will bring about a substantial repatriation of flight capital, because millions of the billions invested by Mexican *sacodólares* are either stolen from the government in one form or another or drug-tainted. Strict regulation of banking statutes would thus serve U.S. security interests by attacking a crucial link in the Mexican drug chain and by replenishing Mexico's ailing economy.

A final border problem is only indirectly related to narcotics, but it merits the utmost attention of American security analysts. If millions of illegal aliens, tons of illicit narcotics, and untold arms shipments can with relative impunity enter the United States and Mexico annually across the border, it would require little imagination to smuggle professional terrorists across the same porous frontier. Groups of illegal Libyans, for example, have already been deported from the Mexican interior. The question is, how many such potential terrorists are waiting to cross? How many have done so already? The prospects are truly sobering.

SUMMARY POLICY IMPLICATIONS

Narcotráfico is today the most diplomatically sensitive issue between Washington and Bolivia, Colombia, Peru, and Mexico. It has, in fact, become a bona fide threat to harmonious relations between Mexico and Washington. Illicit drugs thus raise several policy questions.

It must first be asked whether the United States does in fact have an international narcotics policy and, second, whether it also has such a policy towards Mexico. The answer is affirmative in both cases. U.S. international narcotics policy has displayed amazing continuity throughout most of this century. It consists of three primary components: eradication at the foreign source, interdiction in the source nation or en route to the U.S., and immobilization of major trafficking networks. At the binational level this translates: keep illicit Mexican drugs out of the United States through eradication, interdiction, and immobilization *in Mexico*! Washington has thus steered a constant course in search of a cure for the nation's drug abuse problem. Only in recent years has it seriously considered the drug ledger's demand side.

Mexico, along with Colombia, is the linchpin of America's international narcopolitics. It is demonstrably the most important country in the world to the State Department's Bureau of International Narcotics Matters. It is therefore unfortunate that U.S. drug policy with Mexico and U.S.-Mexican narcotics relations have been cyclical in nature, often unilateral, incident-prone, and highly acrimonious. *Narcotráfico's* impact on relations between the neighboring states has been decidedly negative as a result.

Since the late 1960s, Mexico-U.S. narcopolitics have been characterized by ebb-and-flow cycles, each determined without exception by America's drug scene and Washington's interpretation of Mexico's role therein. The relationship's tone depends on Mexico's share of the U.S. illicit drug market. The larger Mexico's share, the greater Washington's pressure. The greater the pressure, the more confrontational U.S.-Mexican narcopolitics and bilateral relations in general. Conversely, when market share indicators are favorable, so too are relations writ, small and large. This interrelationship has remained constant for many years, the nature of leadership in either country notwithstanding.

A second constant of U.S. narcopolitics with Mexico has been a propensity for unilateral decision making within a bilateral, cooperative framework. Washington generally pursued a cooperative approach during the "peaks" of the relationship. Consultation and mutual decision making typify harmonious times. But, when Mexico's share of America's drug market increases, or in the wake of unfortunate personal incidents, Washington tends to forgo cooperation and act unilaterally. While consistent with the prerogatives of an independent nation and generally effective in the short term, such unilateral actions do little in the long run to benefit Washington's narcopolitics, U.S.-Mexican relations, or America's security interests.

A third constant in the relationship involves personal incident or tragedy followed by diplomatic acrimony and deteriorating relations. During the last two decades this has included everything from the defaming of Mexico's national flag by a San Diego newspaper to the torture of one DEA agent in Mexico and murder of another. The result is remarkably similar in each unfortunate case: diplomatic acrimony and deteriorated narcopolitics.

It is particularly disconcerting from a policy viewpoint how little both nations have learned through the years, from incident after incident. Neither Washington nor Mexico has developed a strategy to minimize the diplomatic damage from such seemingly inevitable events. It is almost as if both sides, in a diplomatically macabre manner, seem to await such events for their cathartic effect. Highly illustrative of this cyclical, incident-prone relationship is the tragic saga of Enrique Camarena, the domestic and foreign policy implications of which continue to haunt relations between Washington and Mexico.

One of the first questions arising from a study of this cyclical, incident-marred relationship involves commitment: how serious is America's determination to solve its drug abuse problem, particularly given its proclaimed security implications? More pointedly for comparative purposes, how determined is its effort vis-à-vis Mexico's? To its credit, the Reagan administration budgeted more funds and assigned more personnel to its antidrug program than any of its predecessors. But considering the threat posed by the problem and its political impact, Reagan, along with Congress, was long on rhetoric and short on both dollars and deeds. The outcome is clear for all to see.

The overall results of Washington's international control program are indeed discouraging. Despite some tentatively encouraging trends, abuse figures are disappointing across the board. Of the three major illicit drugs, none is in short supply. The cocaine market, in particular, is glutted, and coke prices continue to fall. Mexico's role in America's drug scene has reached major status. As a result, critics and *curanderos* abound.

For Washington, the most logical U.S. policy option involves a balancing of priorities between supply and demand. It must place more emphasis on the problem's demand side. This need not mean neglecting the role of source countries such as Mexico, but it will clearly require far more funding, less rhetoric, and new ways of conceiving the nation's abuse problem. The Mexicans, along with a crescendo of voices from other source countries, have long reminded Americans of the glaringly obvious: *No hay tampolina sin piscina.* A second politically feasible option would couple demand reduction efforts with stepped-up law enforcement in the United States. Its backers argue for a tougher "get tough" approach to trafficker *and* user.

Mexican officials favored the Reagan administration's *in-country* law-and-order policies over those of previous governments. They have always prodded U.S. officials to "practice what they preach," to do unto their narcotics law breakers what they demand that the Mexican officials do unto theirs. They reason that if Washington couples a concerted demand reduction program with accelerated law enforcement efforts against grower, trafficker, and abuser, America's narcotics problem will be substantially reduced and with it the threat posed by drug abuse to the U.S. national interest. There would then be no reason for Washington's international politics of pressure regarding America's drug abuse problem.

As regards the two policy options, several caveats are in order. First, there can be no doubt regarding the demand side of the question. U.S. law enforcement officials themselves, particularly those along the border, are very pessimistic about the interdiction component. They reason correctly that personnel, equipment, and technology notwithstanding, demand must be reduced, for as long as the profit incentive remains so great, illicit drugs will traverse the frontier. While the suggestion of coupling demand reduction with stepped-up law enforcement is perhaps logical, it is also fraught with danger, particularly for Mexico and other Latin American source countries.

Such an approach would by definition result in greater emphasis on demand reduction and domestic law enforcement, but it would also involve greater emphasis on eradication, interdiction, and immobilization in source countries and far greater interdiction efforts along the border. Given the realities of civil liberties, criminal procedure, and Gramm-Rudman-Hollings, it is likely that "get tough" legislation in the United States, including the Anti-drug Abuse Act of 1988, will ultimately mean "get tough" with border traffickers and more stringent border inspections, not more arrests and convictions of small-scale marijuana growers and users. There simply are not enough night courts, jails, or prisons to accommodate them.

Assuming, as does the author, that U.S. drug policy will remain essentially intact under the Bush administration, what options, other than equal status for the demand component, will improve, particularly as regards the Mexican components. The first suggestion involves "narcorhetoric," which, like narco statistics, has a way of escalating out of control at the worst times in U.S.-Mexican relations. The program's rhetoric must be toned down. To note that corruption has seriously hampered Mexico's *campaña* is one thing, to call all Mexican officials "totally corrupt" is something else.

Stated goals and expectations for both countries should be reduced. American narcotics officials should set realistic goals and standards for their own programs and for Mexico's. In this regard, it is crucial that Americans deal with Mexicans and Mexican reality *as they are*, not as we might like them to be. The same holds true for Mexican officials, especially when it comes to such Americanisms as "free press," "separation of powers," and "federalism."

Serious attention must be given to the near and distant future of the drug phenomenon. Both governments must plan ahead, devising strategies for changing drug scenarios. The U.S. scene has always been marked by fluctuations and new problems. Cocaine, today's major issue, was ten years ago a problem on the horizon, while crack was unheard of. Marijuana used to be deemed a "soft drug"; today's *sinsemilla* is assuredly "two-toke dope." Heroin maintenance was once a feasible alternative; the British experiment, "black tar," and "China white" render it unworthy of emulation.

Mexico's drug scene is also changing. Abuse was once a problem for a minority of poor *campesinos* and slum dwellers. Today, official denials aside, it is a serious, escalating problem, particularly in the use of inhalants in the nation's sprawling urban ghettos. More to the point from a political perspective, drugs now pose an undeniable threat to the middle class, the elite, and their children. Virtually no cocaine was smuggled through the country in the 1970s; today tons are seized annually. If, through some miracle, American demand declines appreciably, what would become of the in-country surplus? The real life tragedies of Colombia, Peru, Bolivia, and Pakistan are undeniable.

From a national interest perspective, the United States should place the issues of illicit Mexican drugs and U.S.-Mexico narcopolitics in proper perspective. To do this, Washington must first assess the relative importance of Mexico in that national interest equation. If it decides that Mexico is in deed, as well as word, crucial to American interests and that drugs play an important part in that relationship, the U.S. should seriously consider the following policy initiatives.

Washington should first begin by thoroughly and impassionately evaluating the current and near future American drug abuse scenario. It must then act immediately to address the problem's root, domestic demand. Third, it should seek a more stable, less confrontational, less acrimonious narcopolitical relationship with Mexico. And Mexico must reciprocate. Together the two nations must find ways to manage the seemingly inevitable narcocrises that prove so damaging to binational relations in general and narcopolitics in particular. These steps may be taken without fundamentally altering Washington's international narcotics control strategy. Its core components need not be changed. Ultimately, however, demand reduction must be given equal status.

Finally, as part of a more harmonious atmosphere, the U.S. should abandon its unilateral policy tendencies, including the sporadic Operation Intercept syndrome. Numerous mechanisms exist for consultation on such matters. And Mexico should be consulted. If it refuses, for whatever reasons, to cooperate, that is Mexico's prerogative. At least it will have been consulted. It is during such talks that Washington may, if it chooses, demand greater cooperation. Each side would then know where the other stands. There would be no surprise actions.

Meanwhile, as one looks beyond the Mexican scene and analyzes the dynamics of cultivation, trafficking, and abuse in the Americas as a whole, the more one comes to realize that the drug-related security interests of the United States lie only indirectly in Peru, Bolivia, Colombia, and Mexico. The cardinal drug threat to American security is glaringly obvious: it is our own enormous substance abuse problem right here at home. For many reasons we Americans have become the world's leading escape artists. We get away from the hassle. By legal prescription or clandestine buy, we get high by the millions every day of the week. We drink booze, smoke pot, snort coke, shoot heroin, and pop pills at a truly staggering rate.

It matters not what came first, the chicken of demand or the egg of production. America's enormous demand for drugs is either one or both, spawning everything from human degradation to prime time television series. Until that craving for illicit and licit drugs is substantially reduced, substance abuse will continue to be a prodigious problem for American society and an increasingly important security issue for the U.S. government.

4

The New Hundred Years War?: U.S. National Security and the War on Drugs in Latin America
Bruce Michael Bagley

INTRODUCTION

No president spoke out more against drugs than President Reagan. No Administration signed more antidrug treaties or spent more money to stem the flow drugs into this country. But as the Reagan years drew to a close, American law enforcement officials acknowledged that they were losing ground in the fight against a new generation of drug smugglers who have the business skill--and capital--to threaten not only the streets of America but even the stability of countries long friendly to the United States.[1]

When President Reagan declared his "War" on drugs in the early 1980s, the United States entered a new era of drug diplomacy in its foreign policy toward Latin America. Control of drug trafficking currently ranks higher than immigration, foreign debt, and communist expansion in Central America as a priority issues in U.S.-Latin American relations. In a March 1988 *New York Times*/CBS News Poll, 48 percent of the respondents indicated that drug trafficking was the most important foreign policy issue facing the nation versus 22 percent for Central America, 13 percent for arms control, 9 percent for terrorism, and 4 percent for Palestinian unrest. Equally revealing, when asked whether it was more important to put a stop to Central American leaders' drug trafficking or to support them against communism, 63 percent expressed the belief that stopping drug dealing was the top priority while only 21 percent felt that stopping communism was more important.[2]

Various factors combined during 1988 to renew concern in the United States about drugs. The exploding crack cocaine epidemic and accompanying increases in drug-related violence and deaths in many American cities was one reason. The attendant rise in media coverage clearly fanned public consciousness. The prominence given to drugs by First Lady Nancy Reagan's "Just Say No" campaign and by Democratic candidate Jesse Jackson during the 1988 presidential campaign lent additional visibility to the issue and prompted many other politicians from both parties to "get tough" on the drug question. The absence of other major issues in the campaign--the U.S. confronted no immediate crises, either domestically or internationally--produced an "issue vacuum" which the drug debate partially filled. The highly publicized arrest, extradition and trial of drug lord Carlos Lehder; the February arrest and subsequent release of another Colombian trafficker, Jorge Ochoa; the indictment against Panamanian strongman Manuel Antonio Noriega handed down by U.S. courts and his on-going defiance of Washington; the "deportation-kidnapping" of Honduran cocaine boss, Juan Ramón Matta Ballesteros, and the ensuing anti-American riots in Honduras; all served to keep public and press attention fixed on the issue as well. Finally, growing awareness in U.S. and Latin American political circles about the destabilizing potential of drug traffickers in Latin America converted drugs into a national security issue in the United States and throughout the hemisphere.[3]

The objective of this chapter is to assess the current status and future prospects of the U.S. "war on drugs" in Latin America. It begins with a brief overview of the scope of the U.S.-Latin American drug trade from both supply and demand sides. The key components of Washington's War on Drugs as formalized in the 1986 Antidrug Abuse Act are then summarized, and the major problems inhibiting effective implementation of U.S. antidrug policies are analyzed. The essay concludes with a review of the principal policy options presently available to the United States in the campaign against drug trafficking.

SCOPE OF THE U.S.-LATIN AMERICAN DRUG TRADE

Supply

Seven Latin American or Caribbean countries account for the bulk of the illegal marijuana, cocaine and heroin smuggled into the United States each year from the Western Hemisphere. Some 90 percent of all the imported marijuana that enters the U.S. market (perhaps 11,650 tons in 1986) originates in one of four Caribbean Basin countries: Mexico (35-40 percent); Colombia (20-25 percent); Jamaica (10-15 percent); or Belize (5-10 percent). The United States itself produces an additional 2,100 tons annually.[4]

Virtually all the cocaine (perhaps 120 tons in 1987) is cultivated in three South America nations: Peru (50 percent); Bolivia (40-45 percent); and Colombia (5-10 percent). Colombia emerged in the mid-1970s as the principal refining country and for more than a decade has controlled roughly 75 percent of all the refined cocaine exported from the Andean region to the United States. These same three countries, again with Colombia in the lead, are also believed to have smuggled approximately 35 tons of cocaine to Western Europe in 1987. In the last three years, several other South American countries -- Venezuela, Brazil, Ecuador, Paraguay and Argentina-- have also surfaced as coca producers, although still on a relatively small scale. This has come about, in large part, because stepped-up U.S. and Latin American enforcement operations have driven some grower-dealers to search for cheaper and safer alternatives for cultivation and processing outside the traditional coca-growing regions.[5]

Mexico is the only heroin producing country in Latin America. About 39 percent of the estimated 6.45 metric tons of heroin smuggled into the United States in 1986 were grown in Mexico; of the rest, 50 percent came from the Golden Crescent (especially Pakistan, the world's largest producer) and the Golden Triangle (especially Burma).

Demand

There are approximately 20 to 25 million marijuana smokers in the United States, 5.8 million regular users of cocaine and 0.5 million heroin addicts.[6] The wholesale value of all illegal drugs smuggled into the United States in 1986 was around $25 billion. At retail or street prices, the U.S. public may spend as much as $150 billion on illicit drugs a year. The profit potential is obviously immense at all levels of the industry, although some 90 percent of the value-added is realized in the distribution process once the drugs have been brought into the United States. Only 8 to 10 percent of the profits accrue to the Latin American source and transit countries. How deeply the major trafficking organizations penetrate and profit from the distribution chain below the wholesale level is not known, but a large-scale transnational criminal organization like the Medellín Cartel in Colombia, for example, probably grosses between $4 and 6 billion annually in the cocaine trade, less than half of which is repatriated.

THE U.S. WAR ON DRUGS

In 1986, after the highly publicized death of basketball star Len Bias from a cocaine overdose, U.S. politicians from both parties jumped on the antidrug bandwagon in the months before the November elections and competed ferociously among themselves to see who could propose the "toughest" drug policies. Caught up in this pre-election, antidrug frenzy, in October the U.S. Congress passed, and President Reagan signed into law, the Antidrug Abuse Act of 1986. Without question, this new law was the most comprehensive effort in modern U.S. history to lower domestic demand for illegal drugs and to reduce the flow of narcotics from the Third World into the United States.

The Act included provisions designed to attack the drug problem on a variety of fronts simultaneously: tougher enforcement in U.S. cities, more and earlier education in the schools, intensified testing in the work place, expanded treatment and rehabilitation programs for users, greater attention to prevention in the home and community, lengthier prison sentences for traffickers, increased federal support for state enforcement efforts, augmented interdiction at the border, and additional resources for eradication, crop substitution and enforcement programs abroad. To finance their proposed full-scale assault against America's drug epidemic, U.S.

lawmakers authorized the Executive to spend an extra $1.7 billion in 1987, in addition to the $2.2 billion previously authorized.[7]

From Fiscal Year (FY) 1981 to FY 1988 authorized federal spending on drug control more than tripled, rising from $1.2 to 3.9 billion. Anti-smuggling funds were increased to $1.37 billion in FY 1987 (35 percent of the total federal drug abuse budget). The U.S. military was also ordered to become more active in the war effort in support of civilian enforcement programs. A General Accounting Office (GAO) report released in June 1987 indicated that the total cost of the U.S. Defense Department's interdiction activities rose from an insignificant $4.9 million in FY 1982 to "an estimated $387 million in fiscal 1987, mostly as a result of direct appropriations in the 1986 antidrug law."[8]

The direction of U.S. aid flows reflect the priority that the Reagan Administration has given to financing the war against drugs during his eight years in office. Between FY 1980 and FY 1987 U.S. allocations for overseas narcotics control efforts more than tripled, surging from some $40 million to over $200 million annually. Congress also moved to tie U.S. foreign aid to country performance in the drug production and trafficking areas. For instance, sanctions were imposed on Bolivia in 1986 and 1987, mainly because Bolivia had not made a serious effort to eradicate its coca crop. In 1988, the Reagan Administration, under congressional pressure, decertified General Noriega and Panama. In addition, several U.S. congressmen initiated efforts to decertify Mexico, Bolivia, Peru, Paraguay, and the Bahamas, despite President Reagan's contention that such punitive measures would damage U.S. relations with those countries and inhibit future cooperative efforts between them and the United States in the war against drug trafficking.[9]

As the Reagan Administration and the U.S. Congress have gotten "tougher" with Latin American source country governments, the U.S."drug warriors" have been able to point to some impressive victories resulting from their increased activities. Cocaine seizures, for example, rose from 2 tons in 1981 to 27 tons in 1986, with local and state enforcement agencies capturing similar amounts. Federal agents also captured a half ton of heroin, 9 tons of hashish, and 1,106 tons of marijuana in the same year. In May 1987 the Drug Enforcement Administration (DEA) completed a three-year, undercover drug enforcement operation (the largest such program in federal drug enforcement history). Dubbed Operation Pisces, this effort resulted in the confiscation of over 19,000 pounds of cocaine worth some $270 million at U.S. wholesale prices. Likewise, Operation Alliance--a multi-agency task force created in 1986 and based in El Paso, Texas--intended to curtail the flow of drugs across the U.S.-Mexican border, reported that seizures of marijuana in FY 1987 doubled the FY 1986 total while cocaine confiscations went up by 400 percent. Moreover, arrests on drug charges rose steeply and average prison sentences became significantly longer.[10]

WHY U.S. POLICIES HAVE NOT WORKED

Despite the increases in resources, manpower, drug seizures, and arrests, however, no one in the U.S. government can realistically claim that the war on drugs is being won. To the contrary, the available evidence indicates that "...worldwide production of illicit opium, coca leaf and cannabis is still many times the amount currently consumed by drug abusers."[11] U.S. narcotics experts believe that interdiction programs catch only 3 percent of marijuana and 10 percent of cocaine imports; thus higher 1987 drug confiscation statistics probably reflect the reality that more rather than less drugs are being smuggled in to the United States. This conclusion is strengthened by the observation that between 1981 and 1988 the price of a kilogram of pure cocaine fell from about $60,000 to under $10,000. The widespread availability of cocaine and other drugs in the United States, the dramatic growth of the crack epidemic, and the notorious expansion of drug-related crime and violence, especially among inner-city teenage gangs, also suggest that America's drug plague is getting worse. However, the most serious accusation is not that the U.S. government is losing the war on drugs, but that the Reagan Administration never really launched a full-scale attack. U.S. policies have been plagued by inadequate resources, lack of bureaucratic coordination, and inconsistent leadership. They have also frequently been subordinated to other U.S. foreign policy interests and priorities, especially security issues. Panama is only one of the most recent examples.

Inadequate Resources

Just three months after signing the 1986 antidrug statute, President Reagan submitted his fiscal 1988 budget in which he proposed to eliminate $1 billion from the FY 1988 drug allocations. Among the key cuts: $225 million from state and local enforcement; half the funds for drug treatment; and $400 million out of drug education (down from $500 to $100 million). Although some protests were voiced by congressional leaders, in practice Congress proved willing to restore only a small portion of Reagan's cutbacks. The Administration's decision not to request reauthorization in FY 1989 for $1 billion in federal funding for local law enforcement, education and rehabilitation programs clearly undermined the war on drugs, both fiscally and psychologically. Given that President Reagan had already lowered federal spending on drug treatment and prevention from $200 million in 1982 to $126 million in 1986, and then deliberately delayed FY 1987 disbursements until the end of the fiscal year, by 1988 many governors, mayors and local officials were frustrated and confused about Washington's real priorities. As Congressman Charles Rangel (D-NY) put it, "these cuts seriously call into question the Administration's commitment to an effective national drug abuse strategy."[12]

Lack of Coordination and Leadership

In 1984 President Reagan created the National Drug Enforcement Policy Board to centralize U.S. government antidrug programs. In March 1987 he broadened the board's authority to include not only enforcement but also prevention, education and treatment activities as well. Headed by Attorney General Edwin Meese and Health and Human Services Secretary Otis Bowen, the seventeen members of the board include all cabinet officers and representatives from the Central Intelligence Agency (CIA), Office of Management and Budget(OMB) and the Vice President's office.

Despite Reagan's formal bureaucratic reorganization, however, separate reports by the GAO and the House Committee on Government Operations in 1987 found that responsibility for U.S. drug policy remains "diffuse and overlapping".[13] The House report was especially critical of the Board's inability to resolve long-simmering interagency "turf battles" and its delayed implementation of mandated studies and programs. One notable example of this problem is the Coast Guard. Although one of its primary missions is to interdict drugs smuggled into the United States, in 1988 the Coast Guard estimated that it would conduct 55 percent fewer patrols than in 1987 as a result of congressionally-mandated cuts of $100 million from its 1988 budget.[14]

For its part, the Pentagon has systematically expressed its reluctance to get involved in the war on drugs, in part because of concern that the drug effort would divert funding away from its central military mission of defending U.S. interests abroad, and in part out of concern that an expanded military role might expose the U.S. armed forces to corrupting influences.[15] Moreover, although the military sporadically supported antidrug operations by Customs and the Coast Guard since 1971, and assumed a more active role since 1981, when Congress revised the Posse Comitatus Act of 1878 to permit military personnel to get involved in law enforcement, the accumulated evidence over the years indicates that military efforts "have been only marginally effective."[16]

Reflecting the pressures at work in Congress during an election year, however, in May 1988, the Senate approved a new military budget that gave the armed forces a much broader role in the antidrug war in spite of the military high command's misgivings. The House had earlier gone even farther, passing a bill that required President Reagan to order the military to "seal the borders to drug smugglers" and to "substantially halt" the flow of illegal narcotics into the United States within forty-five days. The discrepancies between these two bills will have to be reconciled by a Senate-House conference committee.[17]

In the face of mounting criticism, Attorney General Edwin Meese has staunchly defended the Reagan Administration's conduct of the war on drugs arguing that "you have seen more progress and you have more cooperative activity taking place now than you have ever had in the history of the government."[18] Nonetheless, various congressmen have begun to agitate for the appointment of a drug "czar" with cabinet-level powers and direct access to the President in order to resolve interagency disputes and better coordinate the federal drug bureaucracy.[19] According to Senate Judiciary Chairman, Joseph Biden (D-Del.) who introduced a bill creating such a position in 1987: "There will never be a war on drugs until we have a full-time, top-level commander."[20] The Reagan Administration has, however, consistently opposed any such move on the grounds that it is more effective "...to let administrators work out policy disputes rather than impose decisions from above" because they are the ones "...who know what is happening out there."[21]

Clashes of Interests and Policy Priorities

Despite the provisions of the 1986 antidrug law requiring the U.S. president to decertify drug-producing and drug-transiting countries that fail to cooperate fully with U.S. authorities, President Reagan has never used his powers to punish a close U.S. ally. In 1988, the Reagan Administration decertified only four nations--Iran, Syria, Afghanistan and Panama--none of which were recipients of U.S. economic or military assistance. Strategically important Turkey is not even mentioned on the State Department's list even though the DEA classifies it as a major heroin-transiting country. In the Asian heroin-producing countries, most of which share borders with Communist nations, the struggle against Communist expansion has always been given diplomatic priority over the antidrug war. It is doubtful that the United States would ever impose sanctions on Pakistan, even though that country is a major source of heroin, or on the Afghan "freedom fighters," despite their deep involvement in opium cultivation and transport. Indeed, when President Reagan met with a group of Afghan guerrilla leaders at the White House in November 1987, he reportedly never broached the topic of drugs with them.[22]

In Latin America, too, the war on drugs has often been subordinated to higher priority U.S. security concerns. Panama, Honduras, the Contras and Jamaica are examples. Both the Carter and the Reagan Administrations tolerated Noriega for years because he was a useful "asset", despite growing evidence that he was involved in the drug trade.[23] U.S. intelligence sources linked General Noriega to drug trafficking as early as 1972. A secret 1985 study written by the U.S. Army's Southern Command charged the Panamanian Defense Forces with involvement in the narcotics trade. According to former National Security Council Economist Norman Bailey the State Department's attitude was "luke warm", the Pentagon did not want to "rock the boat," and the CIA actively opposed doing anything: "He's an important asset."[24]

In Central America, the U.S.-backed Contras have repeatedly been accused of involvement in drug trafficking, although no hard evidence implicating the principal Contra organization, (the Fuerzas Democráticas Nicaraguenses, FDN), has ever been made public. The CIA did have suspicions that other Contra factions may have been involved but did not pursue them aggressively because of the Reagan Administration's heavy commitment to the Contra movement. In contrast, with less-than-conclusive evidence, Washington has repeatedly accused the highest levels of the Sandinista government of active participation in the drug trade.

As with the Contras, numerous allegations of Honduran military involvement in the narcotics trade have surfaced in recent years. A DEA agent based in Honduras between 1981 and 1983 reported that Honduran army and navy officers were involved in the transshipment of drugs through Honduran territory and in the protection of drug traffickers. DEA Chief

John Lawn later explained that the evidence was too "weak" to merit investigation. The DEA office in Honduras was finally closed in 1983 because it had not been "productive". According to one Reagan Administration official: "It wasn't that there was a coverup. It's that people knew certain questions shouldn't be asked."[25]

DRUG TRAFFICKING AND U.S.-LATIN AMERICAN RELATIONS

In practice, American drug diplomacy has achieved little besides raising levels of friction in U.S. relations with Latin America during the 1980s. "There has been too much pressure and too few incentives, too much fingerpointing and too little cooperation."[26] Washington has neither provided Latin American governments with the economic or technical wherewithal required to combat drug trafficking nor developed a coherent drug-fighting strategy in the region.

Adequate resources are the *sine qua non* of any effective drug-control program. While billions have been spent (or misspent) at home, U.S. drug-control expenditures annually in the Andean coca-producing countries total only $40-50 million. Perhaps another $20-30 million is put up by the countries themselves, principally Colombia. The cocaine industry earns a conservatively estimated $3 billion a year in U.S. wholesale markets alone and employs close to a million people (including coca farmers and laborers). Furthermore, by equally conservative calculations, the cocaine trade returns between $1 billion and $1.5 billion a year to the Andean economies. These resources allow the drug lords to buy a lot of protection--firepower, fast aircraft and boats, informants and intelligence networks, and compliant government officials.[27]

There is now widespread consensus in Latin America that the United States must curb demand for drugs at home. If the history of alcohol and tobacco is any indicator, however, it is sure to be a lengthy process and possibly a quixotic one. Meanwhile, the cocaine industry has become a serious political threat to various governments in South America. For example, Colombia's Medellín Cartel has, for all practical purposes, demanded veto power over national policy on drugs, especially with regard to extradition to the United States, and it backed its demands with a campaign of kidnapping, extortion and murder.[28]

Colombia and Mexico are cornerstones of the U.S. war on drugs in Latin America. Despite some achievements (like Mexico's successful but short-lived antidrug campaign of the 1970s, herbicide spraying of marijuana in Colombia in the 1980s, and Colombia's extradition of kingpin Carlos Lehder), however, there have also been multiple setbacks such as the suborned release of drug baron Jorge Ochoa after only a month in jail. U.S.-Colombian and U.S.-Mexican drug diplomacy has been cyclical, unilateral, and incident-prone. Drug trafficking has repeatedly surfaced as an acrimonious issue between Washington and these countries at least since the early 1970s. In practice, this "ebb-and-flow pattern" has been determined by Washington's perceptions of these countries' roles in the U.S. drug trade. In other words, "the tone of bilateral relations has depended on the share of the U.S. illicit drug market filled by each country. The larger the share, the greater Washington's pressure and more confrontational bilateral relations in general; conversely, when market share indicators are favorable, so too are relations writ small and large."[29]

U.S. policy toward Colombia provides a particularly revealing case study of the inconsistencies in the current U.S. war on drugs in Latin America. One of the most glaring deficiencies of the current U.S. strategy is the tendency toward non-consultative, unilateral decision-making within a bilateral or multilateral consultative framework. Typically, Washington has pursued a cooperative strategy during the "peaks" of its dealings with Colombia. But during the "valleys" in the relationship, those periods when Colombia's share of America's drug market increases, during electoral campaigns, or in the wake of dramatic incidents, Washington frequently abandons its cooperative approach and acts unilaterally without consulting or even warning Bogotá. In short, during "times of exasperation over perceived Colombian inaction, American officials--all too often those not directly involved in the day-to-day antidrug program--shift to a go-it-alone and damn-the-torpedoes mode."[30] While consistent with the sovereign rights of an independent nation and, at least at times, effective in the short term, in the long run such an approach probably reduces the chances for bilateral cooperation in Washington's drug war, and thus weakens rather than strengthens U.S. national security.

From a policy perspective, it is astonishing how little has been learned by either party in this "peak and valley" relationship. Neither the U.S. nor the Colombian government has developed a strategy to anticipate, much less resolve, these crises. "Sequentially, the pattern is roughly as follows: worsening narcorelations, unilateral American initiative and/or damaging incident, charge-countercharge, spillover into relations in general, escalating rhetoric from officials and media, mediation by cooler heads, binational conferences followed by words of praise for one side by the other, and improved cooperative efforts."[31] Then, the cycle is repeated again.

President Reagan has unquestionably assigned more financial and human resources to antidrug programs than any of his predecessors. But given the scope of the drug trafficking problem, the U.S. response under President Reagan has clearly been inadequate. In a very real sense, the Colombian government has been drafted to man the front lines of the drug war without the proper resources, training or equipment. The results have been fatal for many Colombian officials and debilitating for the political system as a whole. Yet, the U.S. government continues to insist that Colombia must take on the drug lords, no matter what the costs. According to Francisco Bernal, head of Colombia's Narcotic's Bureau within the office of the Attorney General: "We're being left to fight this war alone. We're supplying the dead, the country is being destabilized and what help are we getting?" [32] Even President Virgilio Barco, who during the first two years of his government supported a crack-down on Colombia's drug traffickers, has publicly expressed concern that Colombia is unfairly "sacrificing" more than other nations.[33]

Many Colombians are incensed by what they consider to be the U.S. government's myopic obsession with extradition. In June 1987, intimidated by violent reprisals ordered by the Medellín Cartel, the Colombian Supreme Court ruled the 1979 U.S.-Colombian extradition treaty to be unconstitutional on procedural grounds. Irritated by this decision and irate about the December 30, 1987, release from jail of Cartel kingpin Jorge Ochoa, Washington ordered sanctions against Colombia, including lengthy customs checks for travelers and products arriving from Colombia. These actions prompted bitter complaints from Colombians, fueled rising nationalist and anti-American resentments, and led many Colombians (both in and out of the government) to conclude that U.S. authorities neither understood the country's precarious situation nor cared that the antidrug war was undermining Colombia "both materially and morally."[34]

Although the Reagan Administration continued to insist that extraditions were an essential antidrug weapon, by early 1988, it had become clear that there was little political or public support in Colombia for a renewal of extraditions. In May, Justice Minister Enrique Low Mutra announced that the Barco government was studying the possibility of repudiating the 1979 treaty unilaterally.[35] U.S. sanctions backfired in Colombia and prompted the Barco government to emphasize the need for a multilateral rather than a purely bilateral approach to the drug trafficking problem.

OPTIONS

To date, the results of Washington's antidrug crusade have been disappointing to say the least. Despite some encouraging signs that drug use in the United States may be tapering off or even declining, drug trafficking remains the fastest growing industry in the world.[36] The consuming population is huge. Total cultivated acreage has continues to expand. New areas and countries are constantly added to the list of producing or transiting nations. The violence, corruption, and destabilization associated with the drug trade continue to increase despite intensified enforcement efforts. And cooperation with key countries like Colombia and Mexico appears to be declining.

What is to be done? One major U.S. tactical option might be to finance mobilization of Latin America's drug-fighting capabilities. The United States could provide source countries with the billions annually required to establish effective control over drug-producing areas--many of which are "occupied" by hostile guerrilla forces or ruthless multinational "mafia" organizations. In practice, this option would require more firepower, helicopters, communications equipment, and intelligence support. In addition, producing countries could be given more advanced technologies for combating the narcotics industries via beefed-up bilateral and multilateral aid programs: herbicides for spraying, radar systems to track the movement of drug smugglers' aircraft, modern anti-aircraft weapons, electronic devices to bug and jam traffickers' communications, and heat-seeking equipment to detect drug laboratories. In many Latin American countries, more sophisticated security systems for top government officials, judges, and witnesses would have to be part of the package. Such escalation, of course, cannot take place unilaterally; politically difficult institutional reforms would have to be made in drug-producing and transiting countries to enable them to cooperate in a reciprocal fashion.[37]

A second U.S. tactical option might be to "Americanize" its antidrug operations in Latin America, which would entail the U.S. government assuming drug enforcement functions source countries do not or cannot perform, if those countries consent. Models of Americanization are the extradition and trial of Colombian drug dealers in U.S. courts and the U.S. Army operation against cocaine laboratories in Bolivia in the summer of 1986 (known as Operation Blast Furnace). The effectiveness of the Americanization model is, however, inherently limited. Operation Blast Furnace paralyzed Bolivia's cocaine industry for a few months, but the introduction of U.S. forces undermined the popularity and nationalist credentials of President Paz Estenssoro's government, was condemned by virtually all factions on Bolivia's political spectrum, and was rejected by most other Latin American countries, including Colombia and Mexico. Extradition is also of limited use. There is no shortage of new aspirants to fill the shoes of extradited drug lords. Moreover, in Colombia, as the result of a successful drug mafia campaign of intimidation and violence that has immobilized the judicial system, extradition has been precluded as an option by the nation's supreme court. Americanization is, therefore, a risky, potentially counterproductive approach that should be applied only under extraordinary circumstances.[38]

A third U.S. option might be to support Latin American governments' efforts to come up with viable economic alternatives to the drug trade. The real costs of drug enforcement involve much more than merely parachuting men and equipment in to raid laboratories and eradicate marijuana, opium, or coca fields. The United States could make a major contribution by helping the economically depressed Latin American nations to provide crop- and income-substitution programs for drug farmers. It could help open new economic opportunities by lowering import barriers for legitimate exports--textiles, sugar, coffee, flowers, and so forth--and by extending the Caribbean Basin Initiative (CBI) system to all South American governments willing to undertake serious antidrug campaigns. It could also alleviate the crushing burden of Latin American debt by taking the lead in devising new formulas of debt relief. Unquestionably, a renewal of economic development in the region is an essential component of any successful, long-term effort to reduce drug trafficking.[39]

A fourth, radically different tactical option would be to abandon the war against drugs and move instead to legalize, or at least decriminalize, drug consumption. Advocates of this option often compare current antidrug policies in the United States and abroad with previous U.S. efforts to prohibit alcohol consumption and predict that the suppression of drug use is likely to be no more successful than was prohibition. "Prohibition of alcohol in the 1920s failed because it proved impossible to stop people from drinking. Our 70 year effort at prohibition of marijuana, cocaine and heroin has also failed. Tens of millions of Americans...have broken the laws against drugs. Preserving laws that are so widely flouted undermines respect for all laws."[40]

Proponents of legalization or decriminalization claim that a distinction should be made between the public health problems caused by drug abuse and the violence and criminality that surround the drug trade simply because it is illegal. They do not condone or encourage drug use; they believe that the best way to curtail drug trafficking is to treat drugs as a public health problem rather than a criminal one. It would be possible to remove the clandestine profits from the drug trade, eliminating the motives of criminal gangs to get involved in the trade, corrupt police and judges, and kill. It would also be possible for the state to control quality and lower sale prices, thereby eliminating the need for users to engage in criminal activity--stealing, muggings, murders--to gain access. Federal, state, and local governments spend approximately $8 billion annually on law enforcement and additional billions on courts, prisons, and prisoner maintenance (one-third of all federal prisoners are in jail for drug-related crimes). Such expenditures could be greatly reduced if drugs were legalized or decriminalized. Moreover, the state could tax the sale of drugs, thereby earning billions in revenue to finance state programs in drug education, prevention, and rehabilitation.[41]

Advocates of legalization often express concern about the implications for civil liberties of an intensified drug war in the United States and abroad: "legalization would remove a severe threat to individual freedom that is posed by widespread drug searches, demands for wholesale testing and the pending use of the military to enforce drug laws."[42]

Those favoring legalization or decriminalization also contend that such policies improve U.S. relations with key Latin American countries like Mexico and Colombia, where "futile" U.S. pressures to rein in drug traffickers at any cost have already seriously damaged strategically important bilateral relationships and undermined fragile democratic institutions throughout the region.

There is, of course, a foreseeable downside to legalization. Even more than with alcohol and tobacco, many Americans consider the idea of legalizing drug use to be morally repugnant. Drug abuse may increase if drugs are legalized--implying additional public health problems--although by how much is not known. Addiction rates, job- and driver-related accidents, worker productivity losses, and medical treatment costs could rise as well. There would undoubtedly be many practical problems in setting up a distribution system for drugs.

Without downplaying such problems, proponents of legalization point out that many of these costs of drug abuse are already present, although often hidden or ignored by the clandestine nature of drug use in contemporary society. They certainly recognize that legalization or decriminalization would be no panacea, but emphasize that current antidrug policies based on eradication, substitution, interdiction, and enforcement have not eliminated drug abuse and are unlikely to do so in the future. Their central point is that the public health and safety aspects of drug abuse can and should be separated from the violence and criminality arising from illegality. Logical or not, however, it is abundantly clear that political winds in the United States are not blowing in favor of legalization; hence this option, at least for the time being, does not appear a viable or realistic. Unless the United

States moves at some point towards legalization, no country in Latin America will be in a position to do so without incurring severe sanctions from Washington.

CONCLUSION

If the legalization option is set aside on grounds that it is not politically viable to destroy or even dent the power of drug traffickers, Latin American countries will need substantial additional assistance from the United States. Unfortunately, Washington's political climate presently seems to be shifting in the other direction. Congress has reduced American economic and military assistance around the world. Many Congresspersons and commentators argue that Washington should demonstrate its "commitment" to the war on drugs by decertifying and punishing Latin American source and transiting countries if they fail to control drug trafficking. It is rarely recognized that, in general, these countries need inducements and not sanctions.

There can be no doubt that the United States needs to rein in demand more effectively for any real success in the war against drugs. As long as the profits remain so great, illicit drugs will be smuggled into the United States. It is also crucial to recognize that linking demand reduction with stepped-up law enforcement at home and abroad, although perhaps logical from the U.S. perspective, is also fraught with danger, particularly for source countries. Such a policy would likely put greater emphasis on demand reduction and domestic law enforcement in the United States, but in all probability, it would also involve at least as much, and possibly more, emphasis on source country governments. Given the realities of U.S. civil liberties, judicial safeguards, and budgetary constraints, "get tough" legislation in the United States will probably mean "get tough" with Latin American and Caribbean governments that do not fully meet U.S. expectations and demands.[43]

Assuming basic continuity in current U.S. antidrug policies--and there are no signs of fundamental change, regardless of controls the White House or Congress--what options are available for its improvement? One potentially fruitful change would be to employ less rhetoric and more diplomacy, which might permit greater U.S. cooperation with the very Latin American countries from whom active support is most needed.

A parallel reduction in stated goals and expectations would be prudent. American drug officials should establish more realistic objectives and standards for their own antidrug programs and for other nations in the region. In this regard, it is crucial that American policy makers recognize that they are dealing with Latin American realities as they are, not as they might wish them to be.

Serious attention must also be given to the medium- and long-term future of the drug phenomenon. U.S. and Latin American leaders must anticipate and plan for a changing drug. The major issue in 1988 was cocaine, especially its derivative, crack. Ten years ago, cocaine was a problem on the horizon; crack was unknown. The principal challenge for

U.S. drug warriors is developing a viable, long-run strategy for both the demand and supply sides, then implementing it consistently. This will necessitate significantly higher levels of U.S. funding both domestically and internationally and sustained efforts to cooperating with Latin Americans. The war on drugs is nowhere close to that goal yet, and it is unclear whether Washington, the American people, or Latin Americans possess either the resources or the political will to reach it. Without such commitments the United States may win some battles from time to time but will almost certainly continue to lose the war.

Postscript: The Omnibus Drug Act of 1988

In late October 1988, visibly frustrated by the lack of tangible progress in curbing drug production, trafficking, consumption, and related violence, and under renewed pressure to "do something" about drugs in advance of the November, 1988, presidential election, Congress enacted a new antidrug initiative: the Omnibus Drug Act of 1988. While retaining the longstanding emphasis in supply-side strategies typical of earlier U.S. legislation, this law also includes a new focus on demand and backs it up by earmarking 50 percent of federal antidrug funding in FY 1989 for domestic demand control programs. The ratio was mandated to rise to 60 percent-40 percent in subsequent years.[44]

Recent Reagan administrative guidelines, the new measures mandated by the 1988 drug act, and President George Bush's well-known anti-drug views suggest that the demand side will receive substantially more attention and resources under Bush than under Reagan. At the same time, considerable ambiguity remains regarding which approaches to demand reduction will be emphasized. In broad strokes, two separate, potentially contradictory policy tracks can be identified amid the welter of demand-side plans and programs currently circulating in Washington: an educational/treatment track and a criminalization/punishment track.

With regard to the first, the 1988 legislation unequivocally recognizes the urgent need to expand and improve federal drug education and treatment programs. It specifically designates treatment "on demand" (within one week of application) as a national priority and authorizes increased federal funding for constructing the facilities required to meet this ambitious goal. The new law also provides expanded federal funding for drug prevention and education programs at the local, state, and national levels, involving both public and private sectors.[45]

Undercutting the rhetorical commitment to the treatment and education track, however, Congress actually appropriated far less funds for these programs in the FY 1989 budget than are required to achieve the objectives outlined in the 1988 legislation. Furthermore, in light of the federal government's severe fiscal deficit, it is uncertain whether the necessary financial commitments will be forthcoming from the 101st Congress.[46]

The second policy track in the 1988 legislation involves heightened emphasis on penalization of both drug users and dealers. For example, the law includes new civil penalties for consumers, authorizes the executive branch to deny federal benefits to citizens convicted of narcotics violations, and establishes a non-mandatory federal death penalty for certain drug-related murders. It also increases federal support for local, state, and federal law enforcement programs, raises the budget for military interdiction efforts, and expands federal authority to prosecute money-laundering operations.[47]

Congressional efforts to reduce demand by more heavily penalizing users were paralleled by new executive measures to identify and punish drug consumers employed by the federal government. Specifically, Reagan authorized expanded drug testing of federal employees. The scope of the testing program was further enlarged in 1988 to include all transportation sector workers--more than four million--because of their responsibility for public safety. Along with expanded testing within the federal bureaucracy, the Reagan administration also promoted the extension of testing programs to state and local levels and to the private sector.[48]

The education/treatment track conceptualizes drug consumption (demand) as a social and a public health problem and seeks to treat it as such. The criminalization/penalization track, in contrast, defines both drug use and drug trafficking as criminal activities and seeks to repress them. Philosophically, these two tracks derive from fundamentally different premises. In practice, they imply alternative public policy priorities and patterns of resource allocation that, at best, will compete with each other for scarce resources and, at worst, may become mutually incompatible.

If both approaches are pursued simultaneously, U.S. budget realities will dictate inadequate resources for both. If personal consumption is severely sanctioned, users will be less likely to undertake treatment voluntarily. If jobs and government benefits are denied to users, the ranks of the unemployed--and potential criminals--will increase, and treatment and rehabilitation will become more difficult. More convictions and stiffer jail sentences will further drain public resources, overload the court system, and overcrowd the jails. Under such circumstances, the already dismal rehabilitation record of the U.S. correctional system will likely get worse.

The heightened priority assigned to demand-side measures in the Anti-Drug Abuse Act of 1988 lends credence to the notion that a conceptual transition away from supply-side approaches is currently underway in Washington. The transition, however, is partial and incomplete.

To begin, the new legislation does not abandon supply-side programs. Instead, it renews funding for these efforts while simultaneously opening a second front directed at demand reduction. The supply-side policies of the past decade have been retained, and there is no indication that the recently-inaugurated Bush administration or Congress intend to modify or redirect them. Unless a significant decline in demand occurs, there is little reason to believe that such policies will be any more effective in the future than they have been in the past. In all likelihood, billions will be spent with only marginal effect. Are the new demand-side measures likely to bring about such a decline? The short answer is no, not soon anyway. Education, treatment, and rehabilitation are at best incremental, long-term policies--if they work at all. Demand may go down among middle class users, but not among the urban unemployed. Criminalization and penalization are more likely to exacerbate drug-related crime and violence--at least in the medium term--than they are to dissuade drug consumption and trafficking. In practice, the contradictions between these two tracks are likely to impede the effective implementation of either. If demand declines at all, it will do so only gradually.

The prognosis for resolving the drug problem, therefore, is bleak. Demand for drugs in the United States will remain high, even if it does not expand further. In addition, demand in Europe is likely to grow. If there is demand, there will be supply. Intensified repression at home and abroad will increase, rather than decrease, drug-related violence. Over the next decade, drug consumption and trafficking are likely to remain as major issues for U.S. domestic and foreign policy.

5

The Cocaine Dilemma in South America*
Rensselaer W. Lee III

INTRODUCTION

This chapter surveys the main economic and political dimensions of the cocaine industry in Bolivia, Colombia, and Peru. Each country's cocaine problem is different; for example, Colombians play a different role on the trafficking chain than do Peruvians or Bolivians. The Colombian economy as a whole is probably less cocaine-dependent than are the Peruvian and Bolivian economies. Colombia does not yet have a large population of peasants who depend on the cultivation of coca for a living. Yet, Colombian trafficking organizations have successfully penetrated parts of the bureaucracy and political system, and they also appear to exercise a veto-by-assassination over national drug policy. In Peru, such organizations do not present a serious challenge to government authority--the cocaine industry in that country is weak, immature, and disorganized. In Bolivia, however, the cocaine mafia, although lacking the financial and logistical capabilities of its Colombian counterpart, has deep political and social roots and appears to have corrupted the government apparatus.

There are, on the other hand, certain common denominators to the cocaine menace. By bringing in foreign exchange, creating employment, and raising the standard of living of some people, the industry has spawned vast and powerful constituencies. Furthermore, Andean governments have more immediately pressing problems than drugs to deal with, for example, fighting inflation, keeping the economy afloat, and combatting guerrillas. For these reasons, U.S. efforts to attack cocaine trafficking at the source are not likely to be very successful in reducing supplies of the drug, although they do help keep the traffic underground. The key to eliminating the cocaine problems lies in wiping out the U.S. market, although changing the habits and preferences of the millions of U.S. citizens now consuming cocaine will be a protracted and difficult process.

ECONOMIC IMPACT

The cocaine industry, like narcotics industries generally, is a symptom of economic ill health. In recent years, the industry has gained a powerful foothold in the economically troubled Andean countries, especially in Peru and Bolivia. The cocaine industry has obviously become an important source of foreign exchange, for example. Viewed in terms of repatriated dollars, cocaine exports are equivalent to an estimated 10 to 20 percent of Colombia's legal exports in 1987, 25 to 30 percent of Peru's, and 50 to 100 percent of Bolivia's (corresponding dollar figures are, respectively, $500 million to $1 billion, $600 to $700 million, and $250 to $450 million). Cocaine is almost certainly the most important export in Peru and Bolivia, although in Colombia it probably accounts for less export income than coffee and petroleum.

Furthermore, the cocaine industry provides jobs. As many as one million South Americans work in the many phases of the industry--cultivation, processing and refining, transportation, and smuggling. In Bolivia, where one-fifth of the population is officially unemployed, cocaine employs an estimated 350,000 to 400,000 people (5 to 6 percent of the population). However, this is just direct employment. There is also an incalculable number of legally employed South Americans--lawyers, accountants, bankers, construction workers, automobile salesmen, and the like--benefitting from the multiplier effect of the cocaine industry by selling goods and services to the industry.

Third, in Peru and Bolivia, especially, the cocaine industry is a kind of economic safety valve, providing jobs, income, and foreign exchange when the formal economy fails to deliver. In Bolivia, for instance, the gross national product declined by 2 to 3 percent per year from 1980 to 1986, and the official unemployment rate from 6 percent to 20 percent. But the coca cultivating land tripled over the same period, and so did the number of Bolivian families in cultivating coca. The collapse of the Bolivian tin industry drove thousands of miners to the coca fields to look for work. Similarly, the hard currency earned from the sale of cocaine compensates for declining inflows of legal foreign exchange. Legal exports from Peru and Bolivia declined, respectively, by 15 percent and 30 percent between 1984 and 1987. Moreover, international commercial lending to the two countries all but dried up in recent years. Moreover, international commercial lending to the two countries all but dried up in recent years.

In Colombia, the national economic impact of cocaine has been less obvious. The rise of the cocaine industry paralleled and partly compensated for the decline of Medellín in the 1970s as a major industrial center. Medellín's leading industrial sector, textiles, nearly collapsed because of Asian competition and punitive import tariffs. The depression lingered into the 1980s. From 1980 to 1985, the unemployment rate in Medellín was consistently higher than that of the other three major cities (Cali, Bogotá, and Barranquilla). In 1986, only Barranquilla suffered a higher unemployment rate. Consequently, many Medellín residents were drawn into the cocaine traffic: "owners of small or middle-sized companies that were bankrupt or on the verge of bankruptcy, unemployed professionals, housewives who had no income, and other unemployed persons, skilled and unskilled."[1] The Colombian economist Mario Arango estimates that approximately 60 billion pesos ($313 million) of proceeds from illegal exports--mostly cocaine--flowed into Medellín's economy in 1987, producing local inflationary effects but also stimulating a mini-boom in textiles, construction, and other industries. As a result, 28,000 new jobs were created in Medellín that year.[2]

Finally--and this is terribly important for understanding the political economy of cocaine--the cocaine industry has generated radically new expectations and aspirations within Andean societies. Coca farmers receive less than of one percent of the final street value of refined cocaine sold to consumers in industrialized countries, yet, farmers typically earn several times the net income they would receive from growing alternative cash crops. According to a December 1986 Agency for International Development (AID) report, a coca farmer in the Bolivian Chapare could net about $2,600 a year from a single hectare of coca--over four times the return from a hectare of oranges or avocados (the most competitive traditional crops) and over four times Bolivia's 1986 per capita income. All along the production-logistics chain, people receive substantially higher wages than they would in the licit economy. For rural dwellers, the industry offers a kind of instant introduction to modern life styles--the chance to enjoy video cassette recorders, high-tech sound systems, or the latest Toyota Landcruiser or Datsun car. For some people, it offers the chance to become fabulously wealthy. As Pablo Escobar remarked in an interview circa 1982:

> Fortunes, large or small, always have a beginning. Most of the great millionaires of Colombia and of the world have begun with nothing. But it is precisely this which converts them into legends, myths, and an example for the people. To make money in a capitalist society is not a crime but rather a virtue.[3]

Cocaine has not been, and is unlikely to be, a catalyst for the economic takeoff of the Andean countries. Most of the profits of South American traffickers are retained abroad, stashed in such tax havens as Panama or the Cayman Islands, or reinvested in real estate, securities, and business. One Congressional source estimates that the Medellín syndicates alone hold $10 billion worth of fixed and liquid assets in North America, Europe, and Asia. Much of the money repatriated does not help the economy, but it is recycled in the production of cocaine, spent on protection (bribes, private armies, and elaborate security systems), or frittered away on imported luxury goods. Because the cocaine trade is not taxed by governments, it produces a schizophrenic development pattern, especially in rural areas. There are coca boom towns well-equipped with banks, Telex machines, discotheques, and stereo and car dealerships that lack basic social services such as paved streets, sanitation facilities, and clean drinking water. Traffickers do invest in legal enterprises, but these funds are seldom channeled into core industries--mining, oil exploration, manufacturing, power generation, and commercial transport.

Mario Arango, the aforementioned Colombian economist, offers some empirical evidence of these financial flows. In late 1987 and early 1988, he interviewed twenty medium- and high-level cocaine capos in Medellín about their legal investment preferences. Although the sample is small, successfully conducting the interviews was an impressive feat in itself. The first investment preferences of the capos are detailed below.[4]

All this does not add up to a balanced investment picture; obviously traffickers are not captains of industry like the Rockefellers, Harrimans, and Carnegies of yore. Moreover, the economics of some drug trafficking investments are suspect. For example, the enormous Posada Alemana hotel complex built by Carlos Lehder in Armenia at a cost of roughly $5 million was touted as a future "tourist epicenter" in Colombia's coffee-growing zone, but lost over a million dollars in its three-year existence. Moreover, traffickers' businesses are sometimes fronts for money laundering. They operate consistently at a loss, but they may thereby force legitimate ventures out of business. For all these reasons, the mafia's legitimate investment activities are unlikely to catalyze the economic takeoff of drug-producing countries in Latin America.

TABLE 1

Colombian Traffickers' Investment Preferences

Preference	Number	%
Real estate (rural and urban)	9	45
Cattle Ranching	4	20
Commerce (wholesale, retail)	3	15
Construction of high-rise office buildings, luxury condominiums	2	10
Services and recreation (sports, gymnasiums, hotel, restaurants, discotheques, clinics)	2	10
TOTAL	20	100

Still, the cocaine industry provides benefits for the ailing economies of the Andean region. In the words of Bolivian president Victor Paz Estenssoro, "Cocaine has gained an importance in our economy in direct response to the shrinking of the formal economy."[5] Mario Arango claims with some exaggeration that drug dollars have not just revived the Medellín economy but have "arrested the social and political deterioration of the country."[6] The Colombian writer Gabriel García Márquez calls narcotics trafficking a "self-defense mechanism of Colombians" and wonders "where would our country be without drugs?"[7] Cocaine may thus be a hedge of sorts against economic and political disaster. Moreover--and this is the most important point--by raising expectations and transforming life styles, the cocaine industry has created new patterns of interest articulation and generated new demands on Andean political systems.

POLITICAL ISSUES

The cocaine industry has amassed significant political clout in the Andean countries because of its large popular base in the upstream phases and its enormous financial and logistical capabilities in the downstream phases. Cocaine's most visible constituency comprises the hundreds of thousands of South American farmers who cultivate coca leaves. Coca farmers are highly organized, sometimes well-armed, and capable of exerting tremendous pressure on governments.

This is in part because coca growing is entrenched in the history and culture of these two Andean countries. Several million people in the Andean altiplano and in parts of the Amazon basin still consume coca leaves, mainly through the practice of chewing or *acullico,* to combat hunger, fatigue, and assorted circulatory and intestinal ailments. More significantly, because cultivation has expanded greatly to meet illicit demand, coca growing is important to the rural economies of Peru and Bolivia. The Bolivian government estimated the aggregate value of coca production at $230 million in 1986, meaning that coca accounted for over 20 percent of total national farm income in that year. In areas such as the Chapare and the Upper Huallaga Valley, that proportion runs well over 90 percent. Including farmers and their families (calculating five to six persons per family), coca cultivation sustains roughly 3 percent of Peru's total population and 6 percent of Bolivia's. In contrast, coca farming supports less than 1 percent of Colombia's population.

The coca lobby in Bolivia and Peru is particularly formidable. Bolivia's 70 thousand coca-farming families are organized into ten regional federations--four in the Yungas and six in the Chapare, the two main growing regions, located in La Paz and Cochabamba departments. These federations receive direct political support from the 1.3 million member Bolivian Workers Union and its main affiliate, the Confederation of Bolivian Peasant Workers. Bolivia has a population of only 6.4 million people, so that country's coca lobby, writ large, encompasses about 20 percent of the national population. In addition, coca farmers are backed by left and far-left political parties that have a combined representation of forty deputies in the Bolivian Chamber of Deputies--one third of the total 120 members in that body. Such backing represents ideological considerations more than any pro-coca sentiment per se--the left is both anti-government and anti-U.S.--yet, it adds to the farmers' overall political clout.

In Peru, coca growers are not the national political force they are in Bolivia. However, they are well entrenched locally. In Peru's Upper Huallaga Valley, where over 90 percent of farm income comes from coca cultivation, growers express their interests through provincial and district self-defense fronts (FEDIPs). FEDIPs apparently are now not only dominated by moderate leftist leaders (representatives of the Izquierda Unida), but also probably infiltrated by the Sendero Luminoso guerrillas.

Sendero now has considerable influence among peasants in the valley, having gained a political foothold in part by exploiting resentment against U.S.-Peruvian eradication policies. Sendero's propagandists are having a field day denouncing controversial plans to spray herbicides on coca. A Sendero leaflet distributed at a roadblock in the Upper Huallaga Valley in August, 1988, proclaimed: "We repudiate and denounce the plan to eradicate coca plantations [by] using insecticides of high destructive power such as "Spike," which not only destroys coca, flora and fauna, but also threatens the lives of animals and humans throughout the region."[8] Sendero also helps coca farmers in another important respect by protecting them against the bullying violence of drug dealers and encouraging them to demand high prices from dealers for their coca leaves.

In defending the right of farmers to cultivate and sell coca leaves, the coca lobby relies heavily on mass mobilization tactics such as sit-ins, demonstrations, and roadblocks. For example, coca farmers in Peru, backed by narcotics traffickers and Sendero Luminoso guerrillas, shut down the main jungle highway in the Upper Huallaga Valley--the Carretera Marginal--for several days in August, 1987, and repeated the performance in August, 1988. Acts of sabotage on these occasions included blowing up bridges, digging trenches, and erecting barriers of boulders, logs, and burning rubber tires. In Bolivia, coca farmers and their worker-peasant allies have blockaded and sealed off Cochabamba, the nation's third largest city, five times since 1983 to protest U.S.-Bolivian antidrug policies. There have been other anti-government demonstrations as well. For example, in May, 1987, hundreds of coca farmers laid siege to a DEA encampment in the Chapare, forcing a temporary withdrawal of the DEA agents from the region. In June, 1988, a contingent of Chapare peasants briefly occupied Bolivian government offices in Cochabamba, taking twelve hostages, including two U.S. advisers. That same month, an estimated 4 thousand to 5 thousand coca growers broke into the offices of DIRECO, Bolivia's coca eradication agency, in the Chapare town of Villa Tumari were searching for evidence to support a rumor that DIRECO and DEA were testing herbicides against coca in the Chapare. UMOPAR (antidrug police) units stationed in the town staged a counterattack that cost ten to fifteen peasants and one policeman their lives.

Pressures from the coca lobby have severely impeded crop reduction, the cornerstone of U.S. anti-cocaine policy in Andean source countries. In Bolivia, the government cannot eradicate a single hectare of coca without consent of the peasants' federations. Bolivia's new anti-coca legislation, enacted in July, 1988, included a prohibition against chemical herbicides, thanks largely to the coca lobby's efforts. In Peru, because of grower opposition and general security problems, eradication in the Upper Huallaga Valley ground almost to a halt in 1987. Only 355 hectares of coca were destroyed, compared to 2,575 hectares in 1986 and 4,830 in 1985. Pressure from the coca lobby and environmental groups compelled the Peruvian government in mid-1988 to suspend a program for the aerial testing of herbicides. Stopping cocaine at the source thus appears an unrealistic hope.

Even more powerful, if less visible than the South American coca lobbies are the criminal syndicates that refine, smuggle, and distribute cocaine. In Colombia, the cocaine mafia has emerged as a significant political force with a strong regional power base including parts of Córdoba, Antioquía, Santander, and other Colombian departments. Mafia influence is also strong in certain cities, such as Medellín, Cali, and the Amazon port city of Leticia. Colombian drug money finances an extensive system of protection and intelligence including accomplices or informants in key national institutions such as the police, the judiciary, government ministries, the legislature, the military, and the news media.

Colombian drug barons do not seek to overthrow the government--they seek a kind of quasi-legitimacy within the political status quo--but they do pursue political objectives. One goal is to shape national policy on drugs, especially extradition. Another objective apparently is to eliminate the influence of Marxist guerrillas in certain regions and neighborhoods. They have pursued both of these goals energetically and sometimes violently. The murders in recent years of prominent supporters of the U.S.-Colombian extradition treaty, leftist leaders (such as the Unión Patriótica's Jaime Pardo Leal), and peasants suspected of collaborating with guerrillas bear testimony to the Colombian mafia's violent political style.

In Bolivia, the cocaine mafia historically has exercised great economic and political influence, at one time virtually running the country. Under the military regime of General Luis García Meza, the cocaine industry and the state apparatus were virtually indistinguishable. Cocaine traffickers financed and manned right-wing paramilitary squads dedicated to repression and terrorism in the service of the state. García Meza's Interior Minister, Luis Arce Gómez--dubbed by CBS' *60 Minutes* the "Minister of Cocaine"--himself participated in the traffic. He was a partner in an air transport company that flew loads of cocaine paste out of Bolivia. He also was said to be the owner of several laboratories in the Beni. At the same time, in his capacity as minister, he collected huge sums in protection money both from coca merchants and cocaine exporters. With the advent of democracy in Bolivia in 1982, the direct political influence of the cocaine mafia receded somewhat. Yet, the dimensions of the cocaine traffic have expanded enormously since García Meza's time. Cocaine traffickers, who account for up to one-half of Bolivia's yearly inflow of foreign exchange, retain widespread influence in government institutions, the military, and the various peasant federations that produce coca. Traffickers probably control local politics in the Beni region. The level of corruption in Bolivia is simply extraordinary, even by Latin American standards. A 1988 report of GAO states: "According to several U.S. and Bolivian officials, corruption exists within all levels of the Bolivian government and very few government officials are to be trusted--corruption is widespread and generally accepted within the Bolivian police, military, and judicial systems."[5] Bolivia's "cocaine superstate" may have passed from the scene, but the narcotics control environment is not fundamentally better than in the early 1980s.

In contrast, Peruvian cocaine dealers have never had the national political clout of their counterparts in Colombia and Bolivia. One reason is that Peru's cocaine industry is relatively undeveloped, producing very little cocaine hydrochloride (CHCL), and only recently have the Peruvians integrated forward from first-stage processing of coca leaves into the production of cocaine base. Peru's traffickers do not represent a self-conscious narcobourgeois class (to borrow from Merrill Collett). There are no great trafficking personalities in Peru comparable to Pablo Escobar or Gonzalo Rodríguez Gacha in Colombia or Roberto Suárez in Bolivia.

Narcowelfare--the sponsorship of charitable and public works projects by drug dealers--is almost nonexistent in Peru, where trafficking organizations are small, highly competitive, and heavily dependent on Colombian traffickers for leadership, technical advice, and armed support. Yet, in the Upper Huallaga Valley, cocaine traffickers are an important political-military force, although the increasing penetration of the Valley by Sendero Luminoso guerrillas in recent years has somewhat diminished the traffickers' influence.

PATTERNS OF CORRUPTION

Drug trafficking in South America--indeed, anywhere--is synonymous with corruption: the purchase of protection from authorities. In its most rudimentary form, protection means bribing law enforcement officials to look the other way. To cite a few examples: During 1986, traffickers in the Bolivian Chapare were reportedly paying police $20,000 to $25,000 for a seventy-two hour window of impunity. All they asked was to be left alone while loading coca paste onto airplanes or while moving major shipments of coca paste by land or by river. In the Upper Huallaga Valley, in the July-August period of 1988, traffickers in the Uchiza district reportedly paid $12,000 in bribes per shipment of cocaine base flown out of the Valley. In one recorded case, $5,000 went to the local military command, $5,000 to the local contingent of the Guardia Civil (national police), and $2,000 to community organizations affiliated directly with Sendero Luminoso. Medellín's former Olaya Herrera International Airport, located in the middle of the city, was for several months in 1986 the scene of a major cocaine smuggling operation apparently carried out with the full knowledge of a twelve-man police commando unit on permanent guard at the airport.

On the rare occasions when leading traffickers are arrested, they can bribe their way out of custody on the spot. For example, a car carrying Pablo Escobar was stopped at a police checkpoint outside of Medellín in November, 1986. Escobar bought his freedom with a $250,000 to $350,000 bribe. When traffickers do, in spite of everything, land in jail, corrupt judges or prison wardens may release them from custody. The release of Jorge Ochoa from Bogotá's La Picota prison in December, 1987, seems to be a case in point. In a March, 1986, incident, one of Latin America's most notorious drug traffickers, Juan Ramón Matta Ballesteros, escaped from the Modelo prison in Bogotá by paying $2 million or $7 million (stories differ) to eighteen of his guards. Matta was given the key to his own cell and walked through seven unlocked jail doors to freedom. "God opened the door for me," the trafficker reportedly commented after his escape.[10]

There is a limit to the mafia's ability to penetrate and corrupt enforcement agencies; it cannot buy immunity for all of its activities. Hence, the mafia needs an intelligence network to supplement the protection network and provide advance warning of planned antidrug operations such as raids on laboratories, customs searches, and police sweeps. The network consists of strategically placed informants in the bureaucracy. For example, documents captured during a Colombian army raid on a traffickers' hideout in Medellín in early 1988 provided solid evidence that traffickers had infiltrated the Colombian Ministries of Justice and Foreign Affairs. Sometimes cocaine traffickers themselves occupy positions of trust and responsibility. In Peru, for example, a trafficker named Reynaldo Rodríguez López was an adviser to the Director of the Peruvian Investigations Police (PIP) while maintaining an office at PIP headquarters. Rodríguez, who was arrested in mid-1985, had some important associates; his drug ring allegedly included several PIP generals as well as Luis López Vergara, private secretary to Luis Percovich Roca, President Belaunde Terry's Minister of Interior.

The U.S. is probably also a target of mafia intelligence gathering. U.S. narcotics experts in Bogotá have speculated that the cocaine mafia might have access to some of the U.S. embassy's cable traffic. According to a 1986 article in Colombia's *Semana* magazine, the mafia's going rate for informants was at least three times that paid by the DEA. Colombian syndicates also were said to maintain a list of DEA agents and their code names, a list that was circulated to counterpart organizations in other South American countries.[11]

This intelligence capability functions within a broader system of social relationships created by the narcomafia. Cocaine traffickers earn friends and supporters within society by spending money within the society. In some cases, traffickers have cultivated a kind of Robin Hood image by donating vast sums to local development projects or giving money and gifts to the poor. The standing that some major capos hold in their communities enables them to co-opt the local populace into their early warning systems. As a result, within major mafia strongholds such as the Beni region in Bolivia and the city of Medellín in Colombia, the "fat fish" of the cocaine trade can operate with relative impunity. With the notable exception of Carlos Lehder, who was arrested in Medellín in February, 1987 and who may well have been betrayed by his colleagues in the cocaine cartel, no major Colombian cocaine trafficker has ever been brought to justice. The July, 1988, arrest of Roberto Suárez at a ranch 35 kilometers from the Beni capital of Trinidad apparently breaks this pattern, although prearrangement is suggested by Suárez's own account of the arrest: "I knew what time they would come--I was ready with my things, dressed, and smoking a cigarette."[12] A Bolivian Ministry of Interior source reports that Suárez gave himself up to get a reduced jail term as well as a guarantee against extradition to the United States. The true story of his arrest, however, will probably never be known.

Drugs and dealers are also an important source of funding for election campaigns. There simply are not very many other sources. Drug money flows rather indiscriminately into party coffers, going to opposing candidates if necessary. For example, Pablo Escobar and Gonzalo Rodríguez Gacha reportedly contributed to the campaign of both Alfonso López Michelsen and Belisario Betancur in the 1982 Colombian presidential election. Yet, traffickers themselves have run for national political office, for example, Escobar in 1982 and Carlos Lehder in 1986. Lehder, of course, founded his own political party, the Movimiento Latino Nacional, which he touted as "a product of the absence of popular power."

In addition, traffickers may strongly favor a particular electoral outcome. In 1983, for example, Suárez allegedly conspired with two members of Hugo Banzer's center-right Acción Democrática Nacional (ADN), a former army general and an ADN congressman, in a vote-buying plot. The plan was to bribe congressperson representatives of the Movimiento Nacional Revolucionario (MNR), the party of Victor Paz Estenssoro, to cast their votes for Banzer in a runoff presidential election that year. Earlier popular elections had failed to give either Paz or Banzer a majority of the popular vote, leaving the outcome to be decided by the congress. The plot was unsuccessful; Paz won the election anyway.

Finally, cocaine dealers have also attempted bribery on a grand scale. In May, 1984, Colombian cocaine barons meeting in Panama with former president Alfonso López Michelsen and attorney general Carlos Jimínez Gómez made a startling proposal. They offered to get out of the cocaine business and repatriate to Colombia the billions of dollars they held in foreign banks. In return, they wanted a government guarantee against being extradited to the United States. Two years later, traffickers offered informally to pay off Colombia's $13 billion foreign debt. The "King of the Beni," Roberto Suárez, offered in a June 1983 meeting with President Siles Zuázo's narcotics adviser, Rafael Otazo, to give the Bolivian government $2 billion in four $500 million installments. If genuine, the offer was possibly underwritten by Colombian trafficking syndicates; it's hard to believe that Suárez could have raised such a sum in Bolivia. Suárez wanted as a quid pro quo a free hand to run his trafficking operations in the Beni. The Otazo-Suárez discussions generated an enormous outcry from Bolivia's political establishment (the Panama discussions aroused a similar reaction in Colombia) and probably hastened Siles' departure from the presidency.

SUPPORT FOR THE SYSTEM

Is the cocaine industry a conservative or a revolutionary force in Latin American societies? Does it threaten democratic systems and values in the Hemisphere? In Colombia and Peru, these questions acquire a special urgency because of the presence of Marxist revolutionary movements. Some U.S. and South American government officials have gone to some lengths to place the narcotics problem within the framework of East-West conflict. The result has been what Merrill Collett calls the "myth of the narcoguerrillas"--an official theory that drug dealers and Communist guerrillas are linked in an alliance against the political status quo.

The narcoguerrilla theory seems particularly inappropriate to the Colombian scene. Most cocaine barons seek legitimacy within Colombia's democratic system. (The exception, of course, was Carlos Lehder, whose fascist-populist program called for radical changes in Colombia's political landscape.) Indeed, cocaine dealers now seem to be allied with elements of the Colombia establishment against the guerrillas. Mafia leaders, traditional landowners, business people, politicians, and elements of the military have apparently made common cause in some areas, for example, the Middle Magdalena Valley, the Uraba region of Antioquía, and parts of Córdoba department. Leftist sources doubtless exaggerate the dimensions of these alliances. A recent clandestine radio broadcast of Radio Patria Libre, for example, reported: "the Narco-Military Republic of the Middle Magdalena Region has control over the mayor's offices in nine municipalities and covers more than 20,000 square kilometers, equal in size to the Guajira Department."[13]

However, certain recent events, for example, the massacres of *campesinos* in the Uraba region of Antioquía and in Córdoba department in the spring of 1988, apparently involved some informal coordination among drug traffickers, traditional landowners, and the military. (The victims had allegedly been members of guerrilla front organizations.) In addition, many authorities believe that the cocaine mafia has been responsible for the murders of hundreds of members of the Communist Patriotic Union (UP), including the October, 1987, assassination of the UP's leader, Jaime Pardo Leal.

There is no more clear evidence of narcoguerrilla hostility than the emerging paramilitary movement in Colombia. Armed self-defense organizations have existed for some time in areas patrolled by Colombia's various guerrilla groups. The purpose of these organizations has been to protect local communities against extortion, kidnapping, and other guerrilla practices. However, the self-defense movement suffered from a lack of equipment, training, and resources, and local landlords often had no alternative but to pay taxes to guerrillas. Yet this situation appears to have changed somewhat. The reason is that Colombian cocaine barons have invested some of their profits in acquiring vast tracts of land in the countryside. Traffickers are said to have bought at least a million hectares of land in the past five years in Córdoba, Antioquía, Meta, and other Colombian departments. Many of these purchases are in "zona rojas"--areas where the guerrilla presence is strong. Traffickers' haciendas, ranches, and farms may house cocaine laboratories or they may be purely legitimate operations--whatever the case, the new narco landed gentry has found itself on the cutting edge of Colombia's guerrilla problem.

The impact of this historically significant process has been to revive and to overhaul the local self-defense forces and to create such forces where none had existed previously. Cocaine barons or their representatives assumed the leadership of and most of the financial responsibility for these organizations.

As a result, self-defense networks have become a significant political and military force in some regions; for example, a paramilitary network centered in Puerto Boyacá (in the middle Magdalena Valley) has its own fleet of planes, helicopter and launches, its own jeeps and bulldozers, a printing press, a clinic and a training school, not to mention vast stores of ammunition and automatic and semi-automatic weapons. Top ranking commanders get paid as much as $4,000 a month (more than double the salary of the President of the Republic). Such elaborate structures of course, are expensive--they have to be funded by contributions from local ranchers, farmers, and businessmen. However, it appears that the narco landholders pay much higher dues than the non-trafficking landholders; in effect cocaine traffickers subsidize the self-defense systems.

What has been the political impact of these trends? To give the devil his due, the narco-paramilitary movement with the tacit or active support of important groups within Colombian society (such as traditional landowners, rightist businessmen and politicians, and some local military commanders) has successfully dislodged communist guerrillas from certain parts of Colombia. One reported consequence is that property values are increasing in the areas where leading traffickers maintain their landed estates. Perhaps the most important example of "sanitization" has been in the Middle Magdalena Valley: the region encompassing the towns of Puerto Boyacá, Puerto Triúnfo and Puerto Berrío--was a FARC stronghold in the early 1980s but the FARC reportedly have been mostly expelled by cocaine traffickers and their allies.

There is, of course, the question of the financial nexus between the drug trade and insurgent groups. FARC guerrillas tax and in certain cases directly manage coca cultivation and cocaine-processing facilities. Yet, the major cocaine trafficking organizations have few ties to FARC. These organizations rely mostly on Peruvian and Bolivian raw materials for manufacturing cocaine hydrochloride. Most of these CHCL labs are probably not taxed by guerrillas; they are located in areas where traffickers have a relatively strong power base (for example, in Antioquía, Córdoba, and Santander) or where guerrillas are almost nonexistent (for example, in the Amazon jungle regions along Colombia's southern border).[14] To put the point somewhat differently, if Colombia stopped cultivating coca tomorrow, the financial base of the FARC would shrink considerably, but the operations of the Medellín-Cali syndicate would not be greatly affected.

In Peru, where the whole cocaine industry is immature and fragmented, traffickers have not developed a common anti-leftist agenda, nor have they been able to establish a close alliance with the propertied classes and with the military. Still, there have been a number of turf disputes over the years between traffickers and Sendero Luminoso guerrillas. To cite one example, in October, 1987, there was a bloody trafficker-guerrilla shootout in the valley town of Paraíso--an episode in which thirty-four people died. The head of the cocaine trafficking gang (who, incidentally, was wounded in the battle and later wound up in police custody) was well known to the police for his effort in organizing local communities against Sendero.

There are, to be sure, instances of collaboration. Drug traffickers pay off guerrillas (and the police and the military) for some shipments of cocaine leaving the Valley. One Peruvian trafficker named "Vampiro" because he lacks all his front teeth except for two upper incisors reportedly allowed his house to be used as a command post for Sendero Luminoso guerrillas when Sendero briefly occupied the Upper Huallaga Valley town of Tocache in April, 1987. Still, the narcoguerrilla relationship is mainly competitive, with each side trying to stake out territories (red and white zones, to use Sendero's terminology) where it can exercise predominant control.

In Bolivia, where there is no revolutionary movement to speak of and where the narco-bourgeoisie traditionally have had rightist leanings, the critical question is: Does the cocaine mafia favor a return to military authority? In Bolivia, the rise of the mafia was symbiotically associated with the military dictatorships of the 1970s and early 1980s. Some leaders of the democratic Siles and Paz administrations see the mafia has having a vested interest in authoritarianism. A former vice president under Siles Zuázo, Jaime Paz Zamora, argued in 1983 that the mafia, far from being "colorless" politically, had a definite goal: to topple democracy and to restore military dictatorship. Some leading traffickers were clearly uncomfortable with the advent of democracy in 1982. Suárez, for example, referred in a 1984 letter to Siles Zuázo to the "fragile foundation" of democracy, its "rotten structure of power," and the "increasing panorama of political confusion and social malaise resulting from the ineffective party system and from anarcho-syndicalism."[15] Clearly, Suárez was no friend of democracy, although he did not openly advocate a return of the military dictatorship to Bolivia. Suárez represents the authoritarian, elitist wing of Bolivia's cocaine elite; he was a major financial backer of García Meza's regime. Yet, his views may no longer be shared by most Bolivian traffickers, who by now are probably comfortable with democracy in Bolivia. After all, the cocaine industry has expanded enormously since the early 1980s, and there are now a lot more actors. Interestingly, Suárez himself has bemoaned the democratization of the industry. Still the possibility of a cocaine-backed military coup should not be dismissed out of hand.

To return to the original question: is the cocaine traffic a destabilizing force? Unquestionably it is, in the same sense that the violence and corruption associated with the drug trade erode public commitment to democratic institutions. The cocaine traffickers are not aligned to any significant degree with the political left. The unfortunate narcoguerrilla stereotype has obscured a more fundamental reality: the increasing penetration by traffickers of established economic and political institutions. The rightward orientation of cocaine traffickers may itself be destabilizing. Consider, for example, García Meza's coup in 1980. Yet, even Bolivia's traffickers today probably prefer to corrupt authorities rather than overthrow them. Arguably, mafia vigilantism in Colombia reduces the chance of accommodation with leftist guerrillas. Yet, some observers, among them this writer, believe that the peace process never had much chance of success anyway.

PROGNOSIS

The prospects of controlling cocaine trafficking within source countries are not particularly promising. The cocaine industry is quite well entrenched in South America. Broad constituencies have developed around the industry, including corrupt officials, people who sell goods and services to traffickers, and beneficiaries of drug traffickers' narcowelfare schemes, not just the people who are engaged in one or another phase of the trafficking cycle. Furthermore, although concern over cocaine is growing in South America, governments and publics still do not see drug trafficking as a survival issue comparable in importance to unemployment, inflation, the general state of the economy, and subversion. Indeed, political elites often view antidrug crusades with apprehension, because such crusades can cause economic hardship (at least temporarily) and can create new and formidable challenges to government authority. In Colombia, the war against drugs is greatly complicated by the fact that the cocaine elite has forged alliances with other "law-and-order" advocates.

Furthermore escalating the drug war may land the United States in a Vietnam-type morass. As of early 1989, there were some thirty to forty DEA agents stationed in the Upper Huallaga Valley spearheading an anticocaine drive that, because the Valley's economy is tied mostly to coca and cocaine, was widely unpopular among the locals. Such a policy cannot succeed either politically or strategically. Indeed, the main beneficiary will be the Sendero Luminoso movement, which has already successfully exploited the issue of coca control to gain converts among the peasantry.

The solution to the U.S. cocaine problem does not lie in the jungles, shanty towns, and cocaine capitals of South America. The emphasis of U.S. drug enforcement policy must be on reducing demand, not supply, focusing especially on education, prevention, and treatment programs. (There are already heartening signs that the U.S. public is becoming alert to the dangers of cocaine use and that consumption of the drug among teenagers and young adults is declining.) This is not to say, however, that U.S. overseas antidrug programs and the programs of Latin American countries themselves are useless. These programs are useful political instruments. They help counter the more outrageous political manifestations of the drug trade; traffickers running for political office, traffickers forming nationalist political parties, cocaine warlordism, the emergence of cocaine superstates, and so on. But discouraging overt political participation by drug dealers is not the same as stopping the drug traffic. We got rid of García Meza and his armies in Bolivia, but the cocaine trade has continued to expand.

However the cocaine trade is ultimately dealt with--education, demand reduction, or legalization--there will be adjustment problems for producer countries. The United States must be prepared to help these countries progress along normal paths of economic growth. The economic stability of the region is an important U.S. national interest. At the same time, U.S. policy makers should endeavor to reduce the now excessively high profile that cocaine has in U.S. relations with the Andean countries, which means, among other things, reducing expectations for the success of supply-side programs. The best way to defeat South American drug lords is simply for North Americans to stop using their products. Changing the habits and preferences of U.S. consumers will take a long time. Meanwhile, the cocaine issue should not be allowed to obscure traditional U.S. diplomatic interests in the Andean region.

III
The Military, Congress, and the War on Drugs

6

The Role of the U.S. Military in the War on Drugs
Donald J. Mabry

Throughout 1988, the public demanded that the military increase its role in the nation's antidrug campaign and Congress responded in the National Defense Authorization Act for FY 1989 and in the Antidrug Act of 1988. These demands varied in scope. One demand was to give search, seizure, and arrest powers outside the United States or outside the land area of the United States to military personnel. More severe was advocacy of using the military to patrol the national borders, including ports of entry, armed with civilian police powers, In May, 1988, the House of Representatives demanded that the military "seal the borders" to drug traffic within forty-five days, an effort that would require both naval and border interdiction. Representative Arthur Ravenel, Jr. (R-SC) demanded that the military shoot down possible drug smuggling aircraft on sight. In addition to demanding that the military interdict drug smugglers, some advocated that the military participate in gang-busting and crop eradication programs inside Latin American countries. Some wanted the Department of Defense (DOD) to replace the Coast Guard as lead agency in interdiction efforts. The smallest demand, which Congress granted, required the military to provide more logistical support and intelligence data. Using the military in the antinarcotics campaign, however, raises serious issues not only of the efficacy of such a policy but also of the long-term implications for future civilian-military relations.[1]

PAST MILITARY DRUG INTERDICTION EFFORTS

The military slowly and reluctantly increased its involvement in the campaign against the Latin American narcotics trade. The Joint Chiefs of Staff yielded to civilian pressure in 1985 and recommended that the U.S. military be involved in fighting the production and trafficking in drugs from Latin America.[2] The 1985 proposal, however, would not have empowered military personnel to be law enforcement officers; they would not conduct searches, seizures, and arrests. Military involvement has steadily increased since 1981, when nothing was spent on interdiction campaigns, to FY 87 when $389 was spent million on drug enforcement.[3] In the latter year, the DOD loaned $303.5 million worth of equipment to drug law enforcement authorities. Indirect support was also provided. To support drug law enforcement agencies in FY 87, DOD flew 16,288 hours of airborne surveillance, reported suspicious ships to the Coast Guard, towed captured vessels, flew helicopters in Operation BAT (Bahamas and Turks), provided ground surveillance radar in Arizona in Operation Groundhog, provided specialized training to law enforcement officials, and sent aerostat radar balloon data to law enforcement officials in Florida.[4] Intelligence data were supplied on a regular basis. For Operation Blast Furnace in Bolivia in 1986, the U.S. Army used six Black Hawk helicopters and 160 soldiers to aid Bolivian narcotics police in destroying cocaine laboratories. U.S. military-owned helicopters and U.S. Army maintenance crews remain in Bolivia.[5]

DEMANDS FOR INCREASED MILITARY PARTICIPATION

For those who do not understand the complexities of the illicit narcotics trade, using the military appears the obvious and easy solution to the failed interdiction campaign. The military, with over two million members, a large budget, vast equipment resources, and sophisticated training, has the installed capacity to turn back this "invasion" of the United States, this national security threat. Some might argue that it is the only *national* institution with such capability. Some argue that, in the absence of war, this installed capacity is idle and thus available at little additional cost for in the antinarcotics effort. Advocates of increased military participation argue, for example, that the Navy in its regular Caribbean and Gulf of Mexico patrols could easily add interdiction to its tasks, and that tracking and capturing this enemy also sharpens wartime skills.[6]

One important demand is to give the military civilian police powers so it can interdict the flow of drugs as quickly as possible and at the least possible cost. Some would allow the military to use these new powers inside the United States, but only at the borders, as well as outside the U.S. Forbidding the use of these powers on land is designed to prevent the military from threatening U.S. civilian government.

Such a proposal, however, would still mean the military would be using civilian police powers *inside* the United States, since it would operate inside the nation's territorial limits. Further, captured traffickers would have to be brought into the United States for trial. For the policy to be fully effective, the military would have to possess the right of "hot pursuit," else traffickers would escape by entering U.S. territorial waters or the land.

DOD POSITION

The DOD has consistently opposed military participation, arguing that the military has a specialized function--defending the nation and its allies against attacks by governments and their armies and weapons of war--and nothing should be done that might impair its ability to accomplish this mission. DOD agrees that the drug problem is a national security issue but points out that other problems, such as the nation's economic health, are national security issues as well but are not solvable by military means. Further, it argues that it cannot afford an additional task without additional funding, unless the nation wants to give up programs such as support of NATO.

In spite of its opposition, DOD joined the war. Its drug interdiction efforts have been limited to aiding civilian law enforcement agencies by lending equipment, providing specialized training, sharing intelligence and sensing data, and allowing Coast Guard personnel to join naval patrols.[7] DOD secretaries Frank Carlucci and Caspar Weinberger argued that military personnel are not police and should not be. Military personnel are not trained in law enforcement techniques, and providing such training and conducting law enforcement activities would detract from military readiness. DOD officials argue that the mission of the armed forces is to protect the nation from foreign armies, not drug smugglers, and that civilian law enforcement agencies, especially the Coast Guard, should be given the resources necessary to do the job. Further, they argue that the military is currently providing material and intellectual resources to law enforcement agencies and will provide more if Congress provides DOD with more funds.[8]

Unless the United States is going to abandon many of its present military commitments, massive resources would have to be added to the already hefty DOD budget. A study done for the Joint Chiefs of Staff estimated that an additional $20 billion would be needed to seal the borders, plus unspecified billions more to supply the estimated ninety infantry battalions, fifty aerostat surveillance balloons, one thousand fighter planes, 160 cruisers, and other necessary equipment.[9] Although these costs may be overstated (after all, the military *does not* want to get involved), they would be high if the military adds a new task to its current functions. Advocates of military force in interdiction campaigns tacitly agree with this point. They do not assert that the military budget is bloated nor that the military should abandon its current commitments.

The military agrees that it is capable of using its war-making powers to interdict drug smuggling if the nation truly wants to go to war or can participate on a basis short of war. No one is seriously demanding that the military go to war, however, so the military emphasizes a more limited participation. Soldiers and sailors could be diverted from their military duties and trained instead in law enforcement techniques over a period of months. Military police forces, whose training resembles that of civilian law enforcement personnel, can be doubled or tripled or quadrupled or multiplied by whatever factor might be necessary. DOD could retrain some existing units and divert them to narcotics interdiction or could dedicate new units to the task. DOD agrees that its sophisticated training, weaponry, and data collection systems outclass those of drug smugglers. DOD argues, however, that deploying all of these would require more funds.

DOD has stressed that the military would do whatever the law requires. The military understands that the Constitution dictates the supremacy of civil authority does not want to abandon its political stance of obeying the Constitution its members are sworn to defend. Rather, in testimony before Congress and elsewhere, military officers have almost pleaded with civilian authorities not to abandon the historic tradition that reins in military power within the United States.

PROBLEMS IN IMPLEMENTING THE NEW DEMANDS

Some serious problems will arise if the military gets directly involved in the antidrug campaign. These include interdiction on the high seas and at the border, use of the National Guard, potential corruption of the military, conflict between military intelligence gathering and civil liberties, arrest powers, implications for civil-military relations, and cost effectiveness. Each of these will be examined in turn.

Maritime Interdiction

Interdiction on the high seas is extraordinarily difficult. The Gulf of Mexico and the Caribbean together comprise 1,664,500 square miles. Every boat or ship passing through these waters is a potential smuggling vessel. Thus total interdiction requires tracking each vessel, for drugs may be aboard not only at the port of departure but later on the high seas transferred from another ship. The challenge is similar to anti-submarine warfare; locating drug-smuggling vessels is akin to finding the proverbial needle in a haystack. In fact, finding enemy submarines in wartime is easier. Drug vessels may range from legitimate cargo or passenger ships, on which a crew member or passenger has been handsomely paid to stow kilos of cocaine, to small pleasure boats. Smugglers have proven extremely flexible in countering interdiction efforts. If the interdiction rate in the Gulf-Caribbean area were raised significantly, smugglers would shift more of their shipments to the Atlantic or Pacific, further complicating the interdiction task.[10]

Identifying and stopping a suspected vessel is only part of the problem. If the vessel is under foreign registry, the government of the nation of registry must give permission before it can be boarded and searched. Searching by trained experts can require from six to fifteen hours. Small packages hidden in specially built compartments are difficult to find and many caches probably never are. Coast Guard figures show that very few searches of suspected vessels ever yield a find. Searchers must follow proper legal procedures to avoid invalidating an arrest, and they also avoid violence. If the ship or boat does contain illicit drugs, it has to be towed to port. Many navy vessels are too large or inappropriately rigged to tow some of these drug vessels, and a smaller vessel must be pulled off station to do the job, thus opening a window of opportunity for smugglers.[11]

The navy does not relish such an assignment. In its view, its current assignment in the Gulf-Caribbean region, with the presence of Soviet submarines and spy ships, requires its full attention. Drug interdiction would require a significant departure, one the navy believes would detract from its primary mission and likely embroil sailors in civil courts when they should be on sea duty. It currently aids the Coast Guard in interdiction through the Law Enforcement Detachment (LEDET) program by carrying a complement of Coast Guard personnel, deviating from its established route when there are grounds to believe that it can help interdict a smuggler, and providing intelligence data to the Coast Guard. Its preference, however, is that the Coast Guard, with its 200-year experience in interdiction, be given the appropriate resources to do the job.

Border Interdiction

The total border, including inlets, is 88,633 miles long and is crossed annually by 290 million people. Given these figures, even with substantial increases in resources, probably the only way that illegal drugs could be stopped at the border would be to create extraordinarily complex and effective system that smugglers would find unpredictable. Such inspections would have to take place along each segment of the border, not just at ports of entry. Customs officials could use military personnel to help them at ports of entry, but these ports are specks on the border. Furthermore, aircraft penetrate the border with great regularity. Even with this worse-case scenario, smuggling would probably succeed. The Soviet Bloc has long exercised maximum border control but has not prevented smuggling. U.S. citizens and trading partners are not apt to tolerate any attempt to replicate Soviet Bloc experience.[12]

Although it is unlikely that policy makers will order the military to seal the national borders, the problems inherent in such a task need to be pointed out. Given the creative nature of drug smuggling, sealing the borders would require more than stationing military personnel in ports of entry and at key entry points. Soldiers would have to be stationed one or two hundred yards apart to insure that no one crossed the border unnoticed. Even with sensors implanted along the border, border guards would have to have quick response mechanisms to get to the violated border point before the smuggler escaped.

One possible use of military force is to deploy National Guard units in addition to or instead of regular military forces. Many National Guard units are trained in techniques useful for drug interdiction, and practicing them in a real situation has merit. This was the reasoning behind Operation Autumn Harvest, when National Guard units were used.[13] Moreover, state governors can deploy National Guard units without violating the Posse Comitatus Act. DOD is neither opposed to nor enthusiastic about using Guard units in this manner because it sees Guard and reserve units as integral parts of the national defense system.[14]

Scheduling is a problem in using the Guard, since its members only serve for short periods during a year. Comprehensive coverage would be difficult, and smugglers could adjust to those limited periods when the Guard is active, as they did during Operation Autumn Harvest. Smugglers knew that the Guard had been deployed and, apparently, adjusted their smuggling activities accordingly.

Bribery

Military men are as susceptible as civilians to bribery by drug dealers but with potentially more serious consequences. A $100,000 or $500,000 offer to a commanding officer for looking the other way while a load of cocaine is being brought into the United States would prove irresistible to some officers. For the smuggler, the cost would be negligible. Such corruption could spread and eventually destroy the morale of the officer corps. Once the officer is hooked, he or she is then susceptible to bribes for espionage purposes. Not only does money talk, but so, too, does blackmail.

This is not an idle concern. The Mexican military, previously one of the nation's least corrupt institutions, has been infected by drug corruption. Portions of the Colombian military have been so corrupted that they have engaged in fire fights with Colombian narcotics police to protect traffickers. Some Paraguayan military officers are deeply involved in the drug trade.[15] This list is not inclusive.

Military Intelligence and Civil Liberties

The use of military intelligence in antidrug campaigns may pose some potential dangers to American freedom. Inevitably, military intelligence agents must collect data on U.S. citizens at home and abroad since some of them would be involved in the international drug business. The amount of data is potentially large since it is impossible to guess who might be involved. As Air Force General Robert T. Herres commented, the U.S. should be wary of asking the military to conduct surveillance of U.S. citizens, some of which would have to be shared with civilian law enforcement officials. A second danger is the validity of such intelligence data in courtrooms, where procedural rights, including probable cause, must be protected. Revealing the source of military intelligence, some of which is politically sensitive, might compromise national security or the sources of the data. Furthermore, drug smugglers have the money with which to buy intelligence data and sufficient incentive to do so. The American Civil Liberties Union (ACLU) has begun to express serious doubts concerning the legality and fairness of using the military in this manner. One would expect the ACLU to challenge as unconstitutional any law excusing arresting officers, be they civilian or military, from testifying in court against drug traffickers or requiring the military to spy on private citizens.[16]

Arrest Powers

Many want military personnel to arrest drug smugglers, a policy that frightens military commanders who see themselves tied up in civilian courts for weeks and months while testifying or embarrassed by dismissals of charges because they or the people under them did not follow proper legal procedures in making arrests. They do not want the frustration with which law enforcement officers must deal on a daily basis, nor the animus that is likely to come their way as drug smugglers beat the charges on technical grounds. More important, they chose the military, not the police, as a career. Furthermore, they believe that involvement in civilian legal proceedings would seriously impair their ability to command since they cannot command troops or sailors or aviators while they are in court.[17]

Implications for Civil-Military Relations

The use of the military in domestic law enforcement would be to reverse a more than 100-year-old policy, the Posse Comitatus Act of 1878. In 1981, Congress did amend the Posse Comitatus Act only so far as to enable the military to assist law enforcement agencies as long as such assistance would not harm military readiness. In spite of the demands to give police power to the military, Congress has consistently remembered that military involvement in civilian affairs threatens civilian rule. The writers of the Constitution of 1787 recognized this potential threat when they specified civilian control of the military and limited the army to annual appropriations to confine its power. This position was reaffirmed in 1878, when Congress passed the Posse Comitatus Act forbidding the use of federal troops in civil matters. The Posse Comitatus Act was one result of the Reconstruction period. From 1867-77, the defeated southern states (except for Tennessee) were divided into five military districts, each under the command of a lieutenant general. The military had several missions during this period of martial law. The first was to maintain peace in a region in which many people had actively tried to kill or maim U.S. citizens during the Civil War. Military occupation was necessary as the Confederate central and state governments collapsed; the military filled the vacuum. The second mission arose from the First Reconstruction Act (1867) and succeeding reconstruction acts when Congress took control of the reconstruction process by using the military to remold the South into a democratic polity. It was not clear then, or now, if using the military in such a manner was constitutional. The framers of the Constitution of 1787 had not anticipated secession efforts; the problem was unprecedented. Within a year after the last troops were withdrawn from occupation duty in the South in 1877, Congress passed the Posse Comitatus Act to prevent such a recurrence. Many military officers understood that the military must have civilian support and did not like the anger directed at them by civilians.[18]

The military has been used domestically on other occasions, as William Taylor notes.[19] To make his case that the military should be used in the antidrug effort, he argues that using the military for domestic security purposes is not unprecedented and not a threat. Taylor cites examples of the military repressing and controlling riots or potential riots in desegregation efforts in Little Rock, Arkansas (1957), the University of

Mississippi (1962), and Alabama (1965), and in urban riot control in Detroit and Newark (1967), and Washington, Baltimore, and Rochester (1968). In some cases the National Guard was federalized; in others, regular troops were also used. In these cases, however, state and local law enforcement officials and/or U.S. marshals, not military personnel, had the task of arresting law breakers. Taylor could also have cited nineteenth century precedents of soldiers in breaking strikes.

There are essentially two possible outcomes to the use of the military in the drug war, be it for eradication or interdiction or sealing the borders or any combination thereof. It can succeed or fail. If DOD were named *lead agency*, the consequences would be more profound than simple success or failure.

If the military were unable to stop the flow of illegal narcotics into the United States, the institution would be severely compromised; it would be defeated. Military leaders are well aware of this possibility and reluctant to assume the risk. They have little desire to be involved in a no-win war. Officers say that they are capable of doing the job but argue that civilians would not like the way they would do it. As General Stephen Olmstead put it, they would use machine guns and not worry about Miranda rights. Merchants and tourists would not like the consequences of search techniques implemented at the borders or on the high seas. Understanding what would be required to have a hope of accomplishing this mission, and also understanding the restrictions civilians would place on them, the military does not want to become the lead agency or become involved in search, seizure, and arrest activities unless the American people clearly understand the price to be paid.[20]

Were the military to succeed where civilians have failed, some military officers and some civilians would conclude that the military is better able to run the country. The fact that civilian politicians demand the military assume a civilian function is a tacit admission of failure. Having proven in this instance that military organization is superior in solving a social problem, the military is likely to be asked to solve other domestic problems. It can easily build upon its greatly enhanced budget and organization and rising self-confidence to enter the civilian arena more fully with or without civilian invitation. The worst case, of course, would be for the military to become the dominant national political institution with control over the civilian population but with no control over the drug trade. The history of military interventions in Latin America and elsewhere certainly provides strong evidence for this view.

LATIN AMERICAN EXPERIENCE

One of the recurring themes of Latin American history since independence has been military coups d'etat and dictatorships. Both the Spanish and Portuguese crowns had recognized the potential threat from armies and purposely kept them in the New World; the wisdom of this policy was validated with the independence wars in Spanish areas, for criollo armies arose which the newly-independent governments could not control, except in rare cases. Militarism was delayed in Brazil, but it was the military that overthrew the Empire in 1889. Power is a potent aphrodisiac, and even professionalization, with its tenet of a non-political military, failed to end militarism. Instead, many military personnel came to believe that they were better able to govern than were the civilians.[21]

The view that civilians are incompetent to govern persists. That most Latin American nations currently have civilian governments does not belie this fact; the region has experienced other periods of civilian rule that were then followed by military rule. For example, both Argentina and El Salvador currently have civilian governments that daily must face the threat of a military coup.

If the military comes to believe that the civilian government cannot preserve what the military believes to be national security or cannot enforce the nation's laws, the military is likely to intervene.[22] The number of instances in which this has occurred are too numerous to list. It has occurred in countries with "democratic" histories as well as in those with chronic political instability. Uruguay, once cited as the "Switzerland of Latin America," is a good example. Uruguayan civilian government officials called upon the military to end the threat of the Tupamaro terrorists/guerrillas when civilian law enforcement failed. The military accomplished the task, but only by destroying Uruguayan democracy and using oppression. Between 1972 and 1985, the Uruguayan military either had veto power over governmental decisions or was the government.[23] Even now, civilian officials continue to look over their shoulders to see how the military will react.

Even precluding eventual military dictatorships, using the military in civilian law enforcement is dangerous. The Colombian armed forces, recently assigned the task of fighting that nation's drug cartels, is abusing the population. One report asserts that the military, in league with right-wing death squads, terrorizes and kills innocent people in Uraba state.[24]

Latin American nations and the United States have very different traditions regarding civil-military relations, of course, but demanding that the U.S. armed forces be given civilian police powers to accomplish a task at which civilians have thus far failed risks an "Uruguayan solution" or, at least, the first major step in that direction. Efforts to prevent this by giving the military only outside the land area of the United States seem doomed to fail. If the military operates within the territorial limits of the U.S. on the ocean or on the high seas, it still would have to conduct surveillance of or collect intelligence on U.S. citizens *inside* the United States, for intelligence is essential for an anti-smuggling program.[25] The military warns against having its personnel conducting surveillance of U.S. citizens. Civilians need to attend to ranking military officers' warnings of the dangers to civilian rule if the military assumes an important civilian function.

COST EFFECTIVENESS

Analysts argue that military interdiction campaigns would not be cost effective. Peter Reuter of the Rand Corporation points out that raising the cocaine interdiction rate from 20 percent to 50 percent would marginally affect supply in the United States, raising the retail or "street" price only 4 percent a kilo.[26] Cocaine and heroin are especially difficult to interdict because of their high dollar value per unit of weight. High dollar amounts of either, but especially cocaine, which is in much greater demand in the U.S., can be hidden inside dolls, cans, or thousands of other items routinely imported by the thousands into the United States. Customs is only able to inspect some 3 percent of the 7.5 million cargo containers entering the U.S. each year. Expensive and sophisticated military equipment such as Airborne Warning and Control System (AWACS) aircraft would not help Customs with this problem.[27] Marijuana, which is bulky and has low dollar value by weight, is easier to interdict. As Captain Gary F. Crosby of the Coast Guard put it, one could often smell the cargo before one saw the ship.[28] In 1987, the Air Force spent $2.6 million on six drug seizures and ten arrests (approximately $339,000 per bust). Under the LEDET program, the Navy spent $27 million and the Coast Guard spent $13 million to capture twenty boats carrying 225,000 pounds of marijuana and 550 pounds of cocaine (approximately $2 million per seizure).[29] In September, 1987, National Guard units joined forces with Customs in Operation Autumn Harvest, an unsuccessful antismuggling effort on the Arizona border, at a cost of $960,000.[30] This is extraordinarily high cost for such a small return, especially when the operation had no effect on the amount of drugs being sold inside the United States. Although one would expect experience to lower costs, the return on investment would continue to be small. The chief beneficiaries would be the drug traffickers, since their profits would rise.

THE NEW MILITARY ROLE

Congress yielded some to the pressure to increase the role of the military in the antidrug campaign. The National Defense Authorization Act for FY 1989 (H.R. 4481)[31] made DOD lead agency for the collection and dissemination of intelligence data on the aerial and maritime transit of illicit drugs into the United States, and commanded DOD to establish a command, control, communications, and technical intelligence (C3I) structure for that purpose. Within the context of other applicable law, DOD may provide relevant intelligence data on possible violations of federal or state law collected during the normal course of training or operations to the appropriate federal, state, or local law enforcement officials, and to do so promptly. To increase the possibility that the military will actually have such data to impart, the act specifies that the needs of civilian law enforcement officials should be taken into account when DOD plans and conducts military exercises. Section 1104 (a) stipulates that the military not conduct domestic intelligence gathering and must respect such laws as the Privacy Act.

Congress also expanded the extent to which military aircraft and ships can be used to supplement civilian law enforcement. Section 373 authorized DOD, with the approval of the Attorney General and the Secretaries of State and Defense, to transport civilian law enforcement personnel and to allow them to use these craft as a base of operations for law enforcement efforts outside the United States. However, these craft can come into the United States when they are in hot pursuit. Section 379 expanded the LEDET program by requiring no fewer than 500 Coast Guard personnel, trained in law enforcement procedures and armed with arrest powers, be assigned to appropriate navy surface ships sailing in drug interdiction areas. Section 7401 of the Antidrug Act of 1988 indemnified the captains of these ships from civil or criminal liability resulting from their having fired on a suspected vessel.[32]

The defense appropriation act carefully stipulated that the military is not to participate directly in civilian law enforcement operations unless otherwise authorized by law (Section 373), and that Air Force, Army, Navy, and Marine Corps members are not to engage in search, seizure, and arrest activities (Section 375). In the conference report accompanying HR 4481, Congress explained that it does not want a radical break with the tradition of keeping the military out of civilian law enforcement.[33]

Nevertheless, the demand for a military solution to the drug war prompted Congress to expand the role of the National Guard. Under Section 1105 of the defense bill, DOD was ordered to provide them with $30 million for operations and equipment and another $30 million for personnel costs specifically for drug interdiction and law enforcement efforts. Guard units must be under the control of state governors (thus avoiding violation of the Posse Comitatus Act), and the antidrug efforts must be in addition to annual training.

To pay for this increased military effort, Congress authorized $300 million, which *must* be used for DOD's antidrug efforts without decreasing the monies DOD had previously allocated, and again required civilian agencies to reimburse DOD for some costs. Of the $300 million, $90 million was transferred from Aircraft Procurement, Navy, 1987/89, and $210 million was new money. To reinforce its desire for increased military reconnaissance of possible drug smuggling activity, $40 million of the total was authorized solely for Army and Air National Guard surveillance efforts. The expanded LEDET program is to be funded by a transfer of $6 million from DOD to the Coast Guard.[34]

As part of the 1988 drug bill, the military was given additional responsibilities outside the United States. One million dollars was authorized to arm foreign aircraft for defensive purposes in narcotics interdiction and eradication campaigns. Two million was authorized for education and training in the operation and maintenance of antinarcotics equipment in Latin America and the Caribbean and, upon the request of a foreign government, to pay for DOD mobile training teams to teach tactical operational skills for narcotics interdiction. Recipient nations must be democratic and their governments must not engage in a "consistent pattern of gross violations of internationally recognized human rights." Another $3.5 million was authorized for military assistance for antinarcotics efforts in Latin America and the Caribbean. Significantly, $15 million was granted to Colombia to support its armed forces' efforts against illicit narcotics production and trafficking.

That the military's role in the national antidrug effort was increased only moderately was the result of successful lobbying by DOD officials and others concerned with preserving civil liberties. The expanded military effort has some inherent dangers. Intelligence data, especially that concerned with smuggling and involving U.S. citizens, is not easily segregated. The easiest, and thus most probable, technique to collect such data is to collect as much as possible and sort it out later. Since the destination of illicit drugs is primarily to U.S. criminal organizations, it seems inevitable that domestic intelligence data will be collected and shared with civilian law enforcement officials. Some of the data collected will not involve law violations.

CONCLUSION

The 100th Congress' actions have brought the military more directly into the civilian arena, the language of defense and drug bills notwithstanding. Using the military to collect intelligence data, transport civilian law enforcement personnel, shoot at suspected smugglers' boats and ships, and engage in hot pursuit into the United States and using the National Guard in civilian law enforcement means that the military will be performing civilian functions. Giving naval commanders the authority to attack and even sink civilian ships, some of which might be innocently used, without legal responsibility is to put those commanders above the law. The initial step in converting military personnel into civilian police has begun. Few military or civilian law enforcement agencies want the military to become police, and neither believe that the military can effectively stop drug smuggling without dramatically changing the nature of American government.

Although the United States is not Latin America with its long tradition of military intervention and military dictatorship, U.S. citizens should heed high-ranking U.S. military officers's warnings that bringing the military directly into the antidrug campaign threatens civilian government. Framers of the Constitution, well aware of Cromwell's military dictatorship in mid-seventeenth century England and of the imposition of martial law on Massachusetts Bay colony by the British in 1774, required a civilian to be commander-in-chief of the armed forces and limited army appropriations to a yearly basis.

The military is being set up to fail. All the available evidence indicates that interdiction efforts by civilians or military or both are doomed to failure. The supply of marijuana and cocaine is so large and smuggling techniques so well developed and so easily changed that Congress is proposing little more than political grandstanding in an election year. The increased role of the military, limited as it now is, will have a negligible effect on the supply of drugs.

The military could conceivably interdict the flow of drugs into the United States by doing what it is designed to do: fight a war. Such a war, however, would be a low-intensity conflict in which the enemy is not easily identifiable and could hide among "friendly" personnel within a gigantic area. Consequently, the most effective strategy would be for the military to take control of U.S. borders by gaining control of the high seas near the coastline, picketing soldiers along the land borders, gaining complete control of airspace near and along the borders, and taking control of ports of entry. Doing this would, of course, disrupt the U.S. and other economies and engender massive anger towards the U.S. Such a strategy also means extensive surveillance of U.S. and other citizens in order to identify potential smugglers and shipments. It means a massive increase in the size and budget of the armed forces so that national defense and the interdiction campaign can occur simultaneously. As long as the military conducts such a war, military personnel will have to leave normal duty to appear in court unless and until the decision is made to suspend constitutional guarantees. In sum, the military would assume a level of importance within the United States not seen since World War II, but to solve a social problem, not meet an obvious and serious threat from foreign militaries.

This worst case scenario will not occur, but the inappropriateness of military involvement in the antidrug campaign raises the question of whether civilian politicians, under fire from their constituents during an election year because they have been unable to curb the supply of narcotics, are intentionally trying to dissipate this anger by providing another potential target--the military. Such a tactic might work. By talking about it, Congress has bought some time from the American people. When, after a few years, the problem persists, Congress can increase military involvement, which can escalate for years. In the meantime, members of Congress will get re-elected and the drug problem will persist until Americans change their drug appetites.

POLICY RECOMMENDATIONS

1. The U.S. Customs Service should be lead agency in the antismuggling campaign, with the Coast Guard serving as one enforcement arm.

2. The Coast Guard and Customs should be given increased funding so they can use their own personnel and equipment to interdict smuggling of any kind at the borders and at sea.

3. The military's mission as the nation's defense against foreign armies and against domestic insurrection should be reaffirmed. The military should fight real wars, not pseudowars such as the so-called "war on drugs."

4. In order to protect constitutional government and civil liberties, the military should not be given civilian police powers. Congress and the Executive branch should insure that its laws do not impair civil liberties, including the Sixth Amendment guaranteeing the accused the right to face their accusers, whether the accusers are civilian or military.

5. If the military is to be involved, it should be restricted to giving logistical support (loans of specialized equipment, communications support, appropriate intelligence information, and specialized training) to civilian law enforcement agencies, and they should be funded appropriately.

6. Congress and the Executive branch should make it clear to the American public that interdiction is no more than a holding action, and that the drug problem will be solved only when Americans decide to quit using illicit drugs. Put another way, expectations that interdiction is a solution should be lowered as quickly as possible.

7. Congress and the Executive branch should make it clear that the United States has no intention of violating the sovereignty of other nations.

8. Congress and the Executive branch should make it clear that the U.S. military will not be used to eradicate or to help eradicate crops in other nations.

9. State governors, with the aid of DOD, should explore possibilities of using their National Guard units to supplement the work of state and local law enforcement.

10. The United States needs to develop better means of border interdiction of all smuggled goods, not just illicit narcotics. Inability to enforce the national importation laws is a more general problem adversely affecting the nation's security and economic well-being.

7

International Narcopolicy and the Role of the U.S. Congress*
Raphael Perl

OVERVIEW

In recent years Congress has expressed growing concern over the problem of drug abuse in the United States. Much attention has been given to international narcotics control through programs primarily aimed at reducing the supply of illicit narcotics in source countries and interdicting supply routes. Funding has been used for crop eradication and control, law enforcement assistance, equipment and materials, training of foreign law enforcement personnel, and development assistance to provide economic alternatives to illicit narcotic crops.

In the past, Congress expressed its concern by enacting legislation authorizing the President to suspend assistance to major illicit narcotic drug-producing or drug-transit countries that did not take adequate remedial action to improve their status as illicit narcotics producers or providers. In addition, Congress established detailed requirements, indicating progress in narcotics control, for continuing of U.S. aid to Bolivia, Jamaica, Mexico, and Peru.[1]

The overall present direction of congressional foreign narcopolicy may be characterized as supply reduction oriented, bilaterally oriented, and more "stick" than "carrot" oriented. Three pieces of noteworthy legislation passed in 1988 may have significant impact on narcopolicy in these three areas. They are the Antidrug Abuse Act of 1988,[2] the Defense Authorization Act for 1989,[3] and the Foreign Assistance Appropriations Act for 1989.[4] A discussion of U.S. international narcotics control policy, the congressional role in antidrug sanctions, and the above-mentioned three legislative enactments follows.

CURRENT U.S. INTERNATIONAL NARCOTICS CONTROL POLICY[5]

The primary goal of U.S. international narcotics policy is to reduce the supply of illicit narcotics flowing into the United States. A second and supporting goal is to reduce the amount of illicit narcotics cultivated, processed, and consumed worldwide. U.S. international narcotics control policy is implemented by a multifaceted strategy that includes the following four elements: eradication of narcotic crops, interdiction and law enforcement activities in drug-producing and drug-transiting countries, international cooperation, and sanctions.

Eradication of Narcotic Crops

Reducing cultivation of illicit narcotic crops through eradication is an official U.S. international narcotics control strategy. In 1988, the United States supported programs to eradicate coca, opium, and marijuana in fourteen countries, efforts conducted by a number of government agencies administering several types of programs. The United States supports eradication by providing producer countries with chemical herbicides, technical assistance and specialized equipment, and spray aircraft. AID funds development projects that promote creation of alternative income for farmers who abandon cultivation of illicit narcotics.[6] U.S. eradication policy receives public relations support from the U.S. Information Agency (USIA), which publicizes the dangers of drug abuse and trafficker violence. In addition, AID sponsors drug education and awareness programs in both Latin American and Asian countries.[7]

Interdiction and Law Enforcement

A second element of U.S. international narcotics control strategy is to help host governments seize illicit narcotics before they reach America's borders. Training foreign law enforcement personnel constitutes a major part of such endeavors. In 1986, the State Department funded antinarcotics law enforcement training programs for foreign personnel from more than seventy countries. In addition, the State Department provides host country antinarcotics personnel with a wide range of equipment, and DEA agents regularly assist foreign police forces in their efforts to destabilize trafficking networks. U.S. efforts to promote effective law enforcement against narcotics traffickers also include suggestions to nations on means to strengthen their legal and judicial systems.

International Cooperation

Essentially all elements of U.S. international narcotics control strategy require international cooperation. By using diplomatic initiatives, both bilateral and multilateral, the State Department encourages and assists nations to reduce cultivation, production, and trafficking in illicit drugs. These bilateral agreements and international conventions have thus far been largely ineffective in reversing the growth of international narcotics trafficking, in part because they lack strong enforcement mechanisms and are not uniformly interpreted by member nations.

U.S. international narcotics control strategy also relies on international cooperation to promote coordinated border operations to interdict traffickers. To this end, the U.S. government has provided technical assistance to coordinated multinational operations in Colombia, Peru, and Ecuador. The United States also participates in multilateral assistance programs through the United Nations Fund for Drug Abuse Control (UNFDAC) and actively enlists the aid and support of other governments for narcotics control projects. UNFDAC currently assists twenty-five developing countries through development, law enforcement, education, treatment, and rehabilitation programs. The 1988 UNFDAC budget totaled $60 million derived from voluntary contributions. For FY 1988, the United States provided $3 million for the U.S. voluntary contribution to UNFDAC.

Sanctions

A fourth element of U.S. international narcotics control strategy, initiated by Congress in recent years, involves applying sanctions against certain drug-producing or trafficking nations. Such sanctions range from suspension of U.S. foreign assistance to curtailment of air transportation to target countries. Current drug sanctions legislation requires the President to give Congress every March 1 a list of major illicit drug-producing and trafficking countries that he has certified as eligible to receive U.S. foreign aid and other economic and trade benefits. This action sets in motion a 45-day congressional review process, during which Congress can override the President's certification.

Certification may be granted because a major illicit drug-producing or trafficking country has "cooperated fully" with U.S. narcotics reduction goals and/or has taken "adequate steps on its own" in tandem with U.S. goals. A country not qualified on the basis of full cooperation or adequate steps taken may escape sanctions if the President certifies that U.S. "vital national interests" preclude implementation of sanctions on that country.

CONGRESS AND ANTIDRUG SANCTIONS[8]

Congress may influence foreign narcopolicy by legislating to establish new programs, to condition and limit spending, to set new objectives and guidelines, and to authorize and direct the executive branch to undertake specified activities. Most noteworthy of such legislative initiatives are the international narcotics control provisions in the Anti-Drug Abuse Acts of 1986[9] and 1988,[10] which link cooperation on international narcotics control issues by major illicit drug-producing or transit countries with their eligibility for U.S. foreign aid and, under certain circumstances, U.S. trade benefits. This process, commonly referred to as "certification," requires the President to withhold 50 percent of U.S. foreign assistance at the start of each fiscal year (October 1) pending a determination of certification on, or after March 1.

Then, on March 1 of each year, the President then sends to Congress a list of major illicit drug-producing and/or transit countries he certifies as eligible to receive full U.S. assistance. Congress has forty-five days of continuous session to evaluate the President's determinations and enact country-specific resolutions of disapproval, should it so choose.

Basically, certification may be justified on two grounds: (1) that United States's *vital national interests* preclude continuing sanctions and that therefore, aid should be disbursed; or (2) that a country has *cooperated fully* with the United States in curbing illicit narcotics and/or has taken *adequate steps on its own* to prevent drug production, processing, trafficking, drug-related money laundering, bribery, and public corruption.[11] In making a determination based on "cooperation," the President "shall consider" whether the government's actions "have resulted in the maximum reductions in illicit production" determined achievable, as well as ten other factors indicating law enforcement cooperation.[12] A country designated in the previous year as a major illicit drug-producing or transit country may not be certified as fully cooperating unless it has in place a bilateral narcotics agreement with the United States, or a multilateral narcotics-related treaty facilitating antidrug programs and cooperation.[13] A major illicit drug-producing or transit country that also produces illicit opium may not be certified unless the country has taken steps to prevent diversion of licit opium cultivation and production into the illicit market, maintains opium stockpiles at (or below) levels of licit demand, and prevents illicit cultivation and production.[14]

If the President does not issue a determination for a major drug-producing or transit country, or if Congress disapproves the President's determination for a specific country, some sanctions will be imposed automatically, and some may be implemented at the President's discretion. Mandatory sanctions include:

- 50 percent suspension of all U.S. assistance for the current fiscal year, exempting certain categories of assistance such as humanitarian assistance and international narcotics control assistance.

- 100 percent suspension of U.S. assistance for subsequent fiscal years, unless the country is certified in the interim.

- Voting against loans to a country in the multilateral development banks.[15]

- Nonallocation of a sugar quota.[16]

Discretionary sanctions include:

- Denial of preferential tariff treatment to a country's exports under the Generalized System of Preferences and the Caribbean Basin Economic Recovery Act.

- Duty increases of up to 50 percent of value on a country's exports to the United States.

- Curtailment of air transportation and traffic between the U.S. and the non-certified country.

- Withdrawal of U.S. participation in any pre-clearance customs arrangements with the non-certified country.[17]

To date, Congress has not decertified any country certified by the President as eligible for foreign assistance under the above provisions. In 1987, resolutions to disapprove certification were introduced against the Bahamas, Panama, and Mexico.[18] Of these, the resolution to decertify Panama, passed by the Senate on April 3, 1987, was the only one to pass either house of Congress. Similarly, in 1988 no country was decertified by the full Congress for narcotics non-cooperation. In 1988, resolutions were introduced to decertify the Bahamas, Bolivia, Mexico, Paraguay, and Peru.[19] Of these, the one to decertify Mexico, which passed the Senate on April 14, 1988, was the only one to pass either house of Congress.[20]

Congress has also imposed requirements for tougher sanctions, including 100 percent suspension of assistance, on a subset of countries posing more difficult problems for the United States. A separate section of the Antidrug Abuse Act of 1986[21] provides *all assistance shall be suspended* (and no U.S. votes shall be cast in multilateral development banks for loans) to a certain subset of more serious major illicit drug-producing or drug-transit countries unless the President certifies the following three items which are not subject to override by joint resolution: (1) overriding national interest requires such assistance, (2) such assistance would improve prospects for cooperation against the flow of illicit drugs, and (3) the government in question has made bona fide efforts to investigate and prosecute what amounts to crimes against DEA agents committed with the complicity of foreign government personnel since January 1, 1985.

Categories of countries subject to 100 percent suspension of assistance include major illicit drug-producing and drug-transit countries that: (1) encourage illegal narcotics production or distribution as a matter of government policy, (2) have a senior government official engaged in such production or distribution, (3) have threatened or inflicted violence on U.S. drug enforcement officials with complicity by government employees; or (4) are not providing reasonable cooperation to U.S. drug enforcement agents.

Provisions listed in categories (3) and (4) above clearly appear to be aimed at Mexico, as many U.S. citizens feel that until Mexico levels jail sentences against those responsible for the murder and torture of DEA agents Enrique Camarena Salazar and Victor Cortez, Mexico is in some respect supporting the wrongdoers. Arguably, many U.S. citizens do not fully appreciate the pride Mexican citizens take in their country's sovereignty and expect U.S. DEA agents to be able to operate in Mexico with at least some authority and freedom. Some analysts go so far as to suggest that this section dealing with a subset of countries posing more difficult problems[22] was written exclusively to apply to Mexico, and that additional ones were added simply so that the provisions applying to Mexico were not so blatantly evident. Other analysts, however, suggest that the section was written to include a broad base of existing and potential situations of concern to U.S. policy makers. Nevertheless, some partisan observers unofficially call this section a "Mexico bashing" amendment.[23]

In acting on a presidential determination of certification, Congress will be centrally concerned that steps taken reduce the overall drug flow into the United States. In addition, Congress may wish to consider the overall effect of sanctions on other (non-narcotics) U.S. foreign policy goals, and the effect of sanctions on U.S. international narcotics policy.[24]

Relevant questions relating to the effect of sanctions on other U.S. foreign policy goals include:

- To what extent might sanctions have a desirable or undesirable effect on domestic political and economic stability of a specific illicit drug-producing or transit country?

- To what extent do demands for narcotics control cooperation with foreign countries have to compete with other foreign policy issues, such as a country's human rights policy, military cooperation, debt repayment, terrorism policy, U.N. voting support, etc.?

- To what extent might imposition of sanctions on a specific country affect U.S. relationships with other neighboring countries in a given region?

Relevant questions relating to the effect of sanctions on U.S. international narcotics policy include:

- What factors influencing the effectiveness of foreign aid sanctions are present in each individual country (e.g., target country's dependence on aid, ability of the foreign government to implement the steps demanded, the presence of international cooperation in implementing the sanctions)?

- If sanctions are employed, to what extent might the United States actually lose the ability to exercise leverage over the offending country? For example, if sanctions are imposed on a major drug-producing or transit country, would this increase the country's dependence on narcotics production to supplement income lost as a result of sanctions?

- If countries do cooperate with the United States in the control of narcotics, does this create a significant U.S. obligation to offset the economic loss incurred by their reduction of the drug flow?

- If sanctions are not used more frequently and decisively, will the mere threat of sanctions still have an effect on the actions of drug producer or transit countries?

● If sanctions are to be fully effective, should they be used in conjunction with additional positive incentives to foster narcotics cooperation by major illicit drug-producing and transit countries?

THE ANTIDRUG ABUSE ACT OF 1988[25]

The 1988 Anti-Drug Abuse Act, passed by the Congress on October 21, 1988, contains provisions relating to all aspects of federal programs curbing the supply, use, and abuse of dangerous drugs in the United States. In total, the act provides for $5.5 billion in new authorizations for 1989--a $2.7 billion increase over authorization levels provided for in regular appropriation levels. Some of these authorizations were partially funded by the supplemental
appropriations title of the drug bill, but nearly $1.8 billion of the total funds authorized remained unfunded when the bill was enacted.

Of the total amount of funds authorized under the Act, 52 percent was for supply reduction measures and 48 percent for demand reduction measures. Of the total funds appropriated for FY 1989 under the act, 56 percent went for supply reduction and 44 percent for demand reduction. Thirty percent of the amount authorized for supply reduction and 38 percent of the amount authorized for demand reduction were appropriated. In previous years, the percentage of funds both authorized and appropriated was roughly 75 percent for supply reduction and 25 percent for demand reduction. Thus, resource allocation under the act indicates a dramatic shift away from primary reliance on supply reduction measures for 1989.

General provisions of the 1988 Antidrug Abuse Act include: authorizing additional funds for law enforcement and drug abuse education and treatment programs, establishing new record-keeping controls over chemicals used in the illicit manufacture of drugs, establishing penalties for diverting of such precursor chemicals into illegal drug manufacture, denying certain federal benefits to drug offenders, prohibiting awards to federal contractors who do not maintain drug-free workplaces, permitting the death penalty against drug kingpins for certain drug related killings, creating a cabinet-level federal "drug czar" position in the Office of the President, enhancing civil and criminal penalties against drug users (including up to $10,000 in civil fines), and overall strengthening of international narcotics control programs.

Title IV of the act is named the "International Narcotics Control Act of 1988." This title contains major provisions relating to: multilateral control efforts; country-specific and country non-specific requirements, authorizations, and earmarkings; annual reporting and certification requirements; international banking and money laundering; and an assortment of miscellaneous provisions. A summary format of the act's major provisions within these categories follows:

General provisions

- Assigns the Secretary of State coordination of all U.S. assistance supporting international efforts to combat illicit narcotics production and trafficking.

- Authorizes for FY 1989 $101 million for international narcotics control programs ($2.5 million over FY 1988), $5 million for rewards for information on narcoterrorists, and $23 million for machine readable visas.

Multilateral control efforts

- Calls on the President to seek creation of a Latin American regional antinarcotics force and to explore the concept of similar forces in other regions of the world.

- Calls on the President and the United Nations to pursue establishment of an international drug force and to begin international discussions towards establishing an international criminal court to try drug traffickers and others who commit international crimes.

- Calls on the President to convene an international conference on combatting illicit drug production, trafficking, and use in the Western Hemisphere.

- Calls on the Secretary of State to consult with heads of other U.S. Agencies and with governments of other Western Hemisphere nations concerning creation of a comprehensive, integrated, multinational plan to combat the international cocaine trade.

- Calls on the Department of State to establish a regional antinarcotics training center in the Caribbean.

- Authorizes $3 million for U.S. contributions to multilateral and regional drug abuse programs ($2 million for UNFDAC and $600,000 for OAS-sponsored projects).

Selected country-specific provisions

Bolivia

- Makes FY 1989 security assistance contingent on presidential certification that Bolivia implements legislation that establishes legal coca requirements, licenses the number of hectares required for legal production, makes unlicensed coca production illegal, and makes unlicensed coca possession and distribution illegal.

- Conditions foreign assistance certification for FY 1989 on presidential certification that Bolivia has entered into a narcotics cooperation agreement with the United States, fully achieved eradication targets of that agreement, and has begun a program of forced eradication of illicit cultivation if voluntary eradication goals are not being met or are not continued.

- Cancels earlier earmarking of $15 million foreign assistance appropriations for narcotics interdiction and control programs.

Peru

- Requires the President, when evaluating Peru's certification, to give special consideration to progress made in meeting eradication targets of the previous year.

Colombia

- Authorizes $15 million in fiscal year 1989 for defense equipment for Colombia, and $5 million to protect officials and members of the press against narco-terrorist attacks.

- Permits (by amendment of the Foreign Assistance Act) more than six members of the U.S. armed forces to be assigned to carry out U.S. international security assistance programs in Colombia.

- Exempts Colombia from Foreign Assistance Act prohibitions on training or financial support to foreign police forces.

Mexico

- Directs the President (when making FY 1989 certifications) to consider Mexico's response to U.S. proposals to establish joint agreements on border air apprehension and surveillance activities.

- Limits narcotics control assistance to Mexico to $15 million.

Pakistan

- Requires the President, when evaluating Pakistan's certification, to consider the extent to which Pakistan is destroying illicit laboratories and prosecuting their owner/operators, putting major traffickers out of business, and changing legal codes to permit more effective prosecution of traffickers (by such measures as new conspiracy and asset seizure laws).

Laos

- Requires periodic reports on the involvement of the government of Laos, or senior officials thereof, in the illicit drug trade, and on any assistance other governments in the region may provide in the distribution of illicit drugs from Laos.

Additional authorizations and earmarkings

- Earmarks $100,000 for testing and using safe and effective herbicides for aerial eradication of coca.
- Earmarks $3.5 million for narcotics-related military assistance programs in Latin America or the Caribbean.

- Earmarks $1 million of military assistance funding for weapons to arm aircraft used in narcotics eradication and interdiction, and not less than $2 million for narcotics-related military education and training.

- Permits military assistance, education, and training funds to be used to provide weapons, ammunition, and training directly to foreign antidrug law enforcement units for antinarcotics use if the recipient countries have democratic governments and do not engage in consistent patterns of gross violations of internationally recognized human rights.

- Authorizes a minimum of $1 million for narcotics control assistance to non-major drug-transit countries.

- Provides for the reallocation of funds from countries not certified to those fully cooperating.

Annual reporting and certification process

- Requires the President to establish numerical standards and guidelines for determining which countries are major illicit drug-transit nations, and to notify Congress each October 1 of the final list of countries likely to require determinations of certification.

- Gives Congress forty-five (instead of thirty days) of continuous session to decertify countries certified by the President as exempt from trade and aviation sanctions.

- Exempts assistance for narcotics education and awareness activities from funding subject to certification sanctions.

- Adds additional criteria (primarily related to antinarcotics law enforcement cooperation) for the President to consider when making determinations of certification.

- Requires that FY 1989 certifications for a major drug-transit country that also produces licit opium be contingent on whether such a government has taken steps to prevent significant diversion of its licit opium crop into the illicit market, to reduce its opium stockpile, and to eliminate illicit cultivation and production. (Although the law does not specifically mention it by name, it appears that this provision is aimed at India).

- Exempts major transit countries from sanctions if money-laundering concerns do not apply to the country, if the country was a former producer country that has eliminated illicit production in the last two years, or if the country is fully cooperating with U.S. antinarcotics efforts. (Although the provision does not mention Turkey by name, it appears that this provision is designed to exempt Turkey from potential application of sanctions.)

International banking and money laundering provisions

- Urges the Secretary of the Treasury to negotiate with foreign finance ministers to establish an international currency control agency that would serve as a central database for international drug enforcement agencies, collect and analyze currency transaction reports filed by member countries, and encourage adoption by member countries of uniform cash transaction and money laundering statutes.

- Urges the Secretary of the Treasury to negotiate international agreements that ensure foreign financial institutions maintain adequate records of large U.S. currency transactions, and to establish mechanisms for U.S. law enforcement officials to obtain such records.

- Requires the President to impose penalties and sanctions against narcotics money laundering countries that have jurisdiction over financial institutions substantially engaged in transactions involving proceeds of narcotics trafficking affecting the United States, that have not reached an agreement with the U.S. on exchanging records of such transactions, and that are not negotiating in good faith to reach such an agreement. Such penalties may be waived or delayed if the President certifies to Congress that the national interest precludes their imposition. Penalties include prohibiting such persons, institutions, or entities from participating in any U.S. dollar clearing or wire transfer system, and from maintaining an account in an institution chartered under U.S. federal or state law. Financial institutions in countries targeted for penalties shall be exempt from their imposition, however, if they "maintain adequate records."

Additional or miscellaneous provisions

- Prohibits the provision of U.S. foreign aid and assistance under the Arms Export Control Act to individuals or entities known or believed to be convicted of any domestic or foreign narcotics violation, and to individuals who have been directly involved in (or who have facilitated) illicit drug trafficking.

• Requires the President to submit to the Congress an annual report on the assets provided by the U.S. Government during the preceding fiscal year to support antinarcotics efforts.

• Provides for reimbursement to the U.S. Department of Defense of the additional cost of services used in providing international narcotics control assistance.
• Denies passports to individuals convicted of drug felony offenses.

• Permits the Export/Import Bank to extend credit for sale of defense articles or services to countries requiring certification which have democratic governments if the President certifies that such sales are in the national interest.

THE DEFENSE AUTHORIZATION ACT FOR 1989[26]

The National Defense Authorization Act for FY 1989 complements programs and provisions of the 1988 omnibus drug act by enhancing the role and contributions made by the military in the nation's antidrug campaign. Title XI of the act, "Drug Interdiction and Law Enforcement Support," contains a number of provisions that:

• establish DOD as "lead agency" for detecting and monitoring aerial and maritime transit of illegal drugs into the United States;

• require DOD to promptly provide civilian law enforcement agencies with relevant drug-related intelligence;

• charge the President to direct that command, control, communications, and technical intelligence assets dedicated to drug control be integrated by the DOD into an effective network;

• permit DOD personnel (with the approval of the Secretaries of Defense and State, and the Attorney General) to transport civilian law enforcement personnel outside the land areas of the United States in connection with law enforcement operations;

• permit increased use of the National Guard in drug interdiction activities; and,

• provide DOD with an additional $210 million for drug interdiction activities.
Noteworthy in the above provisions is what appears to be an ongoing trend to enhance direct military involvement in the nation's antidrug campaign, as well as to enhance military support to civilian antidrug enforcement activities. In addition, integrating DOD antidrug intelligence assets into an operational network--if effectively implemented and

integrated into the antidrug networks of other intelligence gathering entities--may have a significant impact on the nation's drug interdiction program.

THE FOREIGN ASSISTANCE APPROPRIATIONS ACT FOR 1989[27]

The Foreign Assistance, Export Financing, Related Programs Appropriations Act of 1989, is the third and final major legislative enactment of 1988 through which the Congress influences U.S. international narcotics policy. The act, through a skillful exercise of the "power of the purse," provides for increased emphasis by the Department of State on programs and policies that: seek to intensify efforts aimed at interdiction and eradication of illicit narcotics, and seek international cooperation on narcotics enforcement matters in such areas as extradition treaties, mutual legal assistance to combat money laundering, and sharing evidence. Title II of the act, "Bilateral Economic Assistance," contains a section under Department of State Appropriations entitled "International Narcotics Control," which appropriates $101 million for international narcotics control activities (at least $7 million of which shall be available for Latin America regional programs).

Title V of the Act:[28]

- provides Economic Support Funds totaling $61 million for narcotics control programs in Bolivia, Ecuador, Jamaica, and Peru (with a $5 million limit on funds for any one country);

- provides Military Assistance Funds totaling $16.5 million for narcotics control programs in Bolivia, Ecuador, Jamaica, and Colombia;

- earmarks $10 million for narcotics education and awareness programs of the Agency for International Development;

- earmarks up to $15 million for narcotics related economic assistance activities;

- waives the existing statutory prohibition that foreign assistance funding for international narcotics control shall *not* be made available for the procurement of weapons or ammunition for Bolivia, Peru, Columbia, Ecuador, or the newly authorized Latin American regional air wing;[29]

- provides for the reallocation of unused funds authorized under the Act *from* countries which have not taken adequate steps to halt illicit drug production or trafficking *to* countries which have met their illicit drug eradication targets, or have otherwise taken significant steps to halt illicit production or trafficking.

Noteworthy among the above-described provisions are those providing positive economic incentives for cooperation with the U.S. narcotics control programs and objectives, and those earmarking funds for narcotics education and awareness programs and narcotics related economic assistance activities.

CONCLUSION

Evidently Congress has taken, is taking, and will continue to take an active role in formulating international narcopolicy. The wide reach of this role is exemplified by the influence Congress exerts over the Executive Branch in determining which major illicit drug-producing and/or transit countries shall be exempt from economic and trade sanctions, i.e., the "certification" process.

In the Antidrug Abuse Act of 1988, Congress has exercised broad reaching powers, established a structure for increased centralization of U.S. drug policy, emphasized regional cooperative efforts, imposed country specific certification requirements, imposed restrictions on money laundering and precursor chemicals, and authorized new highs in funding levels for the war on drugs. Perhaps even more important, the act shifted the overall proportion of resource allocation between supply reduction and demand reduction from previous levels of approximately 75 percent for supply reduction and 25 percent for demand reduction to a level roughly approaching fifty-fifty.

In the Defense Authorization Act of 1989, Congress assigned the military a key role in the nation's antidrug interdiction effort--that of lead agency in the effort to interdict air and sea traffic in illicit drugs--and expanded the role of the National Guard in drug interdiction activities.

In the Foreign Assistance Appropriations Act of 1989, Congress, by exercising power of the purse, earmarked funds as positive incentives to certain cooperative major illicit drug-producing or transit countries, and waived certain restrictions on providing weapons to countries where drug barons are gaining in power.

How will Congress continue to shape the overall character of U.S. international drug policy? Will future policy, as recent legislation may indicate, focus more on multilateral and regional cooperative efforts? Will U.S. policy focus more on law enforcement cooperation as a factor in the certification process? Will the U.S. gradually shift the lion's share of its antidrug resources from supply reduction programs to demand reduction programs? And will U.S. international narcotics policy begin to emphasize more of a "carrot" approach of positive incentives and earmarkings of funds, rather than a "stick" approach of sanctions alone? If the antidrug legislation enacted by Congress in 1988 is a continuing trend, an affirmative conclusion might well be warranted.

IV
The View from Mexico

8

Rethinking Hemispheric Antinarcotics Strategy and Security
Samuel I. del Villar

The premises and consequences of U.S. narcotics control nowadays have generated a most disruptive relationship between the United States and Latin American countries that appears to endanger as no other threat the regional security of the Western Hemisphere, including that of the United States. The root of the problem is the U.S. narcotics control strategy's erroneous assumption that foreign drug producers and their governments, instead of domestic consumers and the U.S. government, are responsible for drug abuse in the United States and for the threat therefrom to its national security.

I have dealt elsewhere with the irrationality and counterproductivity of such an assumption for curtailing the U.S.-Mexico illicit drug market, and discussed the premise of a new conceptual framework for a rational and more effective antidrug strategy within this bilateral context.[1] The purpose of this chapter is to review it in the context of U.S. and Latin American illicit drug markets, and to explore new avenues for a badly needed alternative and more effective Hemispheric antinarcotics strategy.

That the issue is perceived in the United States as only a question of "The Latin American Narcotics Trade and U.S. National Security" reflects the equivocal assumptions underlying the current approach of antinarcotics strategy. The implication is that the national security of the U.S. is endangered by foreign narcotics trading, while in fact the massive illicit drug consumption and trading within the U.S. States national boundaries are is the major threat to the national security not only of the United States but also of Latin America and the Western Hemisphere as a whole. The U.S. international narcotics control program and Latin American cooperative efforts to implement it have been defeated in their "war on drugs" because, along with the foreign drug interdiction programs, they are the major extensions of such erroneous and counterproductive strategy eluding the core of the threat posed by illicit drug markets and are based upon its secondary effects.

THE U.S.-LATIN AMERICA ILLICIT DRUG MARKETS

There is no single illicit drug market between the United States and Latin America. Markets differentiate along different drug lines and along the roles that different countries play in their structure. Marijuana, cocaine, and heroin are sufficiently distinguishable commodities--as are tobacco and alcohol--in terms of consumer preferences, production, and distribution patterns to establish autonomous markets. There may be substitution and complementary effects among them, but these effects operate on the margin.

On the other hand, fifteen of the twenty-three countries that "joined the United States in eradicating their drug crops, destroying 283 metric tons of opium, 5,046 metric tons of coca leaf, and 17,585 tons of cannabis" in 1987 are in the Western Hemisphere, and they participate in different ways in the illicit drug business,[2] very much in the same fashion as the entities of the United States do. There are some other Western Hemisphere countries that have not joined U.S. eradication initiatives, but drug-producing, trafficking and/or money-laundering activities are carried out in their territories. Mexico, Colombia, Jamaica, Belize, Guatemala, Costa Rica, Honduras, Venezuela and Brazil produce marijuana, as do most states in the U.S. Colombia is the most significant processor of coca leaves--largely imported from Peru and Bolivia--and coca paste into cocaine, as any major city in the United States processes cocaine into crack. Argentina, Brazil, Venezuela, Panama, Honduras, Costa Rica, Guatemala, Belize, the Bahamas, Cuba, the Dominican Republic, Haiti, Jamaica, Puerto Rico, and Mexico are cocaine transit countries, as are Florida, Georgia, Louisiana, Texas, California, and other U.S. border states. However, there are some distinctions.

The Andean countries (and Brazil to some extent) are the significant producers of coca leaves. Mexico is the significant producer of opium poppy in the Western Hemisphere. What distinguishes the United States across the board is that its people are the significant consumers, retailers, and importers of marijuana, cocaine, and heroin, the common national denominators that integrate the various illicit drug markets within the U.S. This common denominator, in turn, leads to the crucial element in the business structure of illicit drugs: more than 90 percent of the illicit value added in those markets is generated in the U.S.[3] In the case of marijuana, the share should be significantly higher since the U.S. is a very significant producer and, for practical purposes, is also the country monopolizing the much more potent and valuable marijuana hybrid, *sinsemilla*.[4]

Distinctions among the illicit drug markets can also be established in light of their size and of the legal controls on them. Marijuana constitutes the largest market, with around 25 million consumers, millions of household producers, and hundreds of thousands of commercial producers in the U.S. It can be produced practically anywhere in the United States, Mexico, Colombia and a number of other Western Hemisphere countries. Its illicit consumption and trade is virtually tolerated in the U.S., and available evidence indicates that it is less toxic than licit alcohol and tobacco. These circumstances render the marijuana business a particularly open market within the United States, so open that a carefully researched monograph contends that it is truly ruled by Adam Smith's "invisible hand."[5] Programs of herbicide spray eradication and of interdiction, especially those in Mexico, Colombia, Guatemala, Belize, and Jamaica, and interdiction efforts at the U.S. border, tend to cartelize foreign supply in the hands of few rings and barons that, through corruption, are capable of overcoming those barriers and profit from them.

The cocaine market is about one-third of the marijuana market in the U.S., but it may be richer in terms of expenditure and revenues due to its higher price. Geography and culture in Andean countries impose barriers to entering coca leaf production, barriers giving them a sort of worldwide monopoly, although a new variety of coca is being developed in Brazil. There is a division of labor within the Andean region. Bolivia and especially Peru, with their centuries-old Inca coca culture, provide most of the coca leaf and paste raw material that is processed in neighboring Colombia, along with its own raw material. Colombia is the gateway to and from South America with shores on the Atlantic, the Caribbean, and the Pacific oceans. Its processing and wholesaling cartels profit from its oligopolistic position to buy abundant supplies of raw material and sell cocaine at the wholesale level, due to their ready sea and air access to the massive U.S. market through different transit routes. U.S.-inspired or -administered eradication and interdiction controls, as well as the destruction of processing facilities, prevent competition in the cocaine processing, transportation, and wholesale business, thereby enhancing rather than undermining the cartel's market power.

On the other hand, cocaine is a much easier commodity to manage and smuggle than marijuana. It is not bulky, much less so relative to its price. It can be stored easily and unnoticed for years without losing its psychotropic power and market value, while stored marijuana requires large, conspicuous facilities, and cannot be stored for more than a year if it is to maintain its natural and commercial attributes. The development of scale economies seems the most significant feature in the marijuana and cocaine import and export business, a consequence of large domestic trafficking to supply massive U.S. demand, and eradication and interdiction efforts. The movement of large volumes of drugs reduces the unit costs of transportation and of corrupting interdicting authorities, reduces the unitary risk of seizure, and facilitates the organization of the illicit business while rendering it more efficient.

Reagan's Commission on Organized Crime found that, besides "La Cosa Nostra," in the United States there are "more than a dozen such organized criminal groups...and all show potential for growth," and that there is "increased concentration of organized crime in drug trafficking operations."[6] The large criminal enterprises organizing drug trafficking in any major U.S. city seem to be the key not only to improved efficiency in the business, but also to the most effective marketing techniques for expanding consumption among the young. Mass production and trafficking developed in response to the boom of massive demand in the United States. The linkage of retail drug trafficking by juvenile delinquents with domestic organized crime in the United States provides an extraordinary structural base for the creation of a mass market, especially the cocaine market. Its efficiency has fostered the development of crack and frequent cocaine gluts (presumably a result of storage capacity) that have kept prices going down at a spectacular rate despite supply reductions.[7] "Cocaine seizures in the United States were up dramatically in 1987.... However, the average price of cocaine dropped to $12,000-$40,000 nationally, down from $22,000-$45,000 in 1986."[8]

The heroin market is much smaller, remaining rather stable at around 500 thousand addicts in the United States, around 5 percent of cocaine users and around 2 percent of marijuana smokers.[9] Mexico seems to be the only Western Hemisphere supplier of this relatively small market. Opium poppy drains are processed into black tar heroin, which, in turn, is exported to the United States. Decades-old eradication and interdiction campaigns seem also to have conveyed cartel market power to heroin producers, although opium poppy cultivation areas seem to have somewhat expanded from their traditional northwestern Sierra Madre location of the border state triangle of Sinaloa, Chihuahua and Durango. The ability of cultivation technologies to manage small, high, and hidden plots has outmaneuvered eradication technologies, concentrating the industry further. Heroin relative to its price is less bulky and easier to store and to manage even than cocaine.

Although Mexican heroin production neighbors the United States, Mexican producers do not enjoy a monopoly as Colombian cocaine producers do. They do not even command the largest share on the U.S. market. Asian heroin producers do, both in volume and in revenue. In fact, the U.S. National Narcotics Intelligence Consumers Committee (NNICC) estimated that Mexico's opium poppy production for 1988 will be of about 1 to 1.6 percent of worldwide production.[10] It should also be pointed out that Mexican production is denied access to the legitimate morphine market in the United States opened to some Asian producers.[11] The comparative advantages that Mexican producers may enjoy for vertically integrating the industry to wholesale levels within the United States seems to be a major concern of U.S. enforcement. The 1987 bust of the very significant Herrera heroin family business, based in Durango and with a wholesale capability in Chicago, might illustrate the barriers Mexican producers are likely to face in the nationally controlled markets of the United States.

CRISIS AND VOLATILITY OF U.S. NARCOTICS CONTROL THEORY

The narcotics control policy legislated by Congress is based on bad economics, whereby the driving force of illicit drug markets are foreign producers and production, not domestic consumers. Its law enforcement corollary is that federal coercive resources should primarily be applied to foreign production, foreign producers, and their governments. The ensuing misallocation of resources has entangled narcotics control policy in a growing Gordian Knot.[12] The basic flaw of U.S. narcotics control theory is the contradiction between virtual tolerance of domestic drug consumption and production of marijuana and the alleged "war on drugs" that generates booming profits for drug rings, corruption, and violence north and south of the Rio Grande. The most recent and dangerous reflection of this contradiction for hemispheric security is the DEA-CIA-Justice-State-White House-Noriega entanglement with the destruction of Panama's economy.

Rational analysis concludes that the only logical way out of the contradiction, and of the Gordian Knot that has been tied on it, is legalization at least of the marijuana market, government monopolies for the heroin markets, and a combination of both for the cocaine market, in order to get "gangsters out of the drug business."[13] This would be accompanied by a structural reallocation of antidrug resources from its current foreign supply emphasis to a domestic demand emphasis on rehabilitation and treatment. Given the irrationality of current political reactions in and out of the United States, there is a prevailing skepticism that domestic and international political processes are incapable of redirecting antidrug strategy along rational lines. This might not be the case.

We are experiencing these days what appears to be the climax of a most acute domestic and international crisis in the Western Hemisphere brought about by an ill-conceived war on drugs. This crisis, in turn, reflects the political desperation within the United States in face of the failure of its government's international enforcement theory of narcotics control. Under extremely critical circumstances, basic political attitudes or prejudices become volatile. The U.S. defeat in Vietnam is illustrative. But the capacity of the political process in the United States to review and to change the premise of a self-destructive war was even more illustrative of an open society's ability to acknowledge the failure of deeply entrenched mistakes and to redirect the course of history in accordance with reason.

The change began with the media presenting balanced reporting and rational editorials of the facts of the Vietnam war, rather than presenting prejudiced and interested political opinions. A similar beginning can already be perceived in the war on drugs. A few years ago, U.S. reporting still conveyed the picture that foreign producers and corruption in their governments were responsible for the mass drug culture in the United States. Now the emphasis is on the futility and corruption of current antidrug strategy.

An influential intellectual landmark was an article published in the Spring, 1988, issue of *Foreign Policy* by a young Princeton professor of political science, Ethan A. Nadelmann; it asserts that U.S. drug policy is a bad export. For U.S. interests lie not only in reducing the costs of drug prohibition policies abroad but also in developing alternatives to a drug control policy that proved both largely unsuccessful and increasingly costly at home."[14] Leading newspapers and commentators are discussing and even advocating legalization. "The unspeakable is debated: should drugs be legalized?" was a front-page story headline of the *New York Times* on May 4, 1988.[15] "Call to debate legalization of drugs becomes louder" was the headline of another front-page *Washington Post* story appearing the same day.[16] "A strange collection of bedfellows--from both ends of the political spectrum, from small towns and major cities--has initiated the call for a national debate on the legalization of narcotics, a dramatic reversal in the nation's drug policy" was its lead-off sentence. The mayor of Baltimore,

Kurt L. Schmoke, produced a breakthrough in the political arena when he acknowledged the self-defeating nature of the current war on drugs, and on April 25, he called for a radical change in dominant perceptions and policies in his address to the conference of U.S. mayors. His proposition was that drugs be treated as a "public health and not a criminal problem."[17] The mayor of Washington D.C., Marion Barry, and on the opposite ideological side, the editor of the *National Review* and influential conservative Republican columnist, William Buckley, Jr., have favored legalization.

Another significant step in this direction appears to be the publication the Surgeon General's report on May 16, 1988. Its basic findings were that tobacco is as addictive as heroin and cocaine, but its addiction produced more than 300 thousand yearly deaths in the United States, while heroin produced around three thousand and cocaine around two thousand. The Surgeon General emphasized in his media presentations of this report that prohibition and criminalization of tobacco smoking would only lead to violence and more death because it would do nothing to stop addiction, and would induce addicts to engage in criminal conduct in an organized illicit drug market.[18] Drawing an analogy with regard to the heroin, cocaine, and especially marijuana markets was inevitable, although the Surgeon General still did not appear prepared to elaborate publicly on the legalization of these markets.

On the other hand, the irrational reactions still prevailing in the United States in face of the accumulative failure of its government's war on drugs have, in turn, polarized the critical scenarios that such war has left in Latin America. Five references are in order: the use of U.S. military personnel in search and destroy missions in Bolivia in 1986; the U.S.-Colombia treaty to extradite Colombian traffickers for prosecution and imprisonment in the U.S.; the indictment of Panamanian general Manuel Noriega in U.S. courts and the disruption of Panama's economy in order to oust him; the abduction in Honduras of transnational drug dealer Manuel Matta Ballesteros; and the 1988 "certification" process of sovereign states under the 1986 U.S. antidrug bill, and its impact on Mexico.

These events indicate an escalating trend of the U.S. government to substitute the sovereignty of Latin American states in order to solve in its territory the domestic drug problem, one that the U.S. government is incapable of dealing with. The extreme irrationality of this policy transcends the merits of drug control. It is *the* most subversive present threat to Western Hemisphere security, particularly if it is carried out without curtailing the domestic U.S. drug market or the flow of narcodollars to drug rings, barons, and corrupt government officials.

U.S. military search-and-destroy missions in Bolivia, conducted under the heading of "Operation Blast Furnace," certainly did not destroy its ancestral coca leaf production. The operation produced some films and photographs of U.S. military choppers landing and destroying deserted jungle laboratories It also produced the Bolivian government's reluctant and humiliating acceptance of such law enforcement "shows," in exchange for the State Department's Bureau of International Narcotics Matters assessment: "the results of the 1986 Blast Furnace Operations were considered temporary."[19]

The implementation of the 1979 extradition treaty, whereby Colombia transferred to the United States its sovereign right to prosecute, convict, and imprison Colombian nationals, produced "the loss of the national State's capacity to guarantee the most elemental human rights,"[20] a devastating wave of violence that further undermined the Colombian government's authority to meet the challenge of its drug cartels, thereby strengthening their power. The Matta Ballesteros abduction did not do much to enhance the Contra-drugs-CIA-shattered national sovereignty and rule of law in Honduras, but led to the burning of the U.S. embassy annex by enraged nationalistic Honduran mobs that demonstrated against the U.S. breach of international law and Honduran sovereignty.

The Panama case was a major qualitative turn in the crisis of U.S. antidrug strategy. It brought to light the confusion and contradiction in Washington's efforts to structure a coherent antidrug policy. On one hand, it was reported that Noriega was a long-lasting element on the CIA payroll, known by the U.S. government as a protector of drug trafficking, and a recipient, at the same time, of letters of commendation from the DEA director praising him for his contribution to the U.S. International Narcotics Control Program. On the other hand, Noriega was indicted in Miami and in Tampa, and the State Department arranged with Panama's president, Joaquín Eric del Valle, a manipulation of Panama's sovereignty whereby Noriega would be removed from command of the National Guard under U.S. economic coercion in violation of Article XIX of the Charter of the Organization of American States.

Again, this U.S. management of Latin American sovereignty failed to break the presumed government-trafficking connection, but in this case there was no charade. Such management was highly successful in wrecking Panama's economy, strengthening Noriega's position, and having Washington ridiculed by an alleged criminal indicted according to U.S. law, with the ensuing loss of credibility and of moral and real authority.

The passing of the 1986 antidrug bill was Congress's attempt to institutionalize a transfer of sovereignty from States subject to yearly "certification" or "decertification" by the President and Congress to this certifying or decertifying transnational powers.[21] A broad range of coercive measures are to be applied to such countries, unless "the President determines and so certifies to the Congress...that during the previous year...the actions of the Government [of said country] have resulted in the maximum reductions in illicit drug production," and provided that "the Congress does not enact a joint resolution of disapproval." Additionally, no criteria for objectively assessing the meaning of "maximum reduction results" is established, and local, state, and federal governments in the United States are not subject to similar standards.

When this bill was passed, it was not given much attention in Latin America in general or in Mexico in particular. Mexico is the critical country in this context for various reasons. A strategic reason is its unique position as Latin America's neighboring country with the United States, and as a very important neighbor with nearly 90 million people in the fourteenth largest industrialized economy in the world and the third largest commercial partner of the United States.[22] A cultural-historical reason stems from the fact that more than half of early Mexico's independent territory in the first half of the nineteenth century was appropriated by the United States, and that Mexican culture nowadays is the foundation of more than ten percent of U.S. nationals. A political-international reason stems from the principle of non-intervention in the domestic affairs of sovereign nations, which had extraordinary weight in framing independent Mexico's national identity in the face of multiple foreign aggressions in the nineteenth century, and continues to be the bottom line of its foreign policy. Finally, Mexican governments have historically followed, more closely than any other country, the guidelines of the U.S. international control programs,[23] currently committing to them nowadays the bulk of its federal enforcement and national security resources.

In February, 1988, President Reagan "determined and certified" that seventeen "major narcotic producing and/or major narcotics transit countries, including Mexico, have cooperated fully with the United States, or taken adequate steps on their own, to control narcotics production, trafficking and money laundering."[24] When the Senate overruled the administrative certification of Mexico in April, 1988, thus adjudicating the performance of Mexican law enforcement and military apparatus, the ultimate expression of Mexican sovereignty, the empowering 1986 legislation captured the attention of Mexicans. There was a qualitative change in the political reaction of Mexico in the face of this unprecedented offense. The presidential candidate of the ruling Partido Revolucionario Institucional, Carlos Salinas de Gortari, charged that U.S. senators were "looking at the speck in the eyes of Mexicans, but not looking at the log in their own eyes."[25] And, in an unprecedented action, all the political parties moved to denounce this illegitimate intervention of the U.S. government in the domestic affairs of Mexico.

After some lobbying by the Mexican attorney general's office and of the State Department, the U.S. House of Representatives did not overrule the certification. Therefore, sanctions were not applied to Mexico, preventing the escalation of another and much more serious crisis in hemispheric relations. However, that was not the basic conflict. The bottom line is the institutional subjection of Mexico's sovereignty to arbitrary adjudication of the President and the U.S. Congress that, in turn, has institutionalized a crisis situation in U.S.-Mexican relations.

Current U.S. antinarcotics control theory and practice have placed its Latin American "partners" in an increasingly tightening sandwich effect. On one hand, its erroneous supply-sided economic assumptions have generated the most formidable illicit drug business with a most formidable corruptive capacity within and without the United States, a business that its government has even protected and contributed to, as the Noriega case has now disclosed. On the other one, when this erroneous and self-defeating theory and practice backfires, Latin American countries are humiliated, blamed, and punished. They are wrecked by both sides: by the drug rings, barons and corruption financed by the U.S.-tolerated demand for drugs and by the confusion and violence with which the U.S. government reacts to the output of such financing and corruption.

Despite recent encouraging developments in the U.S. media and breakthroughs of the mayor of Baltimore and the Surgeon General, the prevailing political antidrug wind in the United States does not seem to blow yet in the direction of righteousness, justice, reason, and effectiveness. Quite significant have been the claims of the chair of the House Select Committee on Narcotics Abuse and Control, Charles B. Rangel, in the sense that the war on drugs has not even begun. "Let's see if we can get a coordinated national battle plan that would include the deployment of military personnel and equipment to wipe out this foreign based national security threat" was his response to the reasons supporting legalization.[26] The most recent administrative and legislative actions continue to be dismaying.

In May, 1988, a new supposedly "zero tolerance" anti-consumption policy was enforced whereby the search of drugs in cars, trucks, and ships within the borders of the United States would be intensified, and these vehicles confiscated in the event that a minimal trace of drugs was found in them. The well-publicized theory was that such harsh penalties would be a new deterrent to drug consumption. Such searches and seizures are not directed towards domestic traffic within the United States, which reflects domestic drug consumption and business. "They claim they are consumers, but in fact they are smugglers," claimed Customs Service Commissioner William Von Raab,[27] suggesting that the "zero tolerance" policy target is merely an additional coercive device against international border traffic that, if continued, should harass bordering countries, namely Mexico, and their commerce with the United States. Its drug-related deterrent effect was deleted a couple of days after the policy was inaugurated, when an expensive boat with traces of drugs was returned to its owners in exchange for a moderate fine. The following week the policy's teeth against U.S. domestic consumers and traffickers were pulled when the confiscatory provisions were deleted by implementing new directives after significant complaints were raised.

During the second week of May, Congress widened the role of the military in the war on drugs, conveying interdiction and search and arrest powers to the Navy with regard to sea trafficking. Again, this reinforcement of the irrational foreign-supply emphasis was received with wide skepticism as to its productivity in reducing the flow of Colombian narcotics into the United States, given its massive demand. Pentagon spokespersons aired this skepticism, and it was reported that Secretary of Defense Frank Carlucci was very reluctant to accept the Congressional determination to widen the military role in drug fighting. There is an understandable concern that such involvement would not only be counterproductive in a self-defeating war, but that it would also expose the U.S. military apparatus to the kind of drug-related corruption and scandal that has already affected other areas of the government, with the ensuing undermining of their moral authority. Paradoxically, just after this new military involvement was announced, scandal broke over a three-year-old cocaine-smuggling operation of one thousand pounds, that involved U.S. military facilities and personnel in the Panama Canal.[28]

AN INTOLERABLE STRATEGY AND NATIONAL SOVEREIGNTY

Further escalation of the current irrational antidrug strategy is morally and politically intolerable for Hemispheric security. From a moral standpoint, the guidelines Pope John Paul II presented in his May, 1988 trip to the Andean countries were most illustrative for rethinking antidrug strategy. He sided with the weakest and most vulnerable party wrecked by the sandwich effect, the poor Latin American peasants exploited by drug cartels who in turn are sheltered by eradication and interdiction campaigns that destroy peasant properties and deprive them of their ancestral freedoms. He also made clear that the source of the injustice done to them is drug abuse outside Latin America and that a demand-sided antidrug approach is the way out of it.

The Pope's words are not supported by coercion, as is the U.S. international narcotics control program. They are supported by moral authority and reason, which the U.S. war on drugs, unfair and poisoned by illegitimate dealings with notorious traffickers, is not. In the future, the Pope's message is likely to carry more weight in Latin America than that of the futile and disruptive U.S. program. It is interesting to remark that the Evangelical-founded political reaction of Mexico's PRI presidential candidate against the U.S. Senate "decertification" of Mexico is similar to the Pope's message. The coincidence is more significant if Mexico's potential weight in the Hemisphere is realized; furthermore, Mexico is the only Latin American country, including Cuba, that does not have diplomatic relations with the Vatican.

Short of regulated legalization of the drug market, a structural reallocation of federal antidrug resources from emphasis on eradication and interdiction to emphasis on rehabilitation and treatment seems to be the fundamental guideline for rethinking a rational antidrug strategy in the United States. Respect for national sovereignty in Latin America is the basic premise for rethinking and rebuilding a rational, fair, and effective antinarcotics strategy. Only with an effective exercise of domestic sovereign powers can an effective international cooperation be built to further hemispheric interest in making law prevail over organized illicit narcotics trafficking and related corruption.

Without rebuilding the moral authority of U.S. antidrug policy to deal with its own and foreign criminal enterprises, the political foundations for an honest and effective regional strategy will remain crippled. The point of departure could very well be the end to undercover illegitimate dealings of U.S. government agencies with drug thugs, and serious and exemplary patterns and actions for dealing with drug-related criminal organizations in U.S. territory. After all, more than ninety percent of the illicit drug business is generated and organized by criminal enterprises in the United States.

U.S. abandonment of legislative attempts to suppress Latin American sovereignty is the *sine qua non* for rebuilding a hemispheric antidrug strategy and security. If local, state, and federal government efforts against drug production, trafficking, and consumption in the United States were subject to the adjudicatory process provided in its 1986 drug bill, the United States would have to be decertified more readily and justifiably than most Latin American countries. However, it is unthinkable that local and state communities, which are not sovereign, and Congress would accept such a offensive process. Consequently, it is not only wrong but also unreasonable for the U.S. government to expect any national sovereign government to accept that kind of subjection, especially when it is purported to support an absurd and unjust antinarcotics strategy.

It would be unfair to blame the U.S. political process alone, or even primarily for the current situation. True, the U.S. government has exerted extraordinary leverage and even coercion to impose the self-defeating international narcotics control program upon a number of Latin American countries, but it is also true that the governments and political processes in these countries have not much resisted the imposition nor proposed a rational and fair alternative consistent with their legitimate national interest and values. Latin American countries cannot expect to be treated with respect and dignity by the U.S. international narcotics control programs if their own governments do not treat them with respect and dignity. Corruption of government processes that uphold national values, interests, and sovereignty leads to national self-disrespect and indignity while dealing both with narco-organized crime and with the United States. As the Noriega case has eloquently shown, there is a wide margin for corrupt accommodation of the irrational U.S. international narcotics control policy and the illegitimate interests of drug criminal organizations, to the detriment of the moral, political, and economic welfare of Latin American and of U.S. citizens.

The cornerstone for building a hemispheric capacity to deal effectively with the challenges of transnational organized crime is effective national sovereignty, which can only be based on national self-respect and dignity. Effective national sovereignty is not based on the absurd pretension that Latin American nations are economically, technologically, politically, or militarily as powerful as the United States to impose their unilaterally defined national interest on others. It is a rational proposition based on the truth that history endowed sovereign nations with an autonomous responsibility to govern their peoples and their territories. It is also based on the truth that such nations are no better, but also no worse, than any other sovereign nation, including the United States, despite their relative unpreparedness to impose on other nations selfish national interests or perceptions. This proposition is the philosophical cornerstone of Western Judeo-Christian civilization. The International Declaration of Human Rights acknowledges that no person is better or worse than any other, despite differences in convictions, race, wealth, and power.

The outcome of this drug crisis could very well be that, in the next few years, the United States will unilaterally legalize and regulate the marijuana, cocaine, and heroin markets, reducing and eventually eliminating in that process the challenges drug-related organized crime poses to its peoples' welfare. However, that will not eliminate transnational organized crime in the Western Hemisphere and the need of international cooperation to deal with it. Meanwhile, drug-related organized crime should be a prime objective of Western Hemisphere cooperative efforts.[29]

The problem, as things stand now, is that the United States and Canada seem to be the only Western Hemisphere countries with developed law enforcement capabilities to deal with organized crime, and that the structure upon which the U.S. international narcotics control program rests prevent the development such national capabilities in Latin American countries. It was built on the erroneous assumption that the Latin American law enforcement apparatus should be subservient to U.S. law enforcement apparatus, and that the former should perform elementary, menial, often irrelevant and counterproductive tasks in the law enforcement process such as finding and eradicating plants, harassing the population in the search of drugs, and arresting their own alleged national criminals in accordance with U.S. national interests, guidelines, and intelligence. At most, Latin American enforcement systems are expected to investigate, prosecute, and imprison drug criminals in whom the U.S. government has a unilateral interest. The extradition treaty with Colombia is perhaps the most extreme example of the disruptive consequences of law enforcement assumptions that pretend to deny the sovereignty of Latin American nations.

U.S. police, soldiers, prosecutors, courts, and prisons are not only theoretically, but also practically, incapable of dealing effectively with crime committed in Latin American nations, no matter how intense the concern of the U.S. government to have the criminals investigated, arrested, prosecuted, sentenced, and imprisoned. Its transnational coercive power might score spectacular isolated operations now and then, as in the abduction of Matta Ballesteros and the prosecution of Carlos Lehder, but such actions greatly disrupt the legal process in Latin America and certainly do not undermine or destroy the power base and business structure of transnational criminal industries.

The only effective alternative is the development of an *in situ* superior effective national law enforcement power that could subdue the national base of transnational criminal organizations. Legitimate, respectful, and dignified cooperation between those national law enforcement powers is the only feasible international option for breaking the structure of transnational organized crime. The current structural problem is that, for different reasons, such *in situ* national law enforcement power is absent or faulty, not only in Latin America but also in the United States, and current U.S.-Latin American cooperation patterns prevent rather that foster its development.

Historically, Latin American societies have not faced major organized crime threats. They never experienced alcohol prohibition and the need, therefore, to develop organized anticriminal law enforcement. They were utterly unprepared for the spectacular development of during the last two decades of organized crime, financed by the demand boom of illicit drugs in the United States. This development, along with the ill-conceived international narcotics control strategy, shattered and corrupted the national law enforcement apparatus in Latin America and, in some cases, their government processes at large. Collaboration with U.S. narcotics control programs brought about more corruption and a technical involution of national law enforcement capabilities in face of expanding organized crime activities.[30]

On the other hand, there is no doubt about the technical capabilities and extraordinary resources of law enforcement in the United States. However, its federalism and a complex fragmentation of federal enforcement jurisdiction thus far have prevented the development of a coherent, rational, and effective antidrug enforcement policy. As Harvard's expert Mark Moore has pointed out with regard to the U.S. "domestic enforcement program," it has been "only occasionally successful in eliminating major trafficking organizations."[31] This provides an unreliable national basis for serious and effective international enforcement cooperation or leadership against drug-related organized crime.

At the same time, U.S. government intelligence dealings with drug barons and rings to raise support and financing for anti-Communist campaigns have further undermined the reliability of U.S. antinarcotics strategy and its consistency in protecting its national security and that of its partners. The U.S. intelligence involvement with Southeast Asian heroin trafficking organizations led Reagan to "determine that it is in the vital national interest of the United States to certify...Laos"[32] in contradiction to the antinarcotics theory of the 1986 bill. Furthermore, the disclosure of the U.S. government's clandestine repetition of this scheme to get financing from and support of the Medellín cartel and of Noriega for the Contras through José Rodríguez, a Cuban exile connected with then Vice President George Bush, undercut the credibility of the U.S. war on drugs. The testimonies of José Blandón, the Panamanian former advisor for political intelligence to Noriega, and of Ramón Millán Rodríguez, the Cuban money launderer for the Medellín cartel exiled in the United States, which were instrumental in bringing the indictments in U.S. courts against Noriega, are also the basis for this alleged U.S.-Medellín-Noriega connection.[33]

Nevertheless, the United States has a fundamental asset for rebuilding its antinarcotics strategy a upon rational, fair, and effective basis. That asset is its political process's capability for airing, acknowledging, and amending clandestine mistakes when they provoke a fundamental crisis endangering its national security and the fulfillment of fundamental national values, no matter the particular interests involved and how deeply they appear to be rooted. There is no reason to believe that this asset will not be productive in this crisis.

We should expect, in the near future, a review of U.S. federal antidrug strategy based on three basic criteria. The first would be a solution to the contradiction between virtual tolerance and formal prohibition to domestic drug consumption and production that puts as much as 3 percent of the U.S. Gross National Product in the hands of the most formidable, dangerous, and violent criminal organizations.[34] The second would be respect for the sovereignty of foreign countries while defining a coherent law enforcement international narcotics control cooperative strategy that would avoid the support, connections, and financing from or to traffickers and their corrupt government protectors. Third would be a reallocation of law enforcement priorities from futile, expensive, and wasteful interdiction attempts to efficient identification, investigation, and conviction of the most significant drug barons and their government accomplices within the United States, to the destruction of their criminal enterprises, and to the recovery of their unlawfully obtained assets.

Likewise, one should expect a profound revision of the antidrug strategy of Latin American countries affected by drug-related criminal organizations. The priority in this case should be the insulation of their law enforcement and security systems from drug-related corruption and the rapid development of national capabilities for subduing drug-related organized crime. The corollary would be a structural reallocation of priorities and resources from futile, wasteful, and corruptive mass eradication and interdiction campaigns[35] to the identification, investigation, and conviction of organized criminals and to the recovery of their unlawfully obtained assets. These criminals are more dangerous to their people and their legitimate government processes. This policy would require reviewing and resetting domestic legal, both substantive and procedural, and administrative frameworks for dealing properly with organized crime.

THE COOPERATIVE AGENDA

Under such a national basis, an effective international cooperative effort could be built in the Western Hemisphere to replace the current disruptive drug entanglement. There are a few critical premises for the effort's success. Symmetrical commitments are crucial and require the abandonment of arbitrary U.S. schemes to coerce Latin American governments into irrational actions conflicting with their national sovereignty and interests that the United States is not prepared to carry out within its own boundaries. Cooperative eradication efforts would have to be reviewed along those lines, and retargeted to cooperative intelligence, investigation, prosecution, and conviction of organized criminals who are a priority not only for the U.S. government, but also for Latin American governments.

Asymmetry in these area greatly distorted the rational selection of the most harmful criminals endangering the security of the Western Hemisphere. A lot of publicity surrounds foreign drug rings, barons, and government corruption operating on the Latin American side of the drug business and affecting U.S. interest, but very little or nothing is said in the cooperative agenda about the same subjects operating on the U.S. side and affecting much more severely Latin American interests. However, more than 90 percent of that business is generated in U.S. territory and largely conducted by U.S. nationals who need to corrupt law enforcement officials at all levels of government. With regard to the investigation and prosecution of drug-related corruption, both the Latin American and the U.S. sides endanger hemispheric security, and should interest the cooperative agenda. For instance, to bring indictments against Panamanian officials for their drug dealings neglecting the criminal liability of U.S. officials unlawfully dealing with those officials, covering those dealings and/or and participating in those conspiracies, is not fair and effective for the destruction of most dangerous drug rings. The Contra-Noriega connection is most relevant in this context.

Another important substantive point in the cooperative agenda is the illicit arms market which seems to be closely tied with the illicit drug market. The arms market operates the other way around. Suppliers, producers, and/or intermediaries (often of Eastern European-made guns) are in the United States, and the consumers are in Latin America. Another difference is that the United States does not supply raw material or semi-processed goods with a small fraction of its market value, but wholly manufactured guns with a much larger share of its high sales price remaining in the U.S. economy. Little is known of this illicit market, but it obviously a major threat to Hemispheric security.

Some procedural and administrative principles and rules are also significant for effective cooperative enforcement efforts. Investigating and prosecuting organized criminal conduct requires multiple diverse actions that need to be coherently and authoritatively integrated.

The target should ordinarily be the destruction of complex, efficient, powerful, resourceful, and violent organizations, firms that are "large scale, enduring, organizations with a well established reputation for irresistible violence," in Moore's terms.[36] The targeting priorities should be a function of the disruptive threat posed by such organizations. The more efficient, powerful, resourceful, and violent an organization is, the higher its destruction should rank in law enforcement priorities. The problem is that the structure of antinarcotics strategy, both at the national and international level, is not ordinarily organized along those lines. It is structured for disjointedly targeting crops, shipments, peasant producers, "burros," marginal dealers, and, eventually, major drug lords and corrupt government officials; even the latter can be replaced for normal conduction of the illicit business. The exception to this proposition was the structure of DEA's Central Tactical Unit (CENTAC). It targeted the destruction of major criminal enterprises, and coherently pulled together, under a responsible single authority, the required intelligence, investigative, prosecutorial, and arrest resources until the target was accomplished. Apparently because of bureaucratic turf, the CENTAC structure was canceled in 1985[37] despite its extraordinary productivity. However, its investigative and prosecutorial concept was maintained in the successful FBI Cashweb Expressway and "Pizza Connection," and the successful DEA Pisces and Cashcrop operations.[38]

Analytically, CENTAC and its operations were a success for U.S. antinarcotics policy because they overpowered the resources, organization, efficiency, and corruptive capacity of the major drug-related criminal organizations targeted. However, from an international hemispherical perspective, it had basic flaws. It was apparently conceived primarily to destroy criminal organizations based outside the United States that had made inroads within U.S. domestic business, or U.S.-based organizations engaged in the importation of drugs. Destroying U.S. drug-trafficking criminal enterprises, that receive 90 percent of the profit from the illicit drug business, has not had the same weight in its priorities.

It also assumed that U.S. police should have the more important role in framing and directing transnational law enforcement efforts, including the control of intelligence and investigative capabilities, and that foreign police should merely follow instructions in search and arrest operations. The quid for the regional cooperative agenda against organized crime would be to develop symmetrically the successful law enforcement *ad hoc* enterprise concept against *ad hoc* organized crime enterprises, balancing Latin American and U.S. legitimate interests, from selecting targets to recovering illegitimate assets and managing the efforts, and controlling intelligence and investigative capabilities.

The focus should be criminal enterprises that regularly carry out complementary and articulated production, processing, transportation, wholesaling, retailing, and consumption of illicit goods, as well as money laundering and corruption of government officials in various nations. The only logical way to respond to their criminal challenge is through cooperative law enforcement enterprises that integrate intelligence, investigation, arrests, prosecutions, and asset recovery in the various nations in which those criminal activities are conducted.

It is erroneously assumed that those criminal enterprises are vertically integrated from agricultural production to retail distribution under a single centralized authority based outside the United States. Quite to the contrary, as was suggested above, there seems to be a highly decentralized structure along national lines whereby national and regional comparative advantages in production, transportation, distribution, and bribery are auctioned and exchanged by autonomous organized criminal entrepreneurs in a relatively open transnational market place. The centralization of control in the United States and/or by its officials has been an inefficient, biased, and disruptive transnational law enforcement response. The quid for successful transnational law enforcement is to jointly target the most significant transnational operations among the most significant national criminal organizations, based on the comparative advantages that cooperative national law enforcement capabilities should have or develop to identify, investigate, arrest, and prosecute them.

The issue in this respect is not how to centralize in a U.S. agency sovereign law enforcement powers of Latin American agencies, but how to develop appropriate national capabilities and centralize national authorities fully able to participate in joint, cooperative law enforcement efforts that could overpower transnational criminal enterprises. Peculiarly enough, some Latin American counties, such as Mexico, with an overriding exclusive federal jurisdiction over drug matters, are in an advantageous situation for integrating a centralized authority, with respect to the United States. In the latter, the national antidrug law enforcement authority is highly fragmented because of concurrent local, state, and federal jurisdictions and because of the extraordinary fragmentation and ensuing turf battles of enforcement powers within the federal jurisdiction. The Attorney General's leading role in federal coordinating committees and the Vice President's role as chair of *ad hoc* task forces were not effective solutions. The creation of a "drug czar" seems to be an even more grandiose solution along the same, and appears to have a rhetorical rather than an analytical approach for sorting out these major structural barriers to effective law enforcement against anti-organized crime.

The fragmentation of U.S. drug enforcement authority is reflected in the international sphere. In a significant U.S. embassy in Latin America there might be agents of the State Department's International Narcotics Control Matters and its Intelligence Service; the Justice Department's Drug Enforcement Administration, FBI, and Immigration and Naturalization Service; the Treasury Department's Internal Revenue Service, Customs Service, and Bureau of Alcohol, Tobacco and Firearms; the CIA, the National Intelligence Agency, and the Defense Intelligence Agency. All of them would have drug-related enforcement powers likely to be necessary for integrating law enforcement enterprises capable of overpowering transnational criminal organizations. The authority of the U.S. ambassador over them is more formal than functional, and in fact has no practical value for managing and conducting a cooperative effort in a law enforcement enterprise. For functional purposes they report to and follow fragmented guidelines from their respective central headquarters in Washington. Additionally, the lack of an effective authority, *in situ*, responsible for the lawful operation of those services and for their respect of the sovereignty of the host country has contributed to the drug-related scandals that have undermined the antidrug moral authority of the U.S. government in Latin America.

The concrete prosecutorial authority responsible for obtaining indictments and convictions before a court of law in the United States and for cooperating with the host country's prosecutorial authority in the same endeavors, which is the requirement to break transnational criminal conspiracies, is the cornerstone under which all those U.S. drug-related enforcement services should be placed. What is required is not a formal bureaucratic "drug czar" in Washington, but an efficient and functional *in situ* comprehensive and responsible U.S. representative authority. Interestingly enough, responsible and functional representatives of the Justice Department as the depository of the government's prosecutorial authority appears to be missing in significant U.S. embassies in Latin America. Such representation is a must if transnational law enforcement cooperative efforts are to be successful.

Likewise, functional law enforcement representation of significant Latin American countries among themselves, and in the United States, would have to be stepped up very considerably to give substance to any effort designed to attain balance and symmetry in hemispheric antinarcotics strategy. International antinarcotics asymmetry stems primarily from ignorance of the international illicit business marketplace and from inappropriate institutional settings for dealing with them and which provide the foundations for building and sustaining a strategy.

Evidently, it is not realistic to assume that Latin American governments could replicate the impressive foreign presence of U.S. law enforcement agencies. However, that is not necessary, nor is it advisable, as the turf-overlapping and counterproductivity of such a scheme shows. It is a problem of quality and structure rather than a problem of quantity. An authoritative unit, logically and efficiently structured and professionally staffed, for interaction with host governments in cooperative enforcement efforts should be much more effective than large, disjointed undercover bureaucracies attempting to spy and/or to take over sovereign responsibilities of host governments.

9

Narcotics as a Destabilizing Force for Source Countries and Non-source Countries
José Luis Reyna

AN ANECDOTE

According to one of his biographers, Sigmund Freud was a drug addict at age 28. He used cocaine because, among other reasons, he wanted "fame." Freud himself thought this drug was the best way to obtain fortune and glory, the miracle solution for all problems. His great enthusiasm led him to send some to his sweetheart, Martha, to give her strength. In one of his love letters to Martha he confessed, "It is right now when I am really a doctor." Freud became euphoric and, in his view, his professional activity increased significantly. He felt neither fatigue nor hunger. In addition, Freud convinced one of his closest friends, Ernst von Fleischl-Marxow, to use cocaine. Fleischl died some time later, probably from drug abuse. Independently of his friend's death, however, Freud later decided that the use of narcotics was a mistake. Freud was but one of many cocaine users who misunderstood the nature of the drug. In Germany, in the last quarter of the nineteenth century, the wave of cocaine users was considered the third plague of humanity.[1]

THE PLAGUE

A little more than one hundred years later, the plague is an international plague, threatening the national security of powerful countries like the United States as well as weak countries like Peru. The Mexican government defines it as a "state problem."[2]

The current narcotics plague has a particular geographic and economic character, one that must be understood in order to understand how poor Andean peasants can threaten U.S. national security or how New York drug users threaten the political stability of Latin American nations. The northern part of the world contains the main consumers of narcotics, the non-source countries. The southern part contains the main producers, the source countries. To put the problem within an economic context: the north controls practically 80 percent of the world economy and has 25 percent of the total population on earth. In contrast, the south only participates in 20 percent of the economy but has 75 percent of the world population. Income per capita is thirty times greater in the north than that of the south.[3]

Obviously, there is a strong correlation between economic prosperity and drug consumption as well as between poverty (underdevelopment) and narcotics production. They are complementary correlations expressing two sides of the same problem.

The magnitude of drug use and broad-scale narcotrafficking has become a new and central component in the conception of national security policies. From a "traditional" viewpoint, national security was mainly conceived as the defense of national frontiers by a structure designed to face any external threat.[4] In recent years, the concept has undergone significant redefinition. During the 1960s and part of the 1970s, guerrilla movements were one of the basic domestic concerns of Latin American governments. The "Cuban effect" preoccupied not only these governments but also that of the United States. The U.S. invasion of the Dominican Republic in 1965 illustrates this point, for the U.S. thought it saw another Cuban Revolution in the making.

The theory, proven false over time, was considered valid and even more, feasible. Through these movements, revolution seemed to represent the best chance for the people to seize power. The fear of popular revolution still exists as the Central American conflict clearly shows. It is not fortuitous that the United States keeps its eyes permanently on the Nicaraguan situation as a barometer of its foreign policy.

National security policy now includes the domestic and international consequences of the illicit narcotics trade as well as the military component. This problem is becoming the primary national security concern in Latin American source countries and the United States, where illicit narcotics usage is part of everyday life, domestic violence is rising, and *traficantes* penetrate U.S. borders at will.[5]

DRUGS AND POLITICS

The central objective of the narcomafias[6] is not to seize power in source countries but to make and increase profits in non-source countries. However, state political power in some source countries is weakening because of the growing strength of the mafias. Colombia is a weak state because the frontal attacks of the narcorings are, in many cases, inevitable and unpredictable. So far there are no means to stop them.

In contrast to guerrilla movements, more easily detectable because of their particular organization and leadership, the narcorings are less detectable because they have both a strong and a diffuse type of organization that includes leadership and bases. By state means (political power), the guerrilla movements were put under control and were practically extinguished. State means have failed to bring the narco-organizations under control even though million of dollars are being invested to combat them. To a certain extent, the reason is the particular organization they have structured. By analogy, the Sendero Luminoso movement is to Peruvian politics what the narcorings are for source and non-source countries. There is a common factor--diffuseness of the organizations. Furthermore, in both cases there seems to be a high degree of societal protection. Sendero Luminoso survives because it has established links with specific segments of society. The survival of narcogangs in source countries may derive from governmental protection. In non-source countries, society protects the gangs through a very simple mechanism--demand for the product. To guarantee access to narcotics implies a kind of protection for pushers and suppliers. One possible conclusion is that society contributes significantly to the survival and expansion of gangs in non-source countries.

Drug use and abuse are central to the drastic change in the system of values of U.S. society and also represent a significant change in the productive system of some source countries. In spite of the fact that Latin America and the United States have made important efforts to bring the problem under control, success is still very far away. Among other things, the narcomafias have better military equipment than their opponents in Latin America, which makes the problem worse if one considers the kinds of organizations outlined above. It is striking, for example, that the Bolivian mafias have more financial resources than the Bolivian state. This is a serious domestic problem for Bolivia that also has serious international implications.

In sum, drugs and politics are linked in many ways and from different perspectives. The state-versus-narcomafia struggle is contradictory and conflicting, while necessary conflict between supply and demand is complementary.

SUPPLY AND DEMAND: TWO CONTRADICTORY PERSPECTIVES

The narcotics plague--a post-modern phenomenon?--is the combination and consequence of supply and demand. Focusing only on one side of the problem means evading the issue; one must analyze both sides. Supply and demand, intimately combined, define the problem both domestically and internationally, although the strategies to face one or the other imply differences if one considers source and non-source countries.

Demand for drugs clearly has a societal neurotic base--a way out of structural stress and social anxiety. It is very likely that this can be a false way out, although the consumption of drugs seems to show the contrary.

Supply does not have a neurotic component; it has an essentially economic basis. Drug production increases economic resources in source countries and strengthens a minority group, the narcomafia. It means profits. Consequently, different strategies have to be implemented for supply and demand even though the overall strategy has to be one addressing both. The overall strategy must be multinational and symmetrical between or among nations. No strategy may be considered a priori minimally successful.

One factor common to both supply and demand is corruption. It is not debatable that corruption only correlates with supply and not with demand. In both cases the correlation is high and positive.

U.S. antinarcotics diplomacy has been unfair and dysfunctional because the U.S. only correlated drugs and supply, ignoring the other side of the coin.[7] Moreover, the U.S. awards certifications for countries that it asserts are truly collaborating in the U.S. fight against narcotrafficking. U.S. policy ignores the correlation between demand and corruption. Consequently the "bad boys" are out while the "good ones" are in.

Certification, if this is a correct procedure, has to start with the consumers and not with the producers. From a "balanced" perspective, it would be much fairer to consider both of them. Put more strongly, displacing the problem to the supply side exclusively is to ignore it and to waste an enormous amount of resources with low chance of success.

A MOST IRRITATING POINT IN MEXICAN-U.S. RELATIONS

The United States is the greatest illegal drug market in the world and, thus, the engine that drives the drug trade, whereas Mexico is mainly a channel for distribution (the country is also a source, particularly of marijuana). The Mexican army and the Attorney General's office destroyed broad zones in which narcotics are produced. The main source countries in Latin America, however, are south of the Mexican border. In spite of Mexico's minor role as a source country and its strenuous effort to reduce the supply of drugs grown there, narcotrafficking and the American illegal drug market have seriously damaged our diplomatic and political relations.

Many Mexican citizens are frequently startled because their government allows the presence and action of U.S. agents--a form of collaboration?--who act almost freely in the national territory under diplomatic cover. From the U.S. viewpoint it would be inconceivable to have Mexican agents traveling freely in U.S. territory searching for drug users. Mexico has accepted practically any condition requested by the U.S. government in order to fight the growing U.S. drug market. In spite of this, Mexico does not qualify for a "good certification," making bilateral relations much more complicated.

The U.S. government, however, seems to ignore the progress of its economy and, therefore, its society. This progress can be associated with this terrible plague of the late twentieth century that tends to grow worse. Estimates of the number of drug users in the United States are impressive: millions of cocaine users, marijuana smokers, and heroin addicts. Approximately 15 percent of the U.S. population, regardless of age, is involved in narcotics use. In other words, one out of six Americans has had some contact with illicit drugs. U.S. society is confronting a new but devastating culture.

Reports indicate that 70 million Americans have used illicit drugs sometime in their lives, with cocaine being the narcotic in first place. Twenty-three million Americans are regular consumers. Additionally, the United States grows 18 percent of the marijuana consumed domestically and produces most of the synthetic drugs. The United States,therefore, is becoming, along with Latin countries, a source for narcotics.[9]

It is difficult to understand why the U.S. charges Mexico with most of the responsibility for trying to solve the American drug problem. If this is a domestic problem, diplomatic and political relations between the two countries must exclude, to a great extent, attributing responsibility to Mexico. Mexico did not promote the use of drugs in U.S. society, nor is it in the center of the drug mafias. A lack of mutual understanding is at the center of this complicated international relations issue. If better understanding is not reached, the most likely outcome is the non-cooperation of the Mexican government in trying to stop the flow of drugs to U.S. territory.

Furthermore, the United States has adopted faulty policies in other parts of Latin America. Broad zones of marijuana production were destroyed, or partially destroyed, using herbicides and toxins. Some of these zones underwent severe ecological problems representing serious danger for the rural population. The result was rather negative to the United States because marijuana production zones grew faster in its own territory.[9] This is an incorrect approach to the problem because the responsibility is placed on source countries, ignoring the neurotic problem of a society that is, essentially, the factor accounting for the drug demand.

Irritation between the United States and Mexico increased significantly in the first quarter of 1988. The New York mayor Edward Koch published a manifesto in the *New York Times* asserting that Mexico, along with other Latin American countries, was practically the nation responsible for the massive consumption and trafficking of drugs in New York City.[10] The charge, extremely naive, worsened Mexican-US relations.

There were some angry Mexican responses and reactions to Koch's point of view. In a press conference, foreign relations minister Bernardo Sepúlveda asked: what was the mayor doing to fight the narcotrafficking in his city, where he is the supreme authority?[11] Sepúlveda's point clearly indicates two things. On the one hand, drug consumption in one of the most important U.S. cities is getting out of control. On the other, the mayor found it necessary to find a scapegoat for the inability of city authorities to solve the problem even partially.

The problem of distribution and consumption in the U.S. is not only concentrated in big cities. The problem is getting worse; it is becoming a component of everyday life in even mid-sized cities.[12]

In 1988, Attorney General Edwin Meese rejected the idea of sending U.S. troops to Colombia to fight Colombian mafias on their own turf. What was the origin of this idea? One more time, it was the mayor of New York City who suggested almost an invasion of Colombia in order to prevent and control the consumption of narcotics in his city and country.[13]

Lorenzo Meyer, a well-known Mexican journalist and political scientist, spoke for millions of his compatriots when he reacted strongly to Koch's statement about Mexico. The title of Meyer's editorial illustrates the tone of his reaction: "To Certify Who Certify." Among other things, Meyer asserted that the illegal drug market has, as a main consequence, created an impressive and complex international organization whose main goal is to satisfy U.S. demand for narcotics, a demand worth over 100 billion dollars. In his editorial, Meyer calls unfair Koch's criticism of source countries alone, neglecting the increasing demand from U.S. society.[14] Frequently, U.S. authorities think that narcotrafficking and drug production are highly positive for source countries. For Mexico, at least, they are more negative than positive. In Colombia or Bolivia, narcopower, by being a parallel power, tends to destabilize their political systems.

So far, Mexico has had a stable political system based on a strong state apparatus. If Mexico overtly promoted these illegal activities, the State would rapidly weaken and the political system become more fragile. Mexican authorities understand that a weak state and an unstable political system, in Mexico's very particular geopolitical situation, would be political suicide.

Corruption associated with drug activities certainly exists in Mexico. Unfortunately, it is impossible to provide the desired empirical evidence on this delicate matter.[15] However, intuitively speaking, Mexican corruption is not as deep nor as broad as that in Colombia or Panama. In those nations, it appears that part of the state apparatus is highly involved in many narcotics matters.

Mexico has narcocorruption problems, but the government is not the main promoter of the production and distribution of drugs going to the United States. Corruption tends to be regionally located and associated much more with middle rank officials than top ones. Assertions have been made in the U.S. that some Mexican governors were involved in illegal drug activities, but no adequate evidence has been presented to authenticate these charges.

SOME MEXICAN EFFORTS AGAINST NARCOTRAFFICKING

The Mexican government has made a significant effort against the distribution and production of drugs. According to data reported in *Excelsior* (March 4, 1988), for its aerial antinarcotics campaign, Mexico spent $15.9 million in 1984 versus the $8.3 million spent by the United States, $20 million versus $9.7 million in 1985, $17.4 million versus $11.6 million in 1986, and spent $18.1 million in 1987 versus the $15.5 million spent by the U.S.

The combined effort of both countries increased during the period considered. It is also clear that the Mexican contribution in this five-year period was greater than the U.S. one. Frequently, U.S. legislators do not take into account these kinds of figures when they deal with that thing called "certification." According to journalistic sources, the Mexican attorney general's office is spending 60 percent of its total budget to fight the drug problem. For example, the number of airplanes belonging to this office increased significantly between 1984 and 1987, especially considering their price and the critical Mexican economic situation. Thus, in 1984 the total number of aircraft was seventy-five while in 1987 it went to ninety-four.[16]

Another indicator of Mexico's effort is the air eradication of amapola (the opium poppy, from which heroin is made) and marijuana. *Excelsior*

(March 8, 1988) reported, using Mexican Attorney General Office figures, that Mexico eradicated 48 percent of the 3.884 million hectares planted in amapola in 1983, 15.7 percent of the 5.238 million planted in 1984, 19.3 percent of the 5.2 million planted in 1985, 33 percent of the 5.2 million planted in 1986, and 41.6 percent of the 5.6 million planted in 1987. For marijuana, Mexico's air campaign eradicated 46.8 percent of the 4 million hectares planted in 1983, 28.2 percent of the 8.734 million planted in 1984, 44.1 percent of the 9 million planted in 1985, 45.8 percent of the 9 million in 1986, and 45 percent of the 9 million planted in 1987.

One striking thing is that estimated production grew significantly during the period considered. Marijuana production more than doubled during these years. Nevertheless, with the exception of 1984, the percentages of amapola eradication were steady but the percentages of marijuana eradication were highly irregular. From 1984 to 1987, however, the percentage tended to grow consistently from 15.7 to 41.6 percent, clearly indicating the important effort made by the Mexican government. Surely, more resources and new strategies must be implemented in order to win this war. What is important is that Mexico is contributing to this war and, therefore, it is unfair to assert that the country is passive in facing the problem.

The effort of the Mexican military is also worth pointing out. According to *Excelsior* (March 4, 1988), from 1983 through 1987, the military increased its eradication of amapola from 4.87 million hectares to 8 million and its eradication of marijuana in that same period from 5.113 million hectares to 10 million hectares. Similarly, the military confiscated 325,000 kilos of cocaine in 1983 but confiscated 9.295 million kilos in 1987.

The achievements are significant. It is outstanding that confiscated cocaine grew almost thirty times between 1983 and 1987. The figures of the other two columns are not as striking but they are consistent with the salient point: the Mexican effort against this big problem has not been insignificant.

In sum, many things are to be done to fight illicit narcotics, but the Mexican government's effort is not contemptuous. It is imperative that all concerned understand that the responsibility for fighting this war has to be *shared*. Mexico is not one of the "bad boys." When one considers the complex organization behind this enormous illegal market, defining Mexico as a principal source of illicit narcotics becomes even more ludicrous.

THE DRUG GANG: A COMPLEX ORGANIZATION

In an important article on U.S. drug gangs, *Newsweek* asked a crucial question: as crime rates rise, can cops fight back? According to *Newsweek*, there are 70 thousand gang members in Los Angeles alone and they significantly outnumber the police and sheriff's departments.

Despite years of experience combating street crime, few L.A. cops will deny that their war against the groups has taken a decisive turn for the worse. The gangs are better armed and more violent than

ever before;...the cops are winning all the battles but [they are] still
losing the war.[17]

For the first time in this century, a real war is taking place on U.S.
territory. Billions of dollars are at the center of the battlefield. Even
though the police, DEA, and other security forces are well organized, they
face an enemy which is as well--or maybe better--prepared to fight back.
The emergence of ghetto-based drug-trafficking organizations is rapidly
expanding not only in Los Angeles but also in the other most populated
American cities. Far worse, the pattern is becoming generalized to smaller
cities, suggesting that this particular kind of war is taking a national scope.
 The war is violent. It is startling to read a newspaper and learn that the
Colombian mafia kills many persons, even government officials (including
the attorney general),[18] but it is also impressive that more than 500 persons
were killed in upper Manhattan just in the last five years.[19] The gangs are
classified by ethnic origin (such as Hispanic or Asian), and the most recent
one to emerge is Jamaican, known as "Posses" (one estimate indicates 5,000
members belonging to this particular gang). This phenomenon suggests a
terrible conclusion: there can be many gangs as well as different leaders,
making the gang organization a complex one based on different and diffuse
leadership.
 Consequently, this is not a conventional war. It is not directed against
an army with a vertical organization. This is a new kind of war in which
there can be many leaders as well as many soldiers (all armed and violent).
It is possible to kill either one soldier or one leader and nothing will
happen. The organization will continue to work. Even more, this drug gang
phenomenon can expand. Such pessimistic views have been expressed by
the president of the Citizens Crime Commission of New York: "If we have
learned anything it is that [if] we let these guys get too big, we've got a
situation that will take decades to control."[20] The situation is almost out of
control now. The gangs are operating efficiently from coast to coast as the
dollar value of the illegal drug market clearly shows.
 The war is even worse than a conventional one because gangs members
are immune to both hope and fear. They can risk every challenge
regardless of the danger. For them, life is not important. What is important
is money and the challenge of facing an "abnormal" life full of risks. If the
leadership is multiple and the organization of gangs highly bifurcated, the
war becomes more complicated. For this reason, the real problem of this
war is not outside United States, but, is already within this country.
 In spite of a diffuse leadership within the United States, it is more
likely that the gang leadership is more vertical and unified outside the
country. Independently of the diffuseness of the U.S. domestic organization,
in this analysis one has to take into account the links of the gangs,
including that of their leadership, with some Latin American governments.
 Drugs and corruption are two highly interdependent phenomena, and
recently the Honduran government declared that the narcomafia had a plan
to take over the government after the incidents produced by the extradition
to the U.S. of Matta Ballesteros, reputedly one of the most important
heads of international narcotrafficking. Panama also helps illustrate this

pattern. Noriega, the outlaw dictator of this country, not only appoints and supports "elected" presidents but also belongs to that international organization (the Medellín cartel) which is supplying narcotics to the U.S.

It is rather difficult to believe that the drug mafia would take over a government. What is more likely is that such a criminal organization can make some Latin American governments much weaker even though the nation receives considerable illicit drug income. For example, the Colombian government has an enviable economic situation because of narcotic production. According to some sources, the parallel power of the narcomafia makes Colombian finances healthier but the State apparatus weaker.

According to The Economist[21], the Colombian gross national product grew consistently during 1987, the exception to the pattern shown by the rest of the Latin America. This growth took place even though its main export product, coffee, underwent a downward price trend in the international market during the same year. The fiscal deficit is low and the external debt is under control. Two billion out of the nine billion dollars that the country earns from the drug trade goes directly to the government, helping to stabilize the economy to a great extent. However, Colombia is not a significant producer but a drug processor and an important link in the international narcotrafficking chain. The important source countries for cocaine are Bolivia and Peru, both of which are even more dependent on drug income and losing state power to the parallel power of narcomafias.

ONE DILEMMA AMONG MANY

The United States is the most prosperous country in the world. Even though its economy has recently shown some ups and downs, its economic power is undeniable. This, in a few words, means an important surplus for U.S. society, a society whose high level of modernization is changing its value system, partially accounting for a significant increase in societal stress. Important economic surpluses combined with increased stress seem to produce a search for "new ways out." One can question what could be "wrong" with this real or false solution? Formally, there is nothing legal against it, only a moral judgment. The illegal aspect of consumption is not well founded.

If one takes into account that the democratic U.S. system means freedom of choice, then U.S. is not choosing inconsistent means because the choices are based precisely on the liberty and openness of a democratic society. The U.S. system supports that kind of "societal decision making". Formally speaking, any drug campaign (or action) oriented to suppress or to control the consumption of narcotics goes against the nature of U.S. democracy, of freedom of choice.

The main questions that have to be raised are: Why does U.S. society demand the drug solution? What is happening to its value system, its morale? How is it possible in an extremely well-organized society and government that drug rings can penetrate them and create an almost insoluble situation? No measure of national security has proven efficient in preventing or stabilizing the level of narcotic consumption in U.S. society. Nevertheless, one must remember that without demand there is no supply problem, while the existence of supply does dictate the existence of demand.

THE PROBLEM OF SUPPLY AND DEMAND

The narcotics problem is twofold: one part is supply and the other is demand, in other words, production and consumption. In consequence, the problem has to be faced in a "balanced" fashion.

To face the problem only from the supply side is, strictly speaking, not to devise a well-structured solution. Let us assume that all narcotics production in Bolivia could be destroyed. The Bolivian supply would stop for a while. However, other production zones would emerge, and more countries would take the role of source countries. In addition, the price would rise to the benefit of the narcomafias. However, the U.S. strategy has not seriously considered a solid repression of demand. To some extent, one can observe a kind of negligence in this aspect. Americans criticize source countries because of the existence of broad networks of corruption within their governments. However, the same is true for governments in the United States; it is inconceivable that the distribution of drugs through very well-organized gangs has no relationship to bribery and corruption. The point is obvious. Corruption is a common denominator both in the consumer and the producer sides of the problem.

One of the first steps in attacking the illicit narcotics problem is to fight corruption. However, the large amounts of money involved in narcotrafficking in both source and non-source countries makes it a very complicated to implement.

Mexico is investing more, proportionately, in the drug war than is the United States.[22] According to the Mexican attorney general, the fight being waged in Mexico benefits the United States much more than Mexico.[23] It deals with the health and morale of U.S. society, but the United States does not understand Mexico's effort nor does it understand that significant parts of Mexico's very limited budget cannot be oriented to such domestic needs as social development because the monies are being spent on the antinarcotics program.

In the short run, a general strategy to drastically reduce the American consumption of narcotics has to be defined. This strategy includes rehabilitation and prevention programs, particularly among young people. It is difficult to predict the potential success of such programs; there is not enough available evidence. However, testing the strategy has to be a U.S. priority. If the outcomes are positive, then the federal government has a new way to solve the problem U.S. society now faces. If the outcomes are negative, another strategy has to be implemented. However, the essential part of the solution is *within* U.S. society, not outside it. Source countries have to support that strategy in a combined effort, not in asymmetrical terms as has happened so far.

AMERICAN INTERVENTION IN MEXICAN POLITICS

On April 14, 1988, the U.S. Senate did not certify the "behavior" of Mexico because, by a 67 to 27 majority, its members asserted that Mexico was not adequately controlling the flow of drugs crossing into the United States. This occurred even though Reagan had recommended not to "sanction" Mexico.[24] Obviously, the U.S. government was divided on the drug issue; the president and twenty-seven senators did not think Mexico was an "indifferent" country in relation to the serious drug problem U.S. society already faces.

Mexico's reaction to this over intervention was strong. Most newspaper editorials and public comments of high officials of the present administration (including Carlos Salinas Gortari, then PRI presidential candidate and now president for the 1982-94 term) expressed anger.

Even though the Senate vote was not binding without a similar majority vote in the House of Representatives, the problem is twofold. On one hand, the United States did not treat Mexico as a sovereign country. It is worth pointing out that Mexico's effort against narcotrafficking is an exclusive matter for Mexico. On the other hand, this kind of political aggression may diminish the Mexican effort against controlling the flow and production of drugs. If this happens, it is very likely that the flow may increase and, turn out more harmful to U.S. society. The U.S. government is not adequately encouraging the possibility of a *real combined effort* between the two countries, but took an action that Americans would not tolerate from any government in relation to any issue.

Aggression and intervention cannot solve the problem. Pressure against Mexico is not functional for this global war. Attitudes have to be changed, otherwise, political irritation will be the main trait of this very complex bilateral relation. It is necessary to prevent anti-American reactions in Mexico. The complexity would turn into conflict.

DRUGS AND POLITICAL STABILITY

The problem of drugs deals not only with health; it has also to do with politics. More specifically, one of its main consequences may be located in the realm of political stability. Drugs (production, consumption, and distribution) can have an important impact on political and social institutions in either source or non-source countries. For example, civil security is really threatened because, among other things, increasing levels of corruption tend to make its efficiency more fragile.

Colombia is a dramatic example of ineffectiveness of those institutions dealing with justice, civil protection, and security. A "dure" power (the informal and the formal but both of them real) threatens the political stability of this country. Similarly, the conflict in Bolivia between the state and the czars of production is also an example of the narcomafias' political power adversely affecting Bolivian political stability. There is an evident growth of non-political power of the mafias that is directly affecting the political power of the state. Honduras and Panama may also be partial evidence for this statement. Top officials apparently are involved in narcotrafficking, and it is clear in those particular cases that the drug problem has some relationship to these countries' instability.

In Panama, where the United States has significant economic and, more importantly, strategic and geopolitical interests, it is striking that political instability may have a direct political effect on the U.S. political system. It may endanger its foreign policy. Drugs can affect political institutions and produce inter-institutional conflicts within countries; drugs are potentially associated with problems of instability.

This possible inter-institutional conflict can alter the functioning of the state and the political system. In 1988, U.S. politicians had to take a campaign stand on the drug issue, including legalization of consumption. One should not ignore that many measures are being implemented against the consumption and distribution of drugs. At the same time, however, suppliers are also devising new measures to assure the distribution and consumption of any kind of narcotic. This is not a phenomenon independent of institutions, but, in general, a phenomenon that goes through some institutions, including those which may be considered political. Instability is a potential problem that may emerge in both source and non-source countries. To ignore this fact is to ignore another consequence of this real plague of the latter years of the twentieth century.

AN ALTERNATIVE?

To clarify the possible alternatives in attacking the illicit narcotics problem, Table 2 presents a matrix of options.

TABLE 2

Consumption of Drugs
(Status)

		Illegal	Legal
Production of drugs (status)	Illegal	1	2
	Legal	3	4

Number 1 (illegal consumption and production as illegal) is the current situation. From it we can derive that the war against drug addiction and the increasing supply of drugs (the essential part of the problem) is getting, to some extent, out of control. Neither source nor non-source countries have had even minimal success in stopping demand and supply, leading to a crucial question: is it worthwhile to continue with the status quo strategy, which has proven unfeasible in bringing the overall problem of drug addiction under control? New ideas have to be implemented.

Number 2 (legal consumption and legal production) is really legalization of consumption. According to some, the legalization of consumption would stabilize the number of drug users. The number may very likely not decrease. But, hypothetically speaking, it can prevent a growing number of users. What is the main reason for not legalizing drug use?

Illegality of drug consumption has created a fabulous multibillion dollar market. Illegality has increased the price of drugs and, with it, the power of the mafias against the Colombian, Bolivian, and Honduran governments, to cite only three examples.

There is one advantage, among others, to legalizing consumption: it will control use among youth. The future of United States is at risk if the drug problem in this group is not controlled.

Alcohol and tobacco are legal even though their harm is impressive in terms of mortality rates, productivity, and the basic value system of U.S. society. The problem is that the production of such drugs as cocaine, heroin, and marijuana remain within the world of illegality. However, legalizing demand could diminish production levels and decrease prices, and control, to some extent, the drug users. In consequence, the power of the drug rings would also diminish, making them easier to fight. Number 2 is not an unreasonable alternative.

Number 3 (legal production and illegal consumption) is not a feasible solution. The problem is more on the supply side rather than the demand side. However, it has an advantage, to identify the producers. It implies both a multinational combined effort and the increased likelihood of fighting them back and decreasing their real power. Although this alternative would seem to allow a census of producers, in fact it would be almost impossible. Therefore, it is not a viable alternative.

Number 4 (legal consumption and illegal production) is unfeasible for some of the same reasons mentioned for Number 3. It is akin to formalizing the drug market, making it part of the economy and the industry.

Number 2 is the best solution. The U.S. government will not adopt it because it is politically unacceptable, even though its adoption might solve the drug-related domestic problems of both source and non-source countries and reduce international tension. But, if Number 1 has proven unsuccessful, why not try a new strategy?

V
Policy Options

10

Antinarcotics Strategies and U.S.-Latin American Relations
Gregory F. Treverton

Narcotics is a major issue in U.S. relations with Latin America; with regard to some countries it is the central issue, overshadowing debt or migration. It is not hard to see why. The American people are alarmed over narcotics, even if that alarm may be superficial. The plethora of antidrug proposals, many quite silly, floating around Congress year reflects that alarm, given concrete expression lest any particular member be out-done by a potential opponent. And most imported drugs reaching the United States come from or through Latin America and the Caribbean.

It also is striking how far apart North Americans and Latin Americans are in conceiving of the issue. The gap was underscored, if inadvertently, by a recent Council on Foreign Relations volume: a chapter on U.S.-Mexican relations by José Juan de Olloqui dismisses the subject in a paragraph with the customary "it's not our problem,"[1] as Congress debated a decertification of Mexico and several other Latin American countries under the 1986 antidrug law.

The "narcotics problem" is in fact two clusters of problems. The first is the social consequence of drug abuse, itself intertwined with the ills that trouble all societies in some measure--poverty, crime, poor schools and erosion of authority. The second is the crime and corruption that result because drugs are illegal, thereby creating huge profits in illicit trafficking. The Presidential Commission on Organized Crime estimates narcotics sales to total more than $100 billion dollars in the United States, or twice what the United States spends on oil and a third of its military budget.[2]

So far it has been the first, abuse, that has been the focus of public attention in the United States, although U.S. police departments and courts are no strangers to drug-related corruption. The emergence of virtual drug wars in major U.S. cities is a vision of the future.

By contrast, it is drug-related crime and corruption that most afflict the Latin American states, although some of them are also becoming familiar with the evils of drug abuse; Colombia has more cocaine addicts per capita than the United States. When narcodollars buy police, courts, and elected officials, the foundations of democracy are shaken even in a stable republic such as the United States. In the struggling democracies of Latin America, where police are offered many times their annual salary to ignore drug dealings, or where honest judges risk death for presiding over drug cases, the threat to representative government is far worse.

THE PROBLEM: THE UNITED STATES

Narcotics use in the United States is staggering in its proportions: 62 million Americans admit having used marijuana and another 22 million report cocaine use. The U.S. public is preoccupied with drug abuse: in a 1986 poll asking what two or three issues people were most concerned about, 26 percent cited drugs, compared with 27 percent for unemployment and 7 percent for U.S. relations with the Soviet Union.[3]

However, attention to the issue has waxed and waned. In 1986, after the death of basketball star Len Bias from a cocaine overdose, Congress passed the Antidrug Abuse Act of 1986, an impressive declaration intending to cut the huge U.S. *demand* for illicit drugs. Cocaine seemed to be losing the image acquired in the 1970s as a clean, safe, even glamorous drug--the choice of rock stars, athletes, and actors.

After the burst of attention in 1986, however, the president quietly cut back his own recommended funding for the war on drugs. Although the ritual denunciations of drug abuse as the ruination of young people continued, politicians moved on to other issues. In the words of an editorialist for the *New York Times*, it is not that the United States lost the war on drugs, it is rather that "we never really decided to get into it."[4]

In the electoral season of 1988, the narcotics issue once again become emotive politics. Latin America has been both a contributing cause and pronounced object of that emotion. When a federal court issued indictments against Panama strongman Noriega for drug trafficking, the indictments and the subsequent inability of the Reagan administration to force Noriega out underscored Latin America's role in the drug trade, never mind that the original indictments were certainly unenforceable and thus almost certainly unwise.

Much of the political debate in the United States has focussed inward on peripheral questions, such as how far to push a reluctant U.S. military into law enforcement, or whether to make some drug crimes punishable by death. Yet, some of the emotion washed directly over U.S. relations with Latin America, most notably so in the instance of Mexico. In 1988 the president "certified" that Mexico was cooperating fully with the United States in the war on drugs, a certification he was required to make under the 1986 act. Subsequently, however, the Senate voted sixty-three to twenty-seven to "decertify" Mexico, which could have denied that country most U.S. aid and access to multilateral bank loans. The decertification was shelved in the House of Representatives, but the episode was illustrative.

Whatever the see-saw in attention, drug abuse peaked in the late 1970s with two exceptions: cocaine use and drug use in general among those over twenty-six, the previous prime age for drug consumption. The special concern now is cocaine, especially the cheap, potent form of smoking it called "crack". Heroin remains a tragedy of inner cities in the United States, but the number of addicts (about 500,000) has remained roughly constant for a decade.

Cocaine has become the drug most often cited in hospital emergency room cases--25 thousand cases and one thousand deaths reported in 1986. Moreover, the demographics of cocaine use differ from other drugs, previously used predominately by 18- to 24-year-olds. That cohort has been declining as a share of the total U.S. population while cocaine use has been increasing, confirming suspicions that cocaine is the drug of choice for those now beyond previous prime ages for drug abuse.

Only recently has there been any evidence that cocaine use may have joined the post-1980 pattern of generally declining drug use among adolescents. Daily marijuana use among high school seniors, for instance, had fallen to just over 3 percent in 1987 from its peak of 11 percent in 1978. Cocaine is now the second most used illicit drug after marijuana. Only in the 1987 survey was the pattern of steady increase in use broken: in 1987, 15 percent of high school seniors had tried it, 10 percent had used in the previous year, and 4 percent in the previous month; for 1986 the numbers were 17, 13 and 6, respectively.

Crack, however, has been on the rise, surely until 1987. The proportion of high school seniors who smoked cocaine remained constant between 1979 and 1983; between 1983 and 1986 it more than doubled, from 2.5 percent to 6 percent--and most of that smoking was crack. In 1987, there was perhaps a levelling-off in crack use. Survey evidence for other drugs, such as marijuana, indicates that use goes down as more people perceive a drug to be dangerous, but not so for cocaine. Its use so far has increased along with the public perception of its danger.

THE PROBLEM: LATIN AMERICA

Chains of drug production and trafficking criss-cross Latin America, involving a shifting set of a dozen-plus countries. Some three-quarters of the cocaine reaching the United States is estimated to come from Colombia.[5] Mexico, a drug control success story in the 1970s, has again become the primary source of heroin and marijuana for the U.S. market, and an estimated one-third of the cocaine reaching the United States transits that country.

A capsule description of the key drug-producing and trafficking countries will underscore the differences in their situations:

Mexico, along with Colombia, is the focal point of U.S. attention to the drug issue in Latin America. It has cooperated, if not always eagerly, with the United States over drugs for longer and more broadly than any other nation, signing some forty-odd cooperation agreements with Washington by 1985. More important, in deciding on the *campaña permanente* (permanent campaign) in the 1970s, Mexico made drug eradication a major army mission. About a fifth of the army of 125 thousand is involved and about a third of the nation's defense budget. More than half the attorney general's 1987 budget of $36 million went to such operations, with the

United States contributing some $15 million. Indeed, Mexico's deputy attorney general asserted in 1986 that "no other country in the world than Mexico does so much for the youth of North America."[6]

Between the mid-1970s and 1983, these eradication efforts produced a nosedive in Mexico's share of marijuana supplied to the U.S., from 70 percent to 10 percent, and its share of U.S. heroin supplies tumbled from 87 percent to 34 percent. While eradication remains major business for the Mexican government, these efforts are failing. Part of the reason surely is Mexico's economic crisis, which encourages small farmers to return to lucrative drug crops even as it strains government resources for attacking the problem. Although the total income to peasant farmers growing marijuana is relatively small--probably less than a billion dollars a year--it may still be significant by comparison to current poverty and alternative crops. By one estimate, of each dollar a marijuana consumer pays, 91 to 93 cents remain in the United States; for cocaine, 97 to 99 cents. Latin American producers thus get a fraction of one cent.[7]

Increasing corruption, especially given the scale of army involvement, is also a culprit for increasing Mexican involvement in drug trafficking; Mexico created a special police force, the Federal Judicial Police, to prosecute the war on drugs while restraining corruption. And, U.S. interdiction efforts in the southeastern United States, while inadequate to bite much into total drug supply, did manage to push traffic westward, through Mexico to the largely invisible Mexican-U.S. border, a fact testified to by the thousands of illegal migrants that cross it every night.

While the Andean countries have become genuinely alarmed by narcotics abuse in their own countries, drug abuse in Mexico is not yet seen as a major social problem. And, while traffickers have corrupted Mexican institutions, nowhere do they pose a direct threat to governmental control as they did in the 1970s in the "critical triangle" of Sinaloa, Durango, and Chihuahua. By moving against drugs there, the central government also regained control where traffickers, perhaps mixed with anti-government guerrillas, had become a law unto themselves.

Thus, Mexicans, including analysts who can hardly be described as reflexively anti-American, feel that Mexico spends too much on the drug war and gains too little. It is periodically coerced into doing still more to help the United States. And, when those efforts fail, predictably, to cut into U.S. drug abuse, Mexico is a convenient scapegoat. As one Mexican study of the problem put it: "Mexico has a drug problem. It is called the United States."

Mexico responds to American pressure more out of need than shared perception of the problem. In 1969, Operation Intercept brought cross-border traffic to a standstill and induced Mexico to mount the permanent campaign. The torture-murder of DEA officer Enrique Camarena in 1985 specifically spurred the 1986 legislation and associated Mexico-bashing. In the wake of the 1988 certification debate, Mexico announced a new cabinet-level task force on drugs.

Moreover, the U.S.-directed war on drugs grates on a Mexican nationalism that is framed in large measure against a history of U.S. dominance. Imagine how Americans would react to DEA agents from another country carrying weapons and conducting independent investigations on U.S. soil, or to the use herbicides and police practices that were banned in that foreign nation.

Peru is the world's largest producer of coca leaf, with annual production in the range of 100 million metric tons; more recent accurate estimates of Peru's production suggest that actual production, post-eradication, has remained roughly constant in recent years. As in Colombia and Bolivia, domestic drug abuse has become a serious social problem.

Peru also illustrates the complexity of relations among narcotics traffickers. The U.S. government has made much of cooperation between traffickers and guerrillas, and there have been instances of that, usually tacit, the result of traffickers and guerrillas occupying the same remote areas and sharing the same enemy--the central government. And guerrillas have engaged directly in trafficking. At least as often, however, traffickers, socially conservative if greedy, have opposed guerrillas, sometimes cooperating with right-wing paramilitary squads in doing so.

In Peru, the Sendero Luminoso insurgency has spread throughout much of the country, but it remains most entrenched in remote areas where the writ of the central government is weak. Some of those areas, particularly northeastern Peru and the Upper Huallaga Valley, are also drug-producing areas, and so insurgents and traffickers fall into tacit alliance. Minimally, the government is triply fearful of mounting anti-trafficker operations: they will be difficult militarily, the army may be corrupted in the process, and destroying the incomes produced by narcotics will undermine the local support on which the anti-guerrilla operations depend.

President Alan García, inaugurated in 1985, has continued brave antidrug efforts. His government has conducted major enforcement operations and, despite increasing violence, has persisted in eradication efforts. Yet, confronted by a collapsing economy and domestic violence, Peru seems to be losing the drug war, at least on the supply side: its coca eradication, 5 thousand hectares in 1985, fell to about half that in 1986.[8] Moreover, Peru also demonstrates that drug-control policies can be self-defeating: the harsher the laws and penalties for drug trafficking, the more incentive they provide to corruption.

The Mexican experience of the 1970s suggests that Latin American governments would be impelled to action against drugs when traffickers pose a significant threat to governmental control of national territory. **Colombia** appears near that point; the power of drug traffickers, who account for perhaps three-quarters of all the cocaine smuggled into the United States, is such that control of the country hangs in the balance. (In terms of coca production, Colombia is a distant third to Peru and Bolivia.) The list of those assassinated by traffickers is a who's of Colombia's antidrug campaigns: the former commander of the special antinarcotics police, a supreme court justice, a premier journalist, and, most recently, the attorney general.

Against these odds, the Barco administration has persisted in its efforts, suggesting that the drug war can retain a high priority across a change in government. That war, however, is at best a draw. One of the most infamous of the traffickers, Carlos Lehder, was arrested, immediately extradited to the United States, and eventually convicted. At the same time, though, other well-known traffickers like Pablo Escobar walk the streets with little effort to conceal their whereabouts. For honest judges to sign extradition orders was to risk giving themselves the death sentence, and, in this atmosphere, Colombia's Supreme Court nullified the extradition treaty with the United States.

In 1986, Colombia increased its eradication of marijuana by about half, to nearly 10 thousand hectares. However, as in Peru, coca eradication slowed because the commingling of drug production and anti-government guerrillas (especially the M-19) simply made it too dangerous. For the same reason, drug seizures also dropped; narcotics police, numbering 1500, suffered fifty-eight casualties in 1986 alone.

Colombia has begun to address its domestic demand for drugs. When cocaine became so plentiful in the early 1980s that international prices dropped, traffickers began dumping coca leaf on the local market. It was then fabricated into a crude, highly addictive drug called *basuco*, all the more dangerous because of the additives--sulfuric acid, kerosene, or gasoline--used in their production. By 1988, as many as a half million of the country's 38 million residents were estimated to be regular *basuco* smokers.[9] In response, Colombia has targeted a program of extracurricular activities on its teenagers, hoping to involve a sixth of its five million teenagers by the end of the year. Yet, whatever the effectiveness of the program, it seems destined to reach middle-class children who attend school and whose parents, like their U.S. counterparts, are alarmed by spiraling drug use--not poor kids, who do not attend school.

Bolivia has made a remarkable rebound from its hyperinflation but has been unable to register much progress in the war on drugs. In 1986, Operation Blast Furnace, involving six U.S. army helicopters with U.S. military and DEA personnel, raided cocaine laboratories in the Beni region. The big operation came as no surprise to the traffickers, so the amount of narcotics actually seized was modest. Still, the short-run disruption was significant: the facilities put out of business had the capacity to process as much as 20 to 40 percent of total U.S. consumption. But longer-term effects were negligible. Coca prices began to rise in Bolivia as U.S. troops moved out, in the expectation that cocaine processing would begin again.

Even the U.S. State Department report acknowledges that "no real progress was made on eradication in 1986."[10] It is not hard to see why. Bolivia's problem seems less the mixing of traffickers and guerrillas--though there is some of that--than simple economics. Trafficking is so lucrative that traffickers can buy the protection they need. Coca is lucrative,too for peasants, if not absolutely then certainly by comparison to the alternatives. One estimate based on prices several years ago reckoned that producers in the Chapare region, where two-thirds of the nation's coca is grown, could earn almost twenty times more money growing coca than the next most profitable crop, citrus.[11] By the same estimate, landless peasants are drawn to the factories to work as *pisadores* (stompers of coca leaf), where they can earn six to eight times the money offered by licit rural employment, and even more than they could earn in the cities. In the process, of course, traditional communal patterns are breaking down.

POLITICS AND ANALYTICS

The shape of the drug problem suggests three broad conclusions relevant to U.S.-Latin American relations. First, the entire range of "police" actions against drugs--from enforcement against traffickers to seizures to crop eradication in producing countries--will have little effect on narcotics supplies in the United States. Even were it possible to seal U.S. borders to drugs, it would not win the drug war, only shift it to so-called "designer drugs" made domestically from chemicals,not foreign crops. Already, the war against imports has been more successful against marijuana than cocaine for obvious reasons: the former is both much bulkier and less lucrative than the latter, so stepped-up seizure has given traffickers an incentive to switch to cocaine. As a result, the United States may produce up to half its marijuana domestically by some estimates (four times the official figure).

In particular, short-term disruptions of drug supplies do not have much long-term effect. For instance, while massive drug eradications succeeded in Mexico in the 1970s, as they did also in Turkey and Bolivia, those policies did not long succeed in reducing the overall supply of illegal drugs to the United States. Drug traffickers were, and are, able to shift their supply base from one country to the next (and, if necessary, from one region to the next), until U.S. drug enforcement programs subside in the chosen area.

Second, the emphasis in U.S. antidrug strategies ought to shift towards demand, as to some extent it already has. Third, however, cutting into demand is a task for the long run, one for which past experience provides some pointers but no guarantees. At a minimum, the time lag between action and effect will be frustratingly large: as with cigarette smoking, the message will take some time to reach home, still more to affect the behavior of those receiving it.

Suffice it to say, however, that these conclusions do not drive the U.S. politics of the war on drugs. Understanding of the issue, in Congress for instance, remains low. The *Times* editorial cited at the beginning represents that lack of understanding; it sounded a clarion call for "stopping foreign drugs flowing into our country...at the source, not at our border or in the streets of American cities." Even inside the U.S. executive branch, "pulling up those coca plants" is a kind of crusade, almost independent of its effect.

Certainly, the conclusion that supply-side policies do not work is counterintuitive. It just seems logical that it ought to be easier to cut drugs off "at the source" than to influence the behavior of millions of potential users. Then, when it turns out that drugs cannot be stopped at the source, Congress is tempted to respond in frustration by punishing supplier countries: witness the 1986 act requiring the president to certify that countries are "fully cooperating" in the war on drugs.

Aid is denied to any country not thus certified, and U.S. representatives are required to vote against multilateral bank loans to that country. Separately, the act denied sugar quotas and imposed up to 50 percent tariffs on the exports of countries whose programs the president did not determine to be adequate; those determinations, moreover, can be overridden by joint congressional resolutions. So far, none of those decertification attempts has succeeded (Panama was not certified by the executive in 1988, although since aid had already stopped, the action had no practical effect).

The act also constrained the president to pressure Latin American drug-producing countries in a number of ways, by requiring him to certify Bolivia's antidrug efforts in order to resume aid to that country, withholding $1 million in drug aid to Mexico until he reported on Mexican progress in bringing Camarena's killers to justice, and suggesting that he "should consider" additional sanctions against Mexico--a travel advisory and other cuts in aid, multilateral bank loan or trade benefits.

Yet, the conclusion that supply-side policies are failing is inescapable. While highly publicized interdiction campaigns, such as the South Florida Task Force, record huge seizures, drugs, especially cocaine, are more and more plentiful in the United States today. Indeed, cocaine prices in the United States are falling. A gram that cost $600 four years ago now goes for $200. As Reagan himself said: "All the confiscation and law enforcement in the world will not cure this plague."[12]

In the State Department's words, coca production still "vastly exceeds cocaine consumption," and the disparity is even more striking in the case of heroin. The world produces some 2,500-plus tons of opium, and the United States consumes only 3-4 percent of that amount.[13] Put more graphically, the U.S. heroin demand could be supplied from a few square miles of opium poppies.

HOW MUCH STRAIN?

Most of pressure the United States puts on Latin American countries is needless, even counterproductive, if it discredits as "made in America" policies Latin American countries ought to adopt in their own interest. Yet, the most that can be said so far is that U.S. policy has moved somewhat in the sensitive direction towards a focus on demand. That seems likely to continue under President Bush, who has not given much prominence to specific antidrug programs but placed the issue high in the litany of national problems when he was campaigning in 1988. However, neither the president nor the broad American body politic has embraced the counterpart logic to more attention on demand, less on supply.

The United States will, as in the past, put pressure on Latin America. As in the past, Mexico is likely to be the focus of that pressure. The United States will expect more of it than of other drug-producing countries: Mexico will loom large as a supplier of the U.S. drug market and will seem to have more economic and political capability to control its territory than Bolivia or Peru.

On the other hand, the simple fact that the United States has large interests in Mexico apart from drugs--ranging from the security of borders to oil to emigration--operates as a check on letting the drug issue drive the entire relationship. By contrast, the Andean drug-producing countries are ones in which tangible U.S. interests apart from narcotics are weak. That makes it especially tempting for Congress and others to vent frustration on those nations, while it means that there are few countervailing interests within officialdom.

Mexico and the United States probably are too important to each other to permit the drug issue to reach a flashpoint, but the mix is explosive-- drug production, plus easy trafficking routes, plus illegal immigration, plus the U.S. perception that Mexico, as a relatively strong government, ought to be able to do better. A nasty accident is entirely possible despite the best efforts of both governments: suppose more celebrated drug deaths in the United States coincided with fresh murders of U.S. agents and an intense bout of concern over illegal immigrants. Pressure to "close the border" or otherwise punish Mexico might then become irresistible, even as doing so remained unwise or impossible.

In Latin America, more generally, there are signs of a backlash against drug-control policies that have become identified with U.S. pressure, all the more so if strong U.S. pressure is not followed by sustained assistance. Earlier this year, Colombia's attorney general, appointed after his predecessor was gunned down by traffickers, talked publicly of, in effect, suing the drug trade for peace, pardoning traffickers, and perhaps legalizing the traffic in exchange for some guarantees. Four years earlier the Colombian president had met with representatives of the Medellín cartel, eventually refusing the cartel's offer to pay off $10 billion in Colombian foreign debt in return for amnesty.

Such a course by any Latin American country is improbable, but suppose the new Mexican administration sought to move in a more nationalist direction to solidify its political coalition, or if domestic events pressed it in that direction. If it did, its hand would be much stronger than Colombia's, but the elements of an implicit deal might be similar: a relatively free hand for cocaine traffickers provided they kept the drug out of Mexico, coupled with reduced eradication of marijuana crops, especially those grown by small farmers. Needless to say, in pursuing this course Mexico would run the risk of a serious reaction from the United States.

More likely, suppose Mexico decided to retarget its antidrug effort in a way that better suited Mexican interests, for instance, away from eradicating marijuana and towards disrupting trafficking networks, especially for heroin. It would reflect judgments that eradicating marijuana is too costly and too inviting of corruption, that cocaine transiting is not yet a serious problem; and that resources would be better spent concentrated on heroin. Marijuana growing would be tolerated so long as the farmers did not move into serious trafficking.[14]

Would Mexico be able to implement such a policy? How would the United States respond if it could? Much would turn on whether Mexico could offer up a stream of traffickers; if it could, the bursts of good publicity would buy some freedom from U.S. pressure. Since the political pressure on Mexico in Congress, for instance, is generally, to "do something about drugs," prosecuted traffickers would serve as well as dead marijuana plants, perhaps better.

Beyond that broad political judgment, there are a host of fine-grain assessments to be made. For Mexico to attack the trafficking networks, it would need U.S. help, principally from the DEA but also from other elements of the Balkanized U.S. antidrug machinery. Could it count on that help if it were less involved in eradication? How would Americans react when more Mexican marijuana began appearing on U.S. streets? And so on.

These questions direct attention to the course of politics and governmental action in the United States with regard to the drug issue. So far, for all the noise, American politicians have been eager to denounce the evils of narcotics and bash the drug-producing countries but not to spend much money on the problem. That ambivalence has been matched by the conflicting stakes of U.S. government agencies. Contrast DEA with, for instance, the general distaste of most of the State Department for the drug issue lest it disrupt other, more traditional diplomatic business (one recent ambassador to Mexico, John Gavin, was a prominent exception, but he was a political appointee, not a careerist). DOD which has also resisted patrolling the border for drug purposes, arguing it is not *its* mission.

If this year's relative good news about cocaine use becomes a trend, however modest, the temperature of the issue in the United States will drop. It may become clearer that there are no definitive battles in the war on drugs, that demand is key, and that the lead-times are long. That perspective is not likely to take hold completely, and so temptations to lash out in frustration at Mexico and other drug producers will remain. But, they should be more manageable.

There do appear to be cycles of attention to the issue in the United States. For instance, Mexico has received sharp U.S. pressure over drugs in 1939, 1948, 1961, 1969, 1975, and 1985--roughly once during each U.S. administration. Specific events, like the Camarena murder, serve as catalysts: during February and March 1985 the *New York Times* ran a total of twenty-four news stories on Mexico, sixteen of which were about Camarena; during this period the only Mexican news on network television was Camarena news.

Over the longer term, the cast of the issue in the United States may change. For instance, as marijuana consumption has levelled off, tolerance for it--now the least of the drug evils--seems to have increased somewhat. Personal possession of marijuana has been decriminalized in ten U.S. states and is legal in Alaska. Young people reflect a different attitude towards it from other drugs: nearly a quarter of 12 to 17 year-olds in 1985 were estimated to have tried marijuana, while less than one-twentieth had done so with cocaine.[15] There has been no change over time in the percentage that has tried heroin (1 to 2 percent). Yet, despite decriminalization, there are some 400 thousand marijuana-related arrests each year in the United States.

In framing policy toward alcohol a half century ago, the United States explicitly separated the problem of abuse from the crime and corruption that resulted from illegality; the costs of prohibition in the coin of the latter were judged too high even, in considering reductions in alcohol use and abuse. Amidst the manifest silliness of recent political antinarcotics rhetoric, legalization became a part of the political agenda. When concern over cocaine first swept the United States, the idea was not even mentioned in whispers; now *The Economist* recommends legalizing cocaine.[16]

Arguments against legalization, often passionate, are of two general sorts. The first is that it would not work: either it would not drive the crime and corruption from the trade, or it would do so but only at the cost of vastly increasing the number of Americans who use and abuse cocaine.

The second argument, more moral in tone, holds drugs to be inherently bad. That alcohol and tobacco are deeply embedded in our society is no reason to accord cocaine the same place. Perhaps cocaine can be kept at the margins of American life. In any case, now is no time to admit defeat and take the irreversible step of legalization.

Both these arguments are weighty. Legalization is a kind of all-or-nothing choice. To have any chance of working, cocaine would have to be available under a system not much more restrictive than that for alcohol currently. A more restrictive system--cocaine only on doctors' certification, for instance--could easily wind up as the worst of both worlds: the threshold of legalization would have been crossed, but the black market for uncertified demand would still exist, with all its attendant crime and corruption.

What we know is that the current U.S. antinarcotics strategy, based on a tactic and a hope, is unpromising. The tactic is to constrain supply through eradication, seizure, and enforcement, thereby driving up the price. In the short run, however, that tactic is self-defeating: if it succeeds in forcing the price up, as it so far has not, that only increases the money to be made from illegal trafficking. If, as seems likely, short-run demand is relatively inelastic--users will try to pay whatever it takes to buy cocaine-- the tactic is a recipe for more, not less crime.

Thus the hope: that over time Americans will be persuaded not to use cocaine no matter what its price. Only if that hope is realized can the current strategy succeed in both reducing use and abuse and containing the crime that exists because the demand is for an illegal substance.

The arguments about legalization, pro and con, are difficult to settle. The U.S. experience with prohibition is ambiguous: alcohol use and abuse did go down, but at the cost of considerable lawlessness, even by ordinary citizens made criminals by their tastes. Perhaps alcohol is different from cocaine, at least in how deep-rooted it is in our society. Nor do small-scale demonstrations--Britain's experience with legalized heroin, for instance--tell us much about what legalization would mean across an entire society.

There is a better way than simply tossing the arguments back and forth. Before seriously considering legalization, suppose the United States decided to give the current antidrug strategy a specified period, say five years. Bench marks of success would be established now, to be measured in five years. Those bench marks should be output measures about which the society cares--data on cocaine use, addiction-related deaths, drug-related killings and the like--not input measures, like drug seizures or narcotics-related arrests.

By those measures of success, it might appear in five years that serious discussion of legalization was unnecessary or premature. In 1987, for the first time, cocaine use declined among high school seniors, although the evidence for crack is more ambiguous. Perhaps that is the first sign that the cocaine epidemic has crested.

If, on the other hand, the evidence five years hence is not so happy, at least the debate should be clearer. If the hope reflected in current antidrug policies turns out to be false, it will be time to confront legalization as a real alternative. It is worth bearing in mind that the costs of current policies--violence and corruption--fall most heavily on Latin America, even as they infect the United States as well.

11

Concluding Observations and Policy Recommendations
Donald J. Mabry
and Raphael Perl

PRODUCTION AND TRAFFICKING AS A SECURITY PROBLEM

The concept of "national security" encompasses more than armaments, military readiness, and espionage; it also includes the political, social, and economic health of a society. Illicit narcotics trafficking threatens the national security of many countries in this hemisphere. To operate effectively, drug traffickers evade or neutralize government officials by intimidation, corruption, and murder. These methods mock the rule of law and destabilize nations, as recent events in Colombia demonstrate. Nor is Colombia alone in this regard. Bolivia and Peru are also unable to exercise effective control over parts of their national territories. When this occurs, one finds two states--the official one and the one ruled by drug traffickers.

In general, corrupt polities are inherently less secure. Corruption weakens the state's ability to carry out one of its fundamental duties--to maintain public order and thereby insure the basic personal security of its citizens. Without effective countermeasures, corruption can become integral to the establishment, endemic, and a threat to national security. Further, large-scale drug smuggling violates national borders, creating unregulated channels through which all manners of persons, goods, and wealth can pour.

Respect for law is the sine qua non of a civil society. Laws are not so much *enforced* as *obeyed*, i.e., most people obey the laws voluntarily because they believe it to be in their self-interest to do so. Widespread disobedience of laws means that the disobedient are creating their own law. By creating a separate code of conduct, drug traffickers and drug users are, in effect, assuming some of the powers reserved for the state. In some countries, this non-elected minority has already redefined the basic rules of society.

At another level, narcotics abuse threatens the ability of a nation to raise an army in times of national crisis. Drug abusers and addicts do not make good military personnel, a fact recognized by the U.S. military's policy of discharging them from duty. The military is necessarily based on discipline and strict obedience to rules, rejected by those who use prohibited substances. Moreover, sophisticated modern military equipment is dangerous to operate while under the influence of narcotics.

The drug trade adversely affects U.S. national security in many ways. It is detrimental to the economic and physical health of the nation and its inhabitants and is detrimental to U.S. industrial productivity. Drug related violence and crime remain the ongoing focus of attention of law enforcement agencies responsible for maintaining U.S. internal security. The drug trade threatens, however, U.S. national security not only by its adverse effects on the American citizenry, but also to the extent that it weakens or destabilizes U.S. allies in Latin America and U.S. bilateral relations in the region. Already, Bolivia, Colombia, and Peru are unable to govern significant parts of their national territory, and while the United States does not want to see them paralyzed or controlled by drug traffickers, the great national security nightmare for U.S. policy makers is the prospect of an unstable Mexico.

The Rise of Narcoterrorism

An even greater national security threat for Latin American nations and the United States is the persistent rise of "narcoterrorism" in the Western Hemisphere. The link between illegal narcotics and terrorism, so-called "narcoterrorism," exists. Guerrillas and drug traffickers coexist in certain areas, with the terrorists sometimes acting as a protective military arm for the "narcomafia." Examples are the M-19 and FARC in Colombia. Drug traffickers have also paid terrorists with weapons brought back from the United States on return trips from carrying drugs. One news report seems to assert this was the case in Mexico in March, 1988, when security forces there seized 360 Soviet-designed AK47 assault rifles, ammunition, airplanes, and land vehicles during raids on drug rings in Agua Prieta, Hermosillo, and Durango.[1]

As Rensselaer Lee notes, basic ideological and economic conflicts of interest exist between left-wing terrorists and drug traffickers. Drug traffickers want a capitalist state, one in which profits are valued, money flows largely unobstructed, and government regulatory and police powers limited. Their dispute with existing governments is over governmental protection of the health, welfare, property, and due process values of its citizenry, which interfere with their business activities. On the other hand, terrorists ideologically aligned with the Left traditionally oppose capitalist forms and values and seek to replace them with state socialist operation of economic activity. Were they to succeed, profit-seeking (capitalist) drug enterprises would presumably be abolished or controlled for political ends. Thus, unless a producing nation were to become a left-wing state and also choose to sell drugs as part of a strategy to destabilize centrist or right-wing states or both, it does not appear likely that the narcotic trade will grow significantly or flourish under left-wing auspices.

To date, most of the attention given to narcoterrorism has focused on links between left-wing groups and terrorists. However, some drug traffickers in Latin America are becoming aligned ideologically with extremist right-wing groups that also engage in terrorist acts. These groups threaten, beat, and murder government officials or "leftists" perceived to get in their way. In addition, some become marginally involved in politics, usually by giving financial support to political candidates. This terrorism is essentially different from terrorist movements that seek to overthrow a state inasmuch as the goal is to intimidate the state into adopting a laissez-faire policy towards the drug business and other established interests. Still, by sponsoring various types of social violence, drug traffickers threaten the rule of law and democracy and the political stability necessary for flourishing, sustained business activity.

One irony in U.S.-Latin American narcotics relations is that U.S. eradication policy, at least on one level, creates a climate favoring the growth of left-wing terrorism and guerrilla movements. Crop eradication, to say the least, is an unpopular measure with farmer groups and affords an opportunity for guerrilla groups to masquerade as friends of local farmers who see their drug crops--their livelihood--destroyed at the behest of the United States.

U.S. NARCOPOLICY IN THE CONTEXT OF PAST RELATIONS

Historians such as Douglas Kinder have carefully traced the origins, implementation, and impact of past narcotics epidemics on the domestic and foreign policy of the United States. From them we learn that the narcotics epidemic of the late nineteenth and early twentieth centuries petered out in the 1920s as a result of declining demand and not declining supply achieved through diplomacy, conferences, reports, and treaties.

The dimensions of the current U.S. narcotics epidemic are magnified by the vast wealth of the U.S., currently the world's largest and most lucrative market for illicit drugs. In the 1980s discretionary income is exponentially higher than it was at the turn of the century, and Americans spend hundreds of billions of dollars annually in the pursuit of pleasure. The ease of travel to, from, and within the United States is a smuggler's fantasy come true. In a matter of hours, cocaine can be moved from jungle laboratories to U.S. streets. Changes in cultural values, what Christopher Lasch calls "the culture of narcissism" and Tom Wolfe the "me generation," have made the use of illicit narcotics and psychotropic substances socially acceptable to many.[2]

Today, the United States faces circumstances dramatically different from those of the past in its relations with Latin America. The United States can no longer unilaterally impose its will on the hemisphere, at least not without adverse consequences. No Latin American government can politically afford to comply openly with U.S. dictates on drugs while ignoring nationalist sentiments. Latin American nations today are stronger and more ready to assert their independence vis-à-vis the United States and are able to find extensive support for such actions in the international community. Finally, the very existence of Cuba and Nicaragua outside the U.S. orbit encourages more independent action for nations so inclined.

Nevertheless, in spite of changed hemispheric realities, many in Latin America believe that the United States continues to follow historically outdated policies when trying to pressure those to the south to cut off the supply of illicit drugs. To many Latins, the certification process, although a new direction in U.S. narcotics diplomacy, smacks of the trade embargoes the U.S. has used with mixed results since the first decade of the nineteenth century and against Latin American countries since 1960. U.S. narcotics foreign policy is seen by many as a nationalistic effort to blame others for a problem the United States will not, or cannot, solve at home.

INTERDICTION AND ENFORCEMENT POLICIES

Illicit drug trafficking is an international problem facilitated by criminal organizations that operate multinationally. In attempting to combat the activities of such multinational criminal enterprises, the producing and consuming nations of the world must increasingly work together to devise a multilateral approach. The current focus of U.S. international narcotics control policy is to eradicate illegal narcotics at their source. In FY 1988, for example, 73 percent of the federal government's antinarcotics funding was used for reduction of supply and 27 percent for reduction of demand.

General agreement exists that interdiction efforts also must be continued and increased even though such activities have a limited payoff.[3] It is important for the nation to regain control of its borders and to make it more difficult to bring such substances into the United States. To accomplish this goal, many believe that additional resources are required for the DEA, Coast Guard, and Customs. Interdiction, though not a solution in and of itself, is clearly a deterrent to traffickers and does raise user prices by taking a portion of drugs out of circulation, as the oft-cited study of Peter Reuter demonstrates.

NEED FOR IMPROVED COORDINATION

A strong need exists for better coordination of U.S. antidrug efforts. The recently abolished National Drug Policy Board, patterned on a cabinet-style format, depended upon the consensus of its members to implement its decisions. Under such a structure, interagency rivalries are prone to obstruct development and implementation of a single, coordinated policy. Yet, creation of a more centralized policy making structure such as the newly created Office of National Drug Policy in the Executive Office of the President may promise to be no more a solution than the creation of past offices headed by "czars" for specific purposes.

There is also a need to improve coordination at U.S. embassies among various agency personnel involved in the antidrug campaign. Many, such as Samuel del Villar, argue that the effectiveness of U.S. personnel operating outside our borders is limited by overlapping jurisdictions; there are too many people making independent decisions.

NEED FOR EFFECTIVE LAWS TO COMBAT MONEY LAUNDERING

As Richard Craig points out, more can be done to interdict drug money transfers by focusing on the proceeds as well as the products. More stringent banking legislation, for example, could help identify laundered money. John Martsh, senior DEA coordinator for Latin America, has argued that the U.S. must increasingly resort to the use of asset forfeiture, for that tactic hits the traffickers where it hurts.[4] Drug traffickers are in business solely for profit. Denying them such profit is thus an effective deterrent. Implementing such policies, however, might considerably inconvenience both bankers and legitimate business clients. Furthermore, a wider grant of police access to banking and business records would be seen by many as an unwarranted invasion of privacy expected in a police state, not a democratic one.

CERTIFICATION

A consensus exists among the scholars contributing to this volume that certification policies[5] need to be closely re-examined. They note that mere use of the term "certification" is offensive to other countries, who see a moral judgment being passed on them by the United States. Both Reyna and del Villar accurately reflect Mexican sensitivity and anger over this process and its very language. They note the Mexican anger provoked in April, 1988, by the U.S. Senate resolution calling for the "decertification" of Mexico. No nation wants someone else publicly passing judgment on it. Compounding the controversy is the fact that the United States, apparently for strategic reasons, continues to certify certain major drug-producing nations such as Pakistan, which could be taking stronger measures to curb illicit drug production or trafficking. From the Mexican perspective, the U.S. message is clear: Mexico is unimportant even though Mexico shares an almost two thousand mile border with the U.S., has common strategic interests, is the U.S.'s third largest trading partner, and is making a serious effort to combat drugs, even though it does not yet have a serious drug problem. Many Mexicans believe that Mexico can ill afford to expend so much of its resources on a U.S. social problem.

Mexicans are now increasingly debating whether to continue the current level of their nation's antidrug efforts. Since Mexico only received approximately $15 million in aid in 1988, it can afford the risk of losing aid through decertification. Although the U.S. could vote against loans to Mexico in international lending agencies, it is unlikely to do so.

Many suggest that the certification process is a punitive approach and that the U.S. would be better served by offering positive incentives to producing and transit nations such as increased military aid, development assistance and crop/income substitution programs, foreign exchange loans, and trade benefits such as lower import barriers. Others have suggested creating a massive foreign aid program, a so-called mini-Marshall Plan. The rationale offered for such proposals is that actions perceived as threats alone are likely to produce hostile responses. Although the United States may have the power to coerce nations such as Bolivia, Peru, Paraguay, Panama, Honduras, and Colombia into implementing policies, the cost of that coercion may be greater than the payoff.

USE OF THE MILITARY

Many people within the general public and the policy making community, upset with the massive importation of illegal narcotics into the United States and the seeming inability of the authorities to stem the flow, demand that the military be increasingly involved in drug interdiction. However, to military leaders generally, whether they be civilians such as former defense secretary Frank Carlucci or uniformed officers such as Lt. General Stephen Olmstead, drug interdiction, a form of law enforcement, is an inappropriate task, one which would erode a valuable barrier between civilian and military functions and draw assets away from and weaken the military's ability to perform its primary mission of defending the nation against other nations. Proponents, however, see military training value in many drug interdiction functions and a great strengthening of resources for the task.

Proposals, such as those made by New York mayor Ed Koch, that the military be sent into Latin America in the absence of invitations of the host governments are seen by many Latin American policy makers as irresponsible. They regard invasion as an act of war likely to provoke resistance not only from the invaded nation and its allies but also from much of the rest of the world. The mere suggestion that the United States invade sends shock waves through Latin America and encourages nationalists of every political leaning to verbally attack the United States. Even if U.S. military units were invited to operate in Latin American nations, nationalistic reactions would, in all likelihood, be severe. Many citizens in Latin American countries are likely to see the presence of foreign troops as an insult and a threat to their national sovereignty. Consequently, DEA assistant administrator David Westrate, at a Congressional Research Service seminar on drug trafficking, has asserted that military actions such as Operation Blast Furnace cannot be attempted again without unwanted political consequences.[6]

NEED FOR INCREASED DEMAND REDUCTION MEASURES

Almost without exception, contributors to this volume agree that the fundamental basis of the U.S. drug problem is the internal market for illicit narcotics in the United States, and that the ultimate solution to the U.S. drug problem lies in effective reducing demand. They suggest, therefore, that U.S. drug policy, first and foremost, concentrate on reducing demand. At present, much of the public perceives the drug problem as being caused by foreign nations. Consequently, they seek to solve the problem abroad and at the borders rather than at home. To date, however, U.S. policies emphasizing supply reduction (i.e., eradication and interdiction) have been marginally successful at best.

In the United States, the use of illegal narcotics can be viewed as part of a larger social phenomenon, Americans' belief that they are entitled to "feel good" instantly. Such an attitude has been fostered by such means as advertisements, economic abundance, and peer pressure. As David Potter argued long ago, American national character has been shaped by Americans being "people of plenty."[7] Thus, the drug problem is directly related to the same factors fostering abuse of legal narcotics, tobacco, alcohol, tranquilizers, designer drugs, and other substances. It is also related to the belief that one can break some laws when done in private and without seeming to infringe on others.

To counter such views, society can continue to send the message that drug usage is socially unacceptable and that the use of mind-altering substances is self-defeating. This message can be sent in a variety and combination of ways. Political and civic leaders can continue to speak out against the use of drugs; laws can be passed and enforced that increase the price, hassle, and risk of drug possession; and education programs can continue to be instituted in schools and expanded to include involvement by voluntary associations such as churches, clubs, youth organizations, and other public oriented service groups. In addition, the entertainment industry can launch major long-term awareness campaigns, and the mass media can more actively promote the antidrug message.

The message can be forcefully sent by adopting practices and laws that ensure civil penalties and disincentives for drug abusers. In some states and nations, conviction of driving under the influence of alcohol or drugs means the automatic suspension of one's driving privileges. Stricter enforcement of such laws would inconvenience the offender's relatives and friends and would encourage them to stop enabling the offender. Testing and job loss for proven illegal drug use and media revelations of convictions are effective though problematic options. Forbidding a student drug user from participating in extracurricular activities such as band and athletic programs unless that person gets rehabilitated sends a powerful message. Firing professional athletes who abuse drugs also sends a strong message.

Finally, the authors believe that the nation must recognize that the use of narcotics is a long-term problem. Historians such as Kinder, H. Wayne Morgan and David Musto aptly demonstrate this point.[8] There is no immediate solution, "no quick-fix."

LEGALIZATION

Varying forms of legalization or decriminalization, of illegal narcotics have been recommended by numerous people including conservative leader William F. Buckley, Jr., city mayors, and scholars. Arguments in favor of legalization include denying profits to criminals, cutting the wave of crimes committed to support expensive habits, increasing revenue sources for governments, redirecting the current billions of dollars spent on drug law enforcement into other sectors of the economy, and recognition that current policies have failed and will continue to fail. If the fundamental problem is the growth of crime and powerful criminal organizations, some suggest the solution is to decriminalize. Analogies are often drawn to the legal tolerance of the largest drug problem in the United States, the use and abuse of alcohol and unsuccessful national attempts to abolish it in the 1920s and early 1930s. Just as the prohibition of alcohol did not work, the argument goes, narcotics prohibition will not work. At another level, however, the argument exists that the use of narcotics is a personal matter: libertarians argue that if people want to harm themselves even to the point of suicide, they should be allowed to do so.

Opponents of legalization offer an equal variety of arguments. They may assert that narcotics users not only damage their own lives, but also those of relatives, friends, and strangers. Opponents argue that addiction to narcotics is different from alcohol dependence both in the rapidity with which it occurs and in the degree of difficulty in ending it. Some oppose narcotics use on moral grounds, perhaps reflecting the "Puritan heritage" of the U.S. Some also believe that narcotics use will not only increase as a result of legalization, but will enslave even more children, who are incapable of making fully informed, rational choices. The issue is further complicated by the fact that no one really knows the consequences of legalization, making it appear a leap into an unknown and conceivably frightening future. Opponents stress that excessive narcotics use, legal or illegal, generally does not lead to societal well-being, but, in fact robs a society of its spark, creativity, and leadership initiative. Legalization is also seen by many as surrender, an admission of the impotence of governments to enforce their will on society. For some, it raises the specter of a society out of control. Opponents of legalization also note that few want to legalize all narcotics use, and that gradations and selective enforcement would cut the promised savings and create general public confusion as to why certain drugs should be permitted and others not.

NARCOTICS AS A FOREIGN POLICY ISSUE IN THE HEMISPHERE

Narcotics policy is an important foreign policy issue, but where should it stand on the scale of U.S.-Latin American relations in the context of other priorities, such as stabilizing the international debt crisis or promoting economic and political stability in Latin America? Many suggest that the drug issue is not the most important one separating the U.S. and Latin America, but stress, however, that it is the most volatile, emotional, and disruptive one, and that takes an inordinate amount of time and attention away from the more serious problems. Consequently, the argument goes that the U.S. does not need to dissipate its energies and "credit" by angering Latin American nations on the drug issue. Instead, U.S. policy might be more effectively devoted to the major problems of the hemisphere.

Many suggest that U.S. demands for more active antidrug campaigns threaten to destabilize some Latin American countries both politically and economically--certainly not an end sought by U.S. policy makers. Nations such as Bolivia, Colombia, Mexico, and Peru have scant resources with which to address serious economic and social problems. No responsible political leader in these nations wants an economy based on narcotics or a polity divided against itself. No such leader wants to return to a version of nineteenth century caudillismo wherein local strongmen with private armies could block the national government from enforcing its laws in their private domains. They are acutely aware that money spent on narcotics or to indulge the whims of traffickers does little to develop their national economies. Moreover, Latin American nations do not want a large scale problem of drug abuse such as the United States faces, but they can do little to combat drugs and the local effects of drug trafficking without additional resources and without some means by which to replace lost income derived from the drug trade. Mexico, in spite of its economic crisis, is healthier politically and economically than the Andean nations; yet, it is debating whether to continue to spend 60 percent of its national attorney general's budget on the antidrug campaign.

Many of the authors contributing to this volume strongly suggest that the current U.S. policy of curbing illegal narcotics at the source be increasingly multilateral in scope. They stress that the U.S. is fond of talking about hemispheric cooperation but reluctant to practice it. As an alternative, the U.S. government should cooperate with source and transit nations as a partner in narcotics control instead of merely as overseer. Furthermore, the U.S. could increasingly help producer and transit nations attack the problem by supplying enhanced funding and training resources. The DEA already operates training programs and works with host country governments to identify their antidrug technological needs.

Those contributing to this volume generally agree that the U.S. has worsened its relations with Latin America by injecting an American social problem into the international arena and by trying to solve it there instead of at home, where it should be solved. In effect, there would be no supply if there were no demand. They suggest that U.S. policy makers must decide which is more important: stable, pro-U.S. Latin American nations, or an international narcotics policy that engenders anti-U.S. nationalistic sentiment and destabilizes Latin American nations.

Latin Americans, like other peoples, do not like hypocrisy, and many see U.S. actions in the drug war exactly as such. Del Villar and Reyna are not alone in demanding that the United States, itself a major drug producer, spray herbicides on its own territory just as it insists be done in Latin America. They want the U.S. to test "Spike," with its unknown environmental dangers, on U.S. agricultural and range land before encouraging its application on coca fields in South America. They suggest that, if the U.S. government is going to use certification procedures, it should apply them to its own states. For example, the U.S. government could withhold federal aid to states that do not meet federal standards for eradicating marijuana crops, prosecuting drug traffickers, or identifying and prosecuting corrupt public officials in league with drug traffickers. Finally, they suggest that, if the U.S. uses certification procedures in dealing with other nations, it should apply them equally and fairly to **all** other nations instead of making exceptions for such countries as Pakistan and Turkey.

OPTIONS FOR CONSIDERATION

Many options exist for U.S. policy makers to consider in their efforts to stem the flow of illicit narcotics into the United States. All of these options either directly or indirectly affect the U.S. relationship with its hemispheric neighbors. Nine major options, which are not mutually exclusive and which could be pursued in various combinations as part of an overall effort, were identified.

• U.S. policy makers must better understand the need to respect the sovereignty of Latin American nations. Too often, U.S. actions (such as the certification program that threatens to cut off aid) are perceived by Latin Americans as coercing their governments into following U.S. policy. Moreover, nationalists often believe that U.S. antinarcotics agents are given free rein to operate in many countries, particularly when drug dealers are kidnapped and whisked to the United States for trial. The riots following the abduction of Juan Ramón Matta Ballesteros in 1988 occurred because many Hondurans believed that the U.S. acted as if it could enforce its laws anywhere, even if this meant disregarding Honduran law. There are limits, however, to the excesses the U.S. should accept in the name of sovereign sensitivity.

• U.S. policy makers might consider more aggressive pursuit of U.S. domestic criminal organizations involved in drug trafficking and the laundering of drug proceeds. By breaking these organizations, the U.S. could reduce the supply of illegal narcotics available domestically to its population.

• U.S. policy makers could consider regaining control of their own national borders, taking the appropriate constitutional measures necessary to achieve this end. The difficulty and cost of this inviting goal should not be underestimated, however.

• U.S. policy makers could increase **multilateral** measures and efforts designed to eliminate the production and trafficking of illicit narcotics. The current glut in the cocaine market and the consequent drop in street prices has not only encouraged the spread of narcotics use in Latin America, but stimulated exports to both Western and Eastern Europe. The international community, regardless of political or economic ideology, could better unite and cooperate in the war on drugs.

• U.S. policy makers could consider the option of committing substantially greater resources to the war on drugs. On the interdiction side, the Coast Guard, DEA, Customs, and state and local law enforcement officials need additional funds to accomplish their mission. Enhanced drug interdiction requires dramatic increases in resources to counteract the virtually unlimited resources traffickers devote to ensuring their continued access to existing markets.

- U.S. policy makers might also consider providing additional resources to law enforcement agencies and criminal justice systems, both domestic and foreign. Additional personnel, training, equipment, and funding are critical if antidrug efforts of producing and transit nations are to succeed, since such nations are often already straining their meager resources to the limit.

- U.S. policy makers could seriously consider adopting a regional mini-Marshall Plan or a superfund to help producing and transit countries break their growing dependence on narcodollars. Economically strapped by low demand for their traditional exports and overburdened with intolerable international debt service, such nations often have little or no real ability to eliminate the local drug economy. Dramatic reduction of drug production and trafficking activities at present might well destabilize many poorer nations unless replacement income is generated to offset the loss of drug-related income. Such economic development would also stimulate Latin American imports of U.S. goods and better enable debtor countries to meet their payment obligations to U.S. financial institutions. Care is warranted, however, to avoid creating incentives for nations to encourage drug exports to the U.S.

- U.S. policy makers and those of other governments might well consider funding more research to analyze the effectiveness of current and potential antinarcotics policies. Kinder and others have suggested that the problem cannot be solved through crop eradication alone, nor can it be solved by law enforcement alone. In spite the expenditure of billions of dollars over the course of years of antinarcotics efforts, very little is actually known about the drug abuse issue and the results or outcomes that can be expected from certain programmatic efforts. Equally, little is known about the drug trade and its political and economic impact on source and consumer countries. Yet, the U.S. continues to follow policies that have failed in the past.

- Finally, U.S. policy makers might well consider concentrating the bulk of their efforts on reducing demand within the United States. Drug testing, both mandatory and voluntary, would be an effective tool, but U.S. citizens must decide if the drug threat is sufficient to authorize governmental and private sector invasion of the privacy of their bodies. Coupled with such efforts would be massive funding for public education and awareness campaigns, orchestrated through professional advertising and public relations firms.

Notes

CHAPTER 1:

1. Amos A. Jordan and William J. Taylor, Jr., *American National Security: Policy and Process* (Baltimore: Johns Hopkins University Press, 1981), 3.
2. See Raphael Perl, *Narcotics Control and the Use of U.S. Military Personnel: Operations in Bolivia and Issues for Congress* (Washington: Congressional Research Service, 1986), CRS-1.
3. Margaret Daly Hayes, *Latin America and the U.S. National Security Interest* (Boulder: Westview Press, 1984), 4.
4. William J. Taylor, Jr., "U.S. Security and Latin America: Arms Transfers and Military Doctrine," in *Population Growth in Latin America and U.S. National Security*, ed. by John Saunders (Boston: Allen & Unwin, 1986), 271.
5. David Westrate, DEA administrator, testimony on the Relationship of Drug Trafficking and Terrorism to the Senate Committee on Foreign Relations and the Committee on the Judiciary, May 14, 1985, mimeographed, copy in possession of the author.
6. Tad Szulc, *Fidel: A Critical Portrait* (New York: William Morrow, 1986).
7. See Rachael Ehrenfeld, "Narco-Terrorism: The Kremlin Connection," paper published by The Heritage Foundation, February, 1987; Rachael Ehrenfeld, "The Drug Terror Connection," unpublished paper; and Joseph D. Douglass, Jr., and General Major Jan Sejna, *International Narcotics Trafficking: The Soviet Connection* (Washington: Security and Intelligence Foundation, 1987).
8. Testimony given before the Senate Subcommittee on Terrorism, Narcotics and International Communications and International Economic Policy, Trade, Oceans and Environment of the Committee on Foreign Relations offers convincing evidence of the validity of these assertions. See the committee's *Drugs, Law Enforcement and Foreign Policy* pt. 1 (May 27, July 15, and Oct. 30, 1987), 100th Congress, 1st sess.; *Drugs, Law Enforcement and Foreign Policy: Panama* pt. 2 (February 8, 9, 10, and 11, 1988), 100th Congress, 1st sess.; and *Drugs, Law Enforcement and Foreign*

Policy: The Cartel, Haiti and Central America pt. 3 (April 4, 5, 6, and 7, 1988), 100th Congress, 1st sess.

9. Lorenzo Crowell, "U.S. Domestic Terrorism: An Historical Perspective," *Quarterly Journal of Ideology* 11:3 (1987), 45-56.

10. Diego Asencio, "Narcotics Trafficking and Western Hemispheric Security," paper presented at the Mississippi State University Center for International Security and Strategic Studies International Conference on The Latin American Narcotics Trade and U.S. National Security, June 16-17, 1988.

11. Diego Asencio and Nancy Asencio. *Our Man Is Inside* (Boston: Little, Brown, 1983).

12. *The Washington Times*, March 23, 1988.

13. Paul Eddy, with Hugo Sabogal and Sara Walden, *The Cocaine Wars* (New York: W. W. Norton, 1988), 306-08, 382. These authors raise the issue of true identity of Vaughn. For newspaper coverage of the issue of Vaughn and the Sandinistas, see *The Washington Times*, July 17, 1984.

14. Douglas Clark Kinder, "Bureaucratic Cold Warrior: Harry J. Anslinger and Illicit Narcotics Traffic," *Pacific Historical Review* 50 (May 1981): 169-91.

15. César Atala, "The Latin American Narcotics Trade: A Peruvian View," speech to the Mississippi State University Center for International Security and Strategic Studies international conference on The Latin American Narcotics Trade and U.S. National Security, June 16-17, 1988.

16. "Combatting Drug Trafficking," *Mexico Today* (October 1986): 3-5.

CHAPTER 2:

1. William O. Walker III, *Drug Control in the Americas* [hereafter cited as Walker, *Drug Control*](Albuquerque: University of New Mexico Press, 1981), 3-6, 9-11, 14-18, 41-45, 50, 56-57. United States law and custom define narcotics as opiates, cocaine, and marijuana. Though pharmacologically distinct, the words "drug" and "narcotic" were used synonymously by the legal community, restrictionists, and the general public in this country until the mid-1960s. As have other historical studies about narcotics, this essay will employ the two terms interchangeably. Drug limitation in the United States has always been closely linked with cultural conflict and nativism. The term "culture" will be used to describe the attitudes, customs, and values that collectively comprise an ethnic or linguistic group's perspective of the world. "Nativism" is both the preference for and the defense of a native culture. On the issue of culture, see Walker, *Drug Control* and Michael H. Hunt, *Ideology and U.S. Foreign Policy* [hereafter cited as Hunt, *Ideology*] (New Haven: Yale University Press, 1987), 12-13.

2. Richard J. Bonnie and Charles H. Whitebread II, *The Marihuana Conviction: A History of Marihuana Prohibition in the United States* [hereafter cited as Bonnie and Whitebread, *Marihuana*] (Charlottesville: University Press of Virginia, 1974), 9-10, 14-18, 20-21, 23, 27-28, 106-11; Norman H. Clark, *Deliver Us from Evil: An Interpretation of American Prohibition* [hereafter cited as Clark, *Deliver*] (New York: W. W. Norton,

1976), 1-5, 221-23; David F. Musto, *The American Disease: Origins of Narcotic Control* [hereafter cited as Musto, *Disease*](New Haven: Yale University Press, 1973), 206-14, 245-48; Arnold H. Taylor, *American Diplomacy and the Narcotics Traffic, 1900-1939: A Study in International Humanitarian Reform* [hereafter cited as Taylor, *Diplomacy*] (Durham: Duke University Press, 1969), 132, 157-59, 171-77, 183-85, 200-24, 230-32, 241, 302-05; H. Wayne Morgan, *Drugs in America: A Social History, 1800-1980* [hereafter cited as Morgan, *Drugs*] (Syracuse: Syracuse University Press, 1981), 88-90; Herbert L. May, "The International Control of Narcotic Drugs," *International Conciliation*, 441 (May 1948), 301-71; Walker, *Drug Control*, 3-6, 9-11, 14-18, 27-35, 41-45, 47-57, 62-74. This study examines the control of opium, morphine, heroin, cocaine, and cannabis. The opiates--opium, morphine, and heroin--are derived from the opium poppy (*Papaver somniferum*). Opium is the refined juice of the poppy; morphine is a crystalline alkaloid obtained from opium; and heroin (diacetylmorphine) is produced from acetic acid and morphine. The coca plant (*Erythroxlon coca*) is the source of cocaine, and the cannabis plant (*Cannabis sativa*) yields hashish (the dried resin) and marijuana (the leaves and flowers). Although opium and coca plants are grown almost exclusively in the Third World, cannabis flourishes both inside and outside the United States. Opiates and cocaine for illicit trafficking can be refined in every country, but medicinal narcotics are usually prepared in the United States or other industrial nations.

3. Douglas Clark Kinder, "Bureaucratic Cold Warrior: Harry J. Anslinger and Illicit Narcotics Traffic," *Pacific Historical Review*, 50 (May 1981), 169-91; Musto, *Disease*, 1-61, 97-120, 135-40, 210-15; Morgan, *Drugs*, 1-63, 118-28; Bonnie and Whitebread, *Marihuana*, 5-15, 20-21, 32-45; Walker, *Drug Control*, 12-20; Charles E. Terry, M.D., and Mildred Pellens, *The Opium Problem* [hereafter cited as Terry and Pellens, *Opium*] (New York: The Bureau of Social Hygiene, 1928), 807-08.

4. Musto, *Disease*, 1-61, 97-120, 135-40, 210-15; Morgan, *Drugs*, 1-63, 118-28; Bonnie and Whitebread, *Marihuana*, 5-15, 20-21, 32-45; Walker, *Drug Control*, 12-20; Terry and Pellens, *Opium*, 807-08; Clark, *Deliver*, 1-5, 218-23; James H. Timberlake, *Prohibition and the Progressive Movement, 1900-1920* [hereafter cited as Timberlake, *Prohibition*] (Cambridge: Harvard University Press, 1966), 39-99; Taylor, *Diplomacy*, 3-122; Rufus King, *The Drug Hang-Up: America's Fifty Year Folly* [hereafter cited as King, *Hang-Up*] (New York: W. W. Norton, 1972), 69-71. Also see David T. Courtwright, *Dark Paradise: Opiate Addiction in America Before 1940* (Cambridge: Harvard University Press, 1982).

5. Musto, *Disease*, 1-61, 97-120, 135-40, 210-15; Taylor, *Diplomacy*, 3-122; Morgan, *Drugs*, 1-63, 118-28; Walker, *Drug Control*, 12-20.

6. Kinder, "Bureaucratic Cold Warrior," 169-91; Musto, *Disease*, 135-40, 210-15; Morgan, *Drugs*, 118-28.

7. Musto, *Disease*, 1-61; Bonnie and Whitebread, *Marihuana*, 1-13; Clark, *Deliver*, 218-20; Morgan, *Drugs*, 1-63; David T. Courtwright, "Opiate Addiction as a Consequence of the Civil War," *Civil War History* 25 (June 1978), 101-11. See also two works by James Harvey Young: *The Medical Messiahs: A Social History of Health Quackery in Twentieth Century America*

(Princeton: Princeton University Press, 1967) and *The Toadstool Millionaires: A Social History of Patent Medicines in America Before Federal Regulation* (Princeton: Princeton University Press, 1961).

8. Morgan, *Drugs*, 1.

9. Musto, *Disease*, 1-61; Courtwright, "Opiate Addiction," 101-11; Morgan, *Drugs*, 1-63; Lawrence Kolb and A. G. DuMez, "The Prevalence and Trend of Drug Addiction in the United States and the Factors Influencing It," *Public Health Reports* 23 (May 1924), 1198; Troy Duster, *The Legislation of Morality: Law, Drugs, and Moral Judgement* [Hereafter cited as Duster, *Legislation*] (New York: The Free Press, 1970), 1-10; Terry and Pellens, *Opium*, 76-83; Alfred W. McCoy, with Cathleen B. Reed and Leonard P. Adams II, *The Politics of Heroin in Southeast Asia* (New York: Harper and Row, 1972), 3-5; Bonnie and Whitebread, *Marihuana*, 1-13.

10. Musto, *Disease*, 1-61; Bonnie and Whitebread, *Marihuana*, 1-13; Clark, *Deliver*, 218-20; Courtwright, "Opiate Addiction," 101-11; Morgan, *Drugs*, 1-63. Cocaine gained much of its popularity among Americans because of Sigmund Freud's reports in medical journals and popular newspapers and magazines. Between 1885 and 1900, coca products, sold as tonics and restoratives, were marketed as extensively as bottled mineral waters. Morgan, *Drugs*, 16.

11. Musto, *Disease*, 1-61; Bonnie and Whitebread, *Marihuana*, 1-13; Kolb and DuMez, "The Prevalence and Trend of Drug Addiction," 1198; Courtwright, "Opiate Addiction," 101-111; Duster, *Legislation*, 1-10; Terry and Pellens, *Opium*, 76-83; McCoy, Reed, and Adams, *The Politics of Heroin in Southeast Asia*, 3-5; Morgan, *Drugs*, 1-63; Clark, *Deliver*, 219-20. By the mid-nineteenth century, some experts believed that morphine was addictive when taken orally but not when hypodermically injected. Morgan, *Drugs*, 27.

12. Clark, *Deliver*, 218-23; Bonnie and Whitebread, *Marihuana*, 5-15, 28, 32-45; Timberlake, *Prohibition*, 39-99; Taylor, *Diplomacy*, 3-122; Musto, *Disease*, 1-61; Walker, *Drug Control*, 13-15; Morgan, *Drugs*, 27-97.

13. Morgan, *Drugs*, 27-97; Walker, *Drug Control*, 13-14; Musto, *Disease*, 1-61; Clark, *Deliver*, 1-5, 220-21; Terry and Pellens, *Opium*, 11, 68, 807-08; Bonnie and Whitebread, *Marihuana*, 5-15, 28, 32-45; Timberlake, *Prohibition*, 39-99.

14. Musto, *Disease*, 6-8; Bonnie and Whitebread, *Marihuana*, 14; Walker, *Drug Control*, 14; Morgan, *Drugs*, 33-97. See also Robert S. Weppner, ed., *Street Ethnography: Selected Studies of Crime and Drug Use in Natural Settings* (Beverly Hills: Sage Publications, 1977); John Helmer, *Drugs and Minority Oppression* (New York: Seabury Press, 1975).

15. Bonnie and Whitebread, *Marihuana*, 32-45; Morgan, *Drugs*, 33-97; Walker, *Drug Control*, 100-02. Also see Bruce Bullington, *Heroin Use in the Barrio* (Lexington: Lexington Books, 1977).

16. Bonnie and Whitebread, *Marihuana*, 14; Clark, *Deliver*, 220-22; Musto, *Disease*, 13-22; Walker, *Drug Control*, 14-15; Taylor, *Diplomacy*, 3-122.

17. Musto, *Disease*, 21-22.

18. "Patent Medicine Crusade," *Nation* 81 (November 9, 1905), 376; "Patent Medicines and Poverty," *Outlook* 83 (June 2, 1906), 253-54; "Creating Customers for Dangerous Drugs," *Outlook* 82 (April 7, 1906), 778-79; Clark,

Deliver, 221-22; Bonnie and Whitebread, *Marihuana*, 14-15; Musto, *Disease*, 22-23.

19. "Patent Medicine Crusade," 376; "Patent Medicines and Poverty," 253-54; "Creating Customers for Dangerous Drugs," 778-79; Clark, *Deliver*, 221-22; Bonnie and Whitebread, *Marihuana*, 14-15; Musto, *Disease*, 22-23.

20. Taylor, *Diplomacy*, 3-19, 28-83, 87-91, 96-120; Musto, *Disease*, 3-6, 22-28, 30-37; Clark, *Deliver*, 219-22; Walker, *Drug Control*, 15; King, *Hang-Up*, 10-11; Bonnie and Whitebread, *Marihuana*, 9-15; Herbert L. May, "The International Control of Narcotic Drugs," *International Conciliation* 441 (May 1948), 308, 310, 314, 320-21. On March 3, 1905, Congress enacted legislation prohibiting the importation, sale, and use of nonmedical opium in the Philippines after March 1, 1908. Taylor, *Diplomacy*, 42-43.

21. Taylor, *Diplomacy*, 3-19, 28-83, 87-91, 96-120; Musto, *Disease*, 3-6, 22-28, 30-37; Clark, *Deliver*, 219-22; Walker, *Drug Control*, 15; King, *Hang-Up*, 10-11; Bonnie and Whitebread, *Marihuana*, 9-15; Herbert L. May, "The International Control of Narcotic Drugs," *International Conciliation* 441 (May 1948), 308, 310, 314, 320-21. For examples of muckraking antidrug reports after 1906, see Harvey W. Wiley, "Another Soothing Syrup Victim," *Good Housekeeping* 60 (June 1915), 709-10; Stuart Chase and F.J. Schlink, "Consumers in Wonderland: What We Get for Our Money When We Buy From Quacks and Vendors for Cure-Alls," *New Republic* 49 (February 16, 1927), 348-51.

22. Musto, *Disease*, 30-40; Taylor, *Diplomacy*, 47-81; Walker, *Drug Control*, 15-16. A "conference" is an international meeting that theoretically binds participating countries to take specific actions; a "commission" is a meeting that only recommends actions to national governments. Musto, *Disease*, 30-35.

23. Musto, *Disease*, 40-8.

24. Taylor, *Diplomacy*, 82-122; Musto, *Disease*, 37-9, 49-53; May, "The International Control of Narcotic Drugs," 321-23; Walker, *Drug Control*, 15-16.

25. Taylor, *Diplomacy*, 82-122; Musto, *Disease*, 37-9, 49-53; May, "The International Control of Narcotic Drugs," 321-323; Walker, *Drug Control*, 15-16.

26. Musto, *Disease*, 40-48, 54-62; Taylor, *Diplomacy*, 127-131; Bonnie and Whitebread, *Marihuana*, 15-17; Walker, *Drug Control*, 16.

27. Musto, *Disease*, 54-62; Bonnie and Whitebread, *Marihuana*, 15-17; *United Statutes at Large* 38, 63rd Congress, 3rd sess., pt. 1, 785-90.

28. Musto, *Disease*, 122-26, 129-32; Bonnie and Whitebread, *Marihuana*, 15-21; Clark, *Deliver*, 222-23; *United Statutes at Large* 38, 63rd Congress, 3rd sess., pt. 1, 785-90; *United States Treasury Department Decisions* 2172 & 2200, March 9 and May 11 ,1915, 124-31 and 173-174.

29. Musto, *Disease*, 122-32; Bonnie and Whitebread, *Marihuana*, 15-21; Clark, *Deliver*, 222-23; *United States v. Jin Fuey Moy*, 241 U.S. 401 (1916); *United States v. Doremus*, 249 U.S. 86 (1919); *Webb et al. v. United States*, 249 U.S. 96 (1919); King, *Hang-Up*, 21; Alfred R. Lindesmith, *The Addict and the Law* [hereafter cited as Lindesmith, *Addict*] (Bloomington: Indiana University Press, 1965), 3-6; Harry J. Anslinger and William F. Tompkins, *The Traffic in Narcotics* [hereafter cited as Anslinger and Tompkins, *Traffic*]

(New York: Funk and Wagnalls, 1953), 187; *United States Statutes at Large* 40, 65th Congress, 3rd sess., pt. 1, 1130-133. Also see "The Superstition of Dope," *Literary Digest* (June 30, 1917), 1990; United States Senate, *Hearings Before the Subcommittee on Improvements in the Federal Criminal Code of the Committee on the Judiciary, Pursuant to S. Res. 67,* 84th Congress, 1st sess., June 2 to December 15, 1955 (hereafter cited as *Daniel Subcommittee Hearings*), testimony of Rufus King, 1380-382; Alfred R. Lindesmith, "Traffic in Dope": Medical Problem," *Nation* 182 (April 21, 1956), 337-38; "Is Prohibition Making Drug Fiends?" *Literary Digest* 69 (April 16, 1921), 19-20; Sara Graham-Mulhall, "The Evil of Drug Addiction," *New Republic* 26 (May 18, 1921), 357.

30. Bonnie and Whitebread, *Marihuana,* 9-10, 14-18, 20-21, 23, 27-28, 106-11; Clark, *Deliver,* 1-5, 221-23; Musto, *Disease,* 206-14, 245-48; Taylor, *Diplomacy,* 132, 200-09; Walker, *Drug Control,* 14-18; Morgan, *Drugs,* 88-90. See also Timberlake, *Prohibition.*

31. Bonnie and Whitebread, *Marihuana,* 9-10, 14-18, 20-21, 23, 27-28, 106-11; Clark, *Deliver,* 1-5, 221-23; Musto, *Disease,* 206-14, 245-48; Taylor, *Diplomacy,* 132, 200-09; Walker, *Drug Control,* 14-18; Morgan, *Drugs,* 88-90.

32. Bonnie and Whitebread, *Marihuana,* 9-10, 14-18, 20-21, 23, 27-28, 106-11; Clark, *Deliver,* 221-23; Musto, *Disease,* 206-14, 245-48; Taylor, *Diplomacy,* 132, 200-09; Walker, *Drug Control,* 14-18; Morgan, *Drugs,* 88-90; "National Menace of the Dope Traffic," *Literary Digest* 76 (February 24, 1923), 34-35; Nicholas and Lillian Segal, "The Drug Evil," *New Republic* 34 (March 7, 1923), 41-43; Stuart H. Perry, "The Unarmed Invasion," *Atlantic Monthly* 135 (January 1925), 70-77. Traditionally, addict population statistics have been very unreliable. According to the best estimates, the United States had about one million drug habitues in 1900 and between 200 thousand and 215 thousand addicts in 1915. A special Treasury Department committee in 1919 discovered, however, that assessments of the total number of American habitues ranged from 200 thousand to four million, and the committee determined that the nation had one million addicts. By the 1920s, the IRB claimed that the Harrison law was operating well and that America had only 100 thousand habitues (the figure officially recognized by the federal government). Yet, at the same time, the New York City health commissioner argued that there were nearly 100 thousand addicts in that area alone, and other observers outside the IRB and later the Prohibition Bureau believed that the national habitue population was large and increasing. Twentieth-century medical and pharmaceutical experts generally have asserted that this country's opiate addicts number at least 400 thousand in each year since the mid-1800s, and they have claimed that punitive narcotics restriction forced habitues into clandestine activities. Walker, *Drug Control,* 13, 17, 19; Musto, *Disease,* 189-90; Taylor, *Diplomacy,* 47; Terry and Pellens, *Opium,* chap. 1 and pp. 469-75; Lindesmith, *Addict,* 99, 105-06, 111; King, *Hang-Up,* 18; U.S.Treasury Department, *Traffic in Narcotic Drugs: Report of the Special Committee of Investigation Appointed March 25, 1918, by the Secretary of the Treasury* (Washington: GPO, 1919), 6-7, 20-25 (hereafter cited as *Report of the Special Treasury Department Committee*); *New York Times,* May 23, 1923.

33. Lawrence F. Schmeckebier and Francis X. A. Eble, *The Bureau of Internal Revenue: Its History, Activities, and Organization* [hereafter cited as Schmeckebier and Eble, *Bureau*] (Baltimore: The Johns Hopkins University Press, 1923), 47-48, 56-62, 116-17; Musto, *Disease*, 59-60, 135, 138-39, 184-90; Anslinger and Tompkins, *Traffic*, 185-86; Lindesmith, *Addict*, 141-42; Terry and Pellens, *Opium*, 49, 90-91; *Report of the Special Treasury Department Committee*, 6-7, 20-25; Walker, *Drug Control*, 18-20, 29-30.

34. Schmeckebier and Eble, *Bureau*, 47-48, 56-62, 116-17; Musto, *Disease*, 59-60, 135, 138-39, 184-90; Anslinger and Tompkins, *Traffic*, 185-86; Lindesmith, *Addict*, 141-42; Terry and Pellens, *Opium*, 49, 90-91; *Report of the Special Treasury Department Committee*, 6-7, 20-25; U.S. House of Representatives, *Report No. 852 of the Ways and Means Committee: Importation and Exportation of Narcotic Drugs*, 67th Congress, 2nd Session, March 27, 1922, 1-11 (hereafter cited as House Report on Importation and Exportation of Narcotics]; *United States Statutes at Large*, 67th Congress, 2nd Session, vol. 42, pt. 1, 596-98; *Linder v. United States*, 268 U.S. 5 (1925); Walker, *Drug Control*, 18-20, 29-30. To enforce the Harrison law, Congress set aside $515,000 in FY 1920. Arrests for Harrison Act infractions went from 3,900 in 1920 to an average of 10,300 in 1924-26 to around 9,000 in 1927-28. Drug law violations caused the incarceration of 2,529 of the 7,738 people in federal prisons at the end of FY 1928. Walker, *Drug Control*, 18-20, 29-30.

35. Walker, *Drug Control*, 18-20. On the concept of cultural conflict and its application to U.S. foreign policy, see Hunt, *Ideology*, 12-13 and William O. Walker III, "Drug Control and the Issue of Culture in American Foreign Relations," 1988 Stuart L. Bernath Memorial Lecture, presented at Society for Historians of American Foreign Relations luncheon, Reno, Nevada, March 26, 1988 (copy in author's possession).

36. Walker, *Drug Control*, 1-11, 35-44; John Edwin Fagg, *Latin America: A General History* (New York: MacMillan, 1977), 3-34, 90-530, 33-562, 658-89; Henry Bamford Parkes, *A History of Mexico* (Boston: Houghton Mifflin, 1969), 3-410; Charles C. Cumberland, *Mexico: The Struggle for Modernity* (New York: Oxford University Press, 1968), 41-323; Arthur P. Whitaker, *The United States and the Southern Cone: Argentina, Chile, and Uruguay* (Cambridge: Harvard University Press, 1976), 27-72; Benjamin Keen, ed., *Latin American Civilization: The Colonial Origins* (Boston: Houghton Mifflin, 1974), 221-24; Lyle N. McAlister, "Social Structure and Social Change in New Spain," in *Readings in Latin American History*, ed. Lewis Hanke (New York: Thomas Y. Crowell, 1966), 154-71; David A. Brading, *Miners and Merchants in Bourbon Mexico, 1763-1810* (New York: Cambridge University Press, 1971), 20-22, 33-7; James W. Wilkie, *The Mexican Revolution: Federal Expenditure and Social Change Since 1910* (Berkeley: University of California Press, 1967), 42-82, 08-209, 215-22; Eyler N. Simpson, *The Ejido: Mexico's Way Out* (Chapel Hill: University of North Carolina Press, 1937), 3-74; Walter F. Boyle to Charles Evans Hughes, October 20, 1921, Decimal File 312.1121/1, Record Group 59, State Department General Records, National Archives, Washington, D.C. [hereafter cited as RG 59, (decimal file)]. In 1950, Mexico's rural inhabitants composed 57 percent of the country's total population. Cumberland, *Mexico*, 367. By 1981, most of the

people in El Salvador, Guatemala, Honduras, Bolivia, Ecuador, and Paraguay still resided in non-urban areas, as did one-third of Colombia's and Peru's populace. Carl Haub, *1981 World Population Data Sheet* (Washington: Population Reference Bureau, Inc., 1981).

37. Walker, *Drug Control*, 35-44; Fagg, *Latin America*, 533-62, 658-89; Parkes, *A History of Mexico*, 285-410; Cumberland, *Mexico*, 190-323; Wilkie, *The Mexican Revolution*, 42-82; League of Nations, Advisory Committee on Traffic in Opium and Other Dangerous Drugs, *Report on the Work of the Committee During its Second Session*, held at Geneva from April 19-29, 1922 C. 233 (1) .1922.XI (Geneva, 1922), 1-3 [hereafter cited as League of Nations, Opium Advisory Committee, *Report on the [number] session*, (date), [file no.], (pages); League of Nations, Opium Advisory Committee, *Report to the Council on the Work of the Fifth Session* (May 24 to June 7, 1923) A.13.1923.XI. 12 [hereafter cited as League of Nations, Opium Advisory Committee, *Report to the Council on the Seventh Session*], 24-31 August 1925, A.28.1925.XI, 9; Boyle to Hughes, October 20, 1921, RG 59 312.1121/1; *Excelsior*, February, 20, June 4, June 10, June 11, and June 15, 1923; O. Gaylord Marsh, Progreso, to Hughes, February 12, 1923, RG 59, 812.114 Narcotics/62; George T. Summerlin to Hughes, July 19, 1923, RG 59, 812.114 Narcotics/79; Mexico, *Diario Oficial*, July 28, 1923; Frederick A. Sterling to Hughes, April 14, 1923, RG 59, 811.114 N 16/107; *Christian Science Monitor*, August 12, 1922; Sterling to Hughes, April 14, 1923, RG 59, 823.114 Narcotics/6; Henry Fletcher to Hughes, April 29, 1923, RG 59, 511.4A1/1814.

38. Walker, *Drug Control*, 1-11; Fagg, *Latin America*, 3-34, 114-26, 128-33, 155-285, 303-433; Keen, *Latin American Civilization*, 221-24. Considerable effort was expended to prepare coca for chewing. Leaves were either mixed with potash or unslaked lime, or a leaf was wrapped around a paste consisting of boiled lime rock and potash. In the latter case, the paste and leaf would be buried for several days before being used. Walker, *Drug Control*, n. 30, p. 213.

39. Walker, *Drug Control*, 3-9, 35-41; Fagg, *Latin America*, 3-34, 90-112, 155-245, 303-72, 391-95, 403-11, 506-30; Parkes, *A History of Mexico*, 3-410; Cumberland, *Mexico*, 41-323; McAlister, "Social Structure and Social Change in New Spain," 154-171; Brading, *Miners and Merchants in Bourbon Mexico*, 20-22, 33-37; Wilkie, *The Mexican Revolution*, 42-82, 208-09, 215-22; Simpson, *The Ejido*, 3-74.

40. Musto, *Disease*, 224-48; Clark, *Deliver Us*; Timberlake, *Prohibition*, 39-99; Dwight C. Smith, Jr., *The Mafia Mystique* (New York, 1975), 87-88; *Washington Star*, March 27, 1951; U.S. Senate, *Hearings Before the Special Committee to Investigate Organized Crime in Interstate Commerce, Pursuant to S. Res. 202*, 81st Congress, 1st sess., pt. 12, 662-68; *Washington News*, November 23, 1953; *New York Times*, June 1, 1962; "Remarks of Harry J. Anslinger, U.S. Representative on the United Nations Economic and Social Committee on Narcotic Drugs," May 8 to June 1, 1962, file 8, box 1, Harry J. Anslinger Papers, Pennsylvania Historical Collections and Labor Archives, The Pennsylvania State University [hereafter cited as HJAP/PSU].

41. *New York Journal-American*, April 1, 1961; Lee Mortimer's column in *New York Mirror*, March 24, 1962; *Baltimore New-Post*, April 3, 1962; Jack

Anderson, "Castro Has a New Weapon," *Washington Post Magazine*, July 29, 1962; "Remarks of Anslinger," 17th session of the United Nations Commission on Narcotic Drugs, May 8-June 1, 1962, file 8, box 1, HJAP/PSU; *New York Times*, June 1, 1962; *New York Journal-American*, June 17, 1962; "Report of the United States Delegation to the 18th Session, United Nations Commission on Narcotic Drugs," April 29 to May 17, 1963, in the International Narcotics Control file, box 1, Harry J. Anslinger Papers, Harry S. Truman Presidential Library.
42. "The Chief Retires," *Newsweek*, July 16, 1962, 28; memorandum from Frederick G. Dutton to A. Gilmore Flues, April 20, 1961, White House central name file, Box 78, John F. Kennedy Presidential Library; Erwin Knoll, "Attack on Drug Policy Brings Narcotics Quiz," *Washington Post*, April 19, 1961.

CHAPTER 3:

*   Portions of this chapter were contained in a paper presented before the Bilateral Commission on the Future of U.S.-Mexican Relations in Querétaro, Mexico, August 17-18, 1987.
1. William O. Walker III, "Control Across the Border: The United States, Mexico, and Narcotics Policy," *Pacific Historical Review* 47 (1978), 92.
2. Richard B. Craig, "Operación Intercepción: Una política de presión internacional." *Foro Internacional* 22 (1981), 203-30.
3. Richard B. Craig, "*La Campaña Permanente*: Mexico's Antidrug Campaign," *Journal of Interamerican Studies and World Affairs* 20 (1978), 107-31.
4. J. W. Van Wert, "Government of Mexico Herbicidal Opium Poppy Eradication Program: A Summative Evaluation," Unpublished Ph.D. dissertation, University of Southern California, 1985.
5. Richard B. Craig, "Operation Condor: Mexico's Antidrug Campaign Enters A New Era," *Journal of Inter-American Studies and World Affairs* 22 (1980), 345-63.
6. Elaine Shannon, *Desperados: Latin Drug Lords, U.S. Lawmen and the War America Can't Win* (New York: Viking Pres 1988).
7. J. D. Lindau, "Percepciones mexicanas de la política exterior de Estados Unidos: el caso Camarena Salazar," *Foro Internacional* 27 (1987), 562-75.

CHAPTER 4:

1. Elaine Sciolino with Stephen Engelberg, "Narcotics Effort Foiled by U.S. Security Goals," *New York Times* April 10, 1988, p. 1y.
2. ibid., 10y.
3. E. J. Dionne, Jr., "Drugs as 1988 Issue: Filling a Vacuum," *New York Times*, May 24, 1988, p. 14y.
4. Rensselaer W. Lee III, "The Drug Trade and Developing Countries," *Policy Focus* 4, June 1987.

5. In Argentina, for example, the statistics on drug cultivation and use indicate that it is not in the same league with the principal producing or consuming nations. It is, therefore, all the more remarkable to note that Argentine authorities seized more than one-half ton of cocaine in 1987 when just three years before (1984) total confiscations had amounted to only twelve kilograms (26.4 pounds). Argentine officials claim they interdict at best 10 percent of cocaine that passes through the country. In addition, during the first three months of 1988, three clandestine coca laboratories, two near the Bolivian-Argentine border and one in Buenos Aires, were raided, revealing that Argentina is not only a transit point but also a budding processing center as well. See Shirley Cristian, "Drug Trafficking and Output Rising Sharply in Argentina," *New York Times*, April 28, 1988.

6. Philip M. Boffey, "Drug Users, Not Sellers, Termed Key Problem," *New York Times*, April 12, 1988, p. 5y.

7. W. John Moore, "No Quick Fix", *National Journal* (November 21, 1987), 2954.

8. ibid., 2955.

9. The 1986 antidrug legislation required the president to certify annually that the twenty-five major source and transit countries are "cooperating fully" with U.S. enforcement agencies. According to the provisions of the new statute, "decertification" automatically obliged the president to withhold half the U.S. economic and military aid package assigned to any country that failed to qualify and to vote against loans for such countries in multilateral institutions such as the International Monetary Fund (IMF), the World Bank, or the Inter-American Development Bank (IDB). In cases where the U.S. executive determined that "over-riding national interests" were involved, these automatic penalties could be waived. For details, see Harry Hogan, et al. "Drug Control: Highlights of P.L. 99-570, Antidrug Abuse Act of 1986." (Washington D.C.: Congressional Research Service, Library of Congress, 86-968 GOV, October 31, 1986.

10. Moore, op. cit, 2956.

11. U.S. Department of State, *International Narcotics Control Strategy Report*, (Washington D.C.: U.S. Department of State, March 1987), 40.

12. Pieter Kerr, U.S. Drug Crusade Is Seen Undermining Itself," *New York Times*, October 26, 1987, 13y.

13. ibid.

14. Sciolino, op. cit., 10y.

15. Caspar W. Weinberger, "Our Troops Shouldn't Be Drug Cops," *Washington Post*, May 22, 1987, c2.

16. Richard Halloran, "In War against Drugs, Military is Found Wanting," *New York Times*, May 30, 1988, 20y; Also Peter Reuter, Gordon Crawford, Jonathan Crane, *Sealing the Borders: The Effects of Military Participation in Drug Interdiction*, (Santa Monica: Rand Corporation, 1988) pp. 122-32.

17. Mark Thompson, "Senate Oks Bill Pitting Military against Drugs," *Miami Herald*, May 28, 1988, 8a.

18. Kerr, op. cit., 13y.

19. William O. Walker III, "Drug Control and National Security," *Diplomatic History* 2 (Spring 1988) 197.

20. Moore, op. cit., 2958.

21. Kerr, op. cit., 13y.

22. Sciolino, op. cit., 10y.

23. On the bipartisan aspects of this double standard, see Seymour M. Hersh, "Why Democrats Can't Make an Issue of Noriega," *New York Times*, May 4, 1988, 31y.

24. Sciolino, op. cit., 10y.

25. ibid.

26. R.W. Lee III, "Thoughts on the Drug War in Latin America." a paper prepared for the seminar on "The U.S.-Latin American Drug Trade" held at the Graduate School of International Studies, University of Miami, Coral Gables, Florida, February 5-6, 1988.

27. ibid., 3.

28. Richard B. Craig, "U.S. Antidrug Policy and U.S.-Colombian Relations," a paper prepared for the seminar on "The U.S.-Latin American Drug Trade" held at the Graduate School of International Studies, University of Miami, February 5-6, 1988.

29. ibid., 2.

30. ibid., 3.

31. ibid.

32. Alan Riding, "Colombians Grow Weary of Waging the War on Drugs," *New York Times*, February 1, 1988, 8y.

33. Bradley Graham, "Drug Killings Cow Colombians," *Washington Post*, February 6, 1987, A14.

34. Riding, op. cit., 8y.

35. EFE News Agency, "Colombia might repudiate Extradition Treaty with U.S." *Miami Herald*, May 17, 1988, 11a.

36. Louis Kraar, "The Drug Trade," *Fortune* (June 20, 1988) 27.

37. Lee, "Reflections...", 3-4.

38. ibid., 4.

39. ibid., 4-5.

40. David Boaz, "Let's Quit the Drug War," *New York Times*, March 17, 1988, 25y.

41. Ethan A. Nadelmann, "U.S. Drug Policy: A Bad Export," *Foreign Policy* (Spring 1988), 97-108.

42. Time, "Thinking the Unthinkable," *Time*, (May 30, 1988), 14.

43. Craig, op. cit., 6-7.

44. C. Mohr, "Drug Bill Passes, Finishing Business of 100th Congress," *New York Times*, October 23, 1988, 1y, 16y.

45. J. Yang, "Congress Passes the Antidrug Bill Including a Death Penalty," *The Wall Street Journal*, October 24, 1988.

46. "The Drug Bill's 2.3 Billion Promise," *New York Times*, October 25, 1988, 26y.

47. Yang, ibid.

48. "Hitting Kingpins in Their Assets," *US News and World Report*, December 5, 1988.

CHAPTER 5:

* This chapter is excerpted from my book, *The White Labyrinth: Cocaine Trafficking and Political Power in the Andean Countries*. New Brunswick, N.J.: Transaction Publishers, 1989.

1. Mario Arango Jaramillo, *Impacto del Narcotráfico en Antioquía*. (Medellín: Editorial J. M. Arango, 1988), 96.
2. Arango, *Impacto del Narcotráfico*, 140-41.
3. Mario Arango Jaramillo and Jorge Child Yelez, *Los Condenados de la Coca*. (Medellín: Editorial J. M. Arango, 1985), 128-29.
4. Arango, *Impacto del Narcotráfico*, 183.
5. Bradley Graham, "Bolivia Runs Risk in Drug Drive," *Washington Post*, July 16, 1986, A1.
6. Arango, *Impacto del Narcotráfico*, 183.
7. "El tráfico de drogas es mecanismo de autodefensa," *El Espectador*, July 3, 1984.
8. "Paro armado de 72 horas," *Bases Huallaga*, August 1988, 1.
9. U.S. General Accounting Office, *Drug Control: U.S.-Supported Efforts in Colombia and Bolivia*. Report to Congress. (Washington: November 1988), 54.
10. Fabio Castillo, *Los Jinetes de la Cocaina* (Bogota: Editorial Documentos Periodistas, 1987), 71.
11. "Quien esta matando a la mafia," *Semana*, April 1, 1986, 32.
12. "'Rey de la Cocaina,' Roberto Suárez. Dice que se entrego para solucionar problemas de narcotráfico boliviano," *Los Tiempos* [Cochabamba], September 25, 1988, 10.
13. "Military-Drug Trafficking Link Alleged," Radio Patria Libre (Clandestine) to Colombia (November 15, 1988).
14. On this point, see Merrill Collett, "The Myth of the Narcoguerrillas," *The Nation* (August 13-20, 1988), 132.
15. "Carta Abierta de Roberto Suárez," *El Diario* [La Paz], October 19, 1988.

CHAPTER 6:

1. See Susan F. Rasky, "Senate Votes 83-6 to Give Military Antidrug Powers," *New York Times*, May 14, 1988, 1; Arthur Ravenel, Jr., "Use Full Military Force in War Against Drugs," *USA Today*, June 21, 1988, 10A.
2. George C. Wilson, "Military Urges Wider Drug War: Training Central American Teams, Blocking Transport Envisioned," *Washington Post*, June 20, 1985, A22.
3. General Accounting Office, *Drug Control: Issues Surrounding Increased Use of the Military in Drug Interdiction*, GAO/NSIAD-88-156, Washington, 1988, 20-21. Of this amount, the military estimated that $75 million was for assistance to law enforcement agencies on a nonreimbursable basis in that it involved expenses incurred during ordinary military activities; the other $314 million were DOD funds designated by Congress to be used for law enforcement purposes. See also Eliot Marshall, "A War On Drugs With Real Troops?" *Science* 241 (July 1, 1988), 13-15. Military contributions represent one seven-hundredth of the DOD budget. For the kinds of value of the equipment, see *Congressional Record-Senate* (May 13, 1988), 100th Congress, 2nd Sess., vol. 134, S5762.

4. *Congressional Record-Senate* (May 13, 1988), 100th Congress, 2nd Sess., vol. 134, S5763-4.

5. Raphael Perl, *Narcotics Control and the Use of U.S. Military Personnel: Operations in Bolivia and Issues for Congress*, Report No. 86-800 F (Washington: Congressional Research Service, 1986).

6. See Susan F. Rasky, "Senate Factions Search for Way to Widen Military Role on Drugs," *New York Times*, May 13, 1988, A1, A19; Edward I. Koch, "War on Drugs? Use the Armed Forces," *Washington Post*, June 20, 1985, A21; Irving Kristol, "War on Drugs? Then Get Serious and Use the Military," *Washington Post*, March 28, 1988, A15; and William J. Taylor, Jr., statements in Congressional Research Service, *Narcotics Interdiction and the Use of the Military: Issues for Congress* (hereafter cited as CRS, *Narcotics Interdiction*). (Washington: GPO, 1988), 10-13, 31-32, 67-72.

7. This involvement was a result of congressional mandate, not DOD desire; amendments to the Defense Appropriation Act of 1982 forced the military to get involved and amended the Posse Comitatus Act to allow it.

8. Frank C. Carlucci III, June 15, 1988 testimony to U.S. Senate and House of Representatives Committees on Armed Services; Caspar W. Weinberger, "Our Troops Shouldn't Be Drug Cops: Don't Draft the Military to Solve a Law Enforcement Problem," *Washington Post*, May 22, 1988, C2. See also George C. Wilson and Molly Moore, "Pentagon Warns of No-Win Mission: Military Says Offensive Against Drugs Would Overstretch Resources," *Washington Post*, May 13, 1988, A4; testimony of Admiral Frank B. Kelso, II, USN, Commander in Chief, U.S. Atlantic Fleet, before the Senate Armed Services Committee, June 15, 1988; and remarks of Lt. General Stephen G. Olmstead, USMC, Deputy Assistant Secretary, Drug Policy and Enforcement, in CRS, *Narcotics Interdiction*.

9. Marshall, "Real Troops?", 13.

10. See the testimony of Admiral Frank B. Kelso II, before the Senate Armed Services Committee, June 15, 1988; Peter Reuter's comments in *Narcotics Interdiction*, 29-30; General Accounting Office, *Drug Control: Issues Surrounding Increased Use of the Military in Drug Interdiction*, GAO/NSIAD-88-156. (Washington: GPO, 1988), 17; and John C. Trainer, "Coping With the Drug Runners at Sea," *Naval War College Review* 40 (Summer, 1987), 77-87.

11. See Kelso testimony, June 15, 1988 and GAO, *Drug Control*, 37.

12. General Stephen Olmstead, USMC, Deputy Assistant Secretary for Drug Policy and Enforcement, DOD, makes this point in *Narcotics Interdiction*, 24. For an analogous look at the problems of "sealing" the U.S.-Mexican border, see Robert J. Shafer and Donald J. Mabry, *Neighbors--Mexico and the United States: Wetbacks and Oil.* (Chicago: Nelson-Hall, 1981).

13. General Accounting Office, *Drug Interdiction: Operation Autumn Harvest: A National Guard-Customs Anti-Smuggling Effort*, GAO/GGD-88-86. (Washington: GPO, 1988).

14. See CRS, *Narcotics Interdiction*.

15. On Mexico, see *La Jornada* [Mexico City], April 11, 1988, 6; on Colombia, see Bruce M. Bagley, "Colombia and The War on Drugs," *Foreign Affairs*, 67:1 (Fall 1988), 80-81; on Paraguay, see Millard Burr, "Narcotics Trafficking in Paraguay: An Asunción Perspective," paper

presented to Center for International Security and Strategic Studies, Mississippi State University seminar on "The Latin American Narcotics Trade and United States National Security," June 16-17, 1988.

16. General Herres made this comment in testimony before the Senate and House Armed Services Committees on June 15, 1988. For the ACLU, see Loren Siegel, "The War on Drugs," *Civil Liberties*, (Spring-Summer), 1988, 4-5.

17. See the June 15, 1988 testimony of General Robert T. Herres, USAF, Vice Chairman, Joint Chiefs of Staff, before the Senate and Armed Forces Services Committees.

18. For the role of the military during Reconstruction, see James E. Sefton, *The United States Army and Reconstruction, 1865-1877*, (Baton Rouge: Louisiana State University Press, 1967); Joseph Dawson III, *Army Generals and Reconstruction: Louisiana, 1862-1877*. (Baton Rouge: Louisiana State University Press, 1982); and William Gillette, *Retreat from Reconstruction: 1867-1879*. (Baton Rouge: Louisiana State University Press, 1979).

19. See William J. Taylor, Jr., in CRS, *Narcotics Interdiction*, 66-72.

20. General Stephen D. Olmstead in *Narcotics Interdiction*, 15.

21. The literature on Latin American civil-military relations is substantial and growing. Abraham Lowenthal, ed., *Armies and Politics in Latin America* (New York: Holmes & Meier, 1976) contains important analytical essays and extensive bibliographies.

22. The reasons for military intervention in politics are numerous and complex, of course, and I am not offering a unicausal explanation. For an analysis of why the military intervenes, see Abraham Lowenthal, "Armies and Politics in Latin America," in *Armies and Politics in Latin America*, 5-27.

23. See Martin Weinstein, *Uruguay: The Politics of Failure* (Westport: Greenwood Press, 1975).

24. Leslie Wirpse, "Taming One of Colombia's Most Violent Areas," *Christian Science Monitor*, October 7, 1988, 9, 11.

25. See testimony by General Herres, June 15, 1988.

26. Peter Reuter, Gordon Crawford, and Jonathan Cave, *Sealing the Borders: The Effects of Increased Military Participation in Drug Interdiction* (Santa Monica: Rand Corporation, 1988), as reprinted in CRS, *Narcotics Interdiction*, 44.

27. Peter Reuter, et al, *Sealing the Borders*, 44-45; on containers, see Patrick O'Brien, special agent in charge of the U.S. Customs Service in Miami, as quoted in Michael Isikoff, "Launching Nuclear Bombs in A Guerrilla War," *Washington Post National Weekly Edition*, August 1-7, 1988.

28. Gary F. Crosby in CRS, *Narcotics Interdiction*, 5.

29. Molly Moore, "Pentagon Almost a Bust in Drug War; Cost of Success Last Year Moves GAO to Ambiguous Conclusions," *Washington Post*, June 3, 1988, A17. See GAO, *Drug Control*, 28-29. Susan F. Rasky, "Senate Votes 83-6 to Give Military Antidrug Powers," *New York Times*, May 14, 1988, reports that DOD spent $91.3 million in 1987 on activities related to the fight against drugs. The discrepancy in the figures might be explained by the cost accounting measures used.

30. GAO, *Drug Interdiction: Operation Autumn Harvest.* Widespread publicity before the joint exercise probably caused smugglers to divert their routes temporarily. The National Guard units reported to GAO that the exercise was valuable training for wartime.

31. National Defense Authorization Act for FY 1989 (PL-100-456), *Congressional Record-House,* 100th Congress, 2nd sess., vol. 134. Future citations to this act will be by section number only.

32. Section 7401, Antidrug Abuse Act of 1988, Title VI, Subtitle C of PL 100-690 of 1988; see HR 5120, *Congressional Record-House,* October 21, 1988. 100th Congress, 2nd Sess. vol. 134.

33. U.S. House of Representatives, *Conference Report to Accompany H.R. 4481, National Defense Authorization Act for Fiscal Year 1989.* Report 100-989. September 28, 1988. p. 452. 100th Congress, 2nd sess.

34. *Conference Report.*

CHAPTER 7:

* The views presented herein are those of the author and should not be understood to reflect positions of the Congressional Research Service.

1. Public Law (P.L.) 99-83, secs. 607, 610, and 612, and P.L. 100-690, secs. 4302-4304.

2. P.L. 100-690, Antidrug Abuse Act of 1988.

3. P.L. 100-456, H.R. 4481, National Defense Authorization Act, FY 1989.

4. P.L. 100-461, H.R. 4637, Foreign Operations Export Financing and Related Appropriations Act, 1989.

5. A more detailed analysis of current U.S. international narcotics control policy and alternative options appears in "Drug Control: International Policy and Options," U.S. Library of Congress, Congressional Research Service Issue Brief No. 88093, updated regularly.

6. $25 million of such projects were funded in 1988.

7. $4.7 million of such programs were funded in 1988.

8. For a detailed analysis of the role of the Congress in the certification process, see: "Congress, International Narcotics Policy, and the Antidrug Abuse Act of 1988" by Raphael F. Perl, *Journal of Interamerican Studies and World Affairs* 30:2 (Summer-Fall 1988).

9. Public Law, 99-570.

10. Public Law 100-690.

11. Sec. 481(h)(2)(A) of the Foreign Assistance Act of 1961, and secs. 802 of the Trade Act of 1974 amended by secs. 4407 and 4408 of the Antidrug Abuse Act of 1988. For the text and detailed analysis of these as well as related provisions, see U.S. Senate, Committee on Foreign Relations, *International Narcotics Control and Foreign Assistance Certification: Requirements, Procedures, Timetables, and Guidelines.* Prepared by Raphael F. Perl, March, 1988.

12. Section 481(h)(3) of the Foreign Assistance Act of 1961 and Section 802 of the Trade Act of 1974 as amended by secs. 4407 and 4408 of the Antidrug Abuse Act of 1988.

13. Section 481(h)(2)(C) of the Foreign Assistance Act of 1961 and sec. 802 of the Trade Act of 1974 as amended by secs. 4407 and 4408 of the Antidrug Abuse Act of 1988.

14. Section 481(h)(2)(e) of the Foreign Assistance Act of 1961 and Sec. 802 of the Trade Act of 1974, as amended by secs. 4407 and 4408 of the Antidrug Abuse Act of 1988.

15. See generally, section 481(h)(1)(A) and (B) and Section 481(h)(5) of the Foreign Assistance Act of 1961.

16. Section 803, of the Trade Act of 1974.

17. Section 802 of the Trade Act of 1974.

18. 100th Congress, 1st Sess., H.J. Res. 202, S.J. Res. 90; for Panama, S.J. Res. 91; and for Mexico, S.J. Res. 92.

19. 100th Congress, 2nd. Sess., H.J. Res. 202, for Bahamas; for Bolivia, H.J. Res. 493; for Mexico, S.J. Res. 268 (the Senate vote was 63 in favor of disapproval, 27 against); for Paraguay, H.J. Res. 495; and for Peru, H.J. Res. 497 and 498.

20. Note that at this time (March, 1988), Panama was not certified by the President. In addition, Congress in December, 1987, had already passed legislation restricting U.S. assistance to Panama, prohibiting funds for joint military exercises, and prohibiting Panamanian sugar exports until the President certifies a number of items including Panamanian progress in assuring civilian control of the armed forces, and until freedom of the press and other constitutional rights are guaranteed. See also, P.L. 100-461, sec. 564 for similar language for FY 1989.

21. P.L. 99-570, Title II, sec. 2013. Sec. 2013 of the Antidrug Abuse Act of 1986 (P.L. 99-570), requires that, not later than six months after enactment and every six months thereafter, the President prepare and transmit to Congress a report on official involvement in narcotics trafficking and other topics. The responsibility for making certifications pursuant to this report has been delegated to the Secretary of State.

22. P.L. 99-570, Title II, sec. 2013.

23. It is interesting to note that an earlier proposed version of the law reveals that this section at one point immediately followed a section entitled "Narcotics Control Efforts in Mexico." See *Congressional Record*, vol. 132, no. 140, pt. II, (October 10, 1986). p. S15940.

24. See "International Narcotics Control: The President's March 1, 1988 Certification For Foreign Assistance Eligibility and Options for Congressional Action," by Raphael F. Perl, U.S. Library of Congress, Congressional Research Service, Report No. 88-175, March 4, 1988. See also U.S. Senate, Caucus on International Narcotics Control, *Narcotics-Related Foreign Aid Sanctions: An Effective Foreign Policy?* Report prepared by the Congressional Research Service on a seminar held June 30, 1987, Senate Report 100-48 (September 1987).

25. P.L. 100-690.

26. The National Defense Authorization Act for FY 1989, P.L. 100-461, H.R. 4481, signed into law September 29, 1988.

27. P.L. 100-461, H.R. 4637, signed into law October 1, 1988.

28. P.L. 100-461, Sec. 578, "Narcotics Control Program".

29. For text of restriction, see: Foreign Assistance Act of 1961, P.L.87-195 as amended, sec. 482(b).

CHAPTER 8:

1. See Samuel I. del Villar, "The Illicit Drug Market between Mexico and the United States: Failure and Alternative" (Mexico, D.F., 1988), scheduled to appear in a book on U.S.-Mexican relations of the School of Advanced Social Studies, Johns Hopkins University).
2. For the latest U.S. official assessment of that participation, see Bureau of International Narcotics Matters (INM), Department of State, "International Narcotics Control Strategy Report" (Washington, D.C., March 1, 1988), pp. 64-173.
3. See Peter Reuter, "Eternal Hope: America's International Narcotics Effort" (Washington: Rand Corporation, 1987).
4. See Roger Wagner, *Invisible Hand: The Marijuana Business* (New York: Beach Tree Books, 1986).
5. ibid.
6. President's Commission on Organized Crime (Washington: GPO, 1986), p. 33.
7. It is estimated that Colombian cocaine exports reached a maximum of 100 metric tons in 1983, and were down to 60 tons by 1985. Alicia Puyana, "El Narcotráfico y la Sociedad Colombiana, Notas para el Estudio del Fenómeno," paper presented in the "El Colegio de Mexico-Harvard on a New Approach to the U.S.-Mexico Antidrug Strategy, held at El Colegio de Mexico, Mexico, D.F. April 28-29, 1988).
8. INM, op. cit., 8.
9. See Mark A. Kleiman and Christopher E. Putala, "State and Local Drug Enforcement: Issues and Practice" (Program in Criminal Justice Policy and Management, John F. Kennedy School of Government, Harvard University, March 1987).
10. It estimated Mexico's 1988 production at a level of 30 metric tons, while worldwide production was estimated between 1,882 to 2,992 metric tons, of which 700 to 1,400 come from South West Asia, and 1,125 to 1,535 come from South East Asia. See INM, op. cit., 15.
11. See Mathea Falco, "The Historical Record: U.S. Narcotics Control Collaboration with Turkey, Mexico and Colombia," Bilateral Commission on the Future of United States-Mexico Relations, Working Documents, Mexico D.F., August 1987.
12. See Samuel I. del Villar, "Drogas: el Nudo Gordiano," *Nexos*, 126, (junio, 1988).
13. *The Economist* (April 2-8, 1988), 9-10.
14. Ethan A. Nadelmann, "U.S. Drug Policy: A Bad Export," *Foreign Policy* 70 (Spring 1988), 108.
15. Peter Kerr, "The Unspeakable is Debated: Should Drugs be Legalized?", *New York Times*, May 15, 1988, 1.
16. Saundra Torry, "Call to Debate Legalization of Drugs becomes Louder," *New York Times*, May 15, 1988, 1.

17. In a *Washington Post* Op Ed article, he summarized his economic and health reasons for his proposal. See Kurt L. Schmoke, "Decriminalizing Drugs, It Just Might Work--and Nothing Else Does," *Washington Post*, May 15, 1988, B1.

18. *MacNeil Leherer News Hour*, Public Broadcasting Service (PBS), May 16, 1988.

19. INM, op. cit., 8.

20. Puyana, op. cit.

21. P.L. 99-570.

22. For the specific overall weight and significance of Mexico to the United States, See Gregory F. Treverton, "U.S. Interests in Mexico Beyond Drugs" (submitted to the "El Colegio de Mexico-Harvard Conference on a New Approach to U.S.-Mexico Antidrug Strategy," held at El Colegio de Mexico, Mexico D.F. on April 28-29, 1988).

23. See Maria Celia Toro, "Acuerdos de Cooperación Fallidos: México y Estados Unidos frente al Narcotráfico" (submitted to the El Colegio de Mexico-Harvard Conference on a New Approach to the U.S.-Mexico Antidrug Strategy, held at El Colegio de Mexico, Mexico D.F. on April 28-29, 1988).

24. *Presidential Determination No. 88-10 of February 29, 1988 concerning Certification for Narcotics Source and Transit Countries under P.L. 99-570*. The certified countries were the Bahamas, Belize, Bolivia, Brazil, Burma, Colombia, Ecuador, Hong Kong, Indian, Jamaica, Malaysia, Mexico, Morocco, Nigeria, Pakistan, Peru, and Thailand. Laos, Lebanon, and Paraguay were certified "in the vital interest of the United States." Afghanistan, Iran, Panama, and Syria were not certified.

25. *La Jornada*, April 16, 1988, 1.

26. Charles B. Rangel, "Legalize drugs? Not on your life," op. ed., *New York Times*, May 17, 1988, A25.

27. NBC Nightly News, May 22, 1988.

28. John Dancy, NBC Nightly News, June 1, 1988.

29. See Ethan A. Nadelmann, "Cops Across Borders: Transnational Crime and International Law Enforcement," unpublished Ph.D. dissertation in political science, Harvard University, 1987.

30. See Juan Ricardo Pérez Escamilla Costas, "La Estructura Administrativa de la Administración de Justicia en México," submitted to the El Colegio de Mexico-Harvard Conference on a New Approach to the U.S.-Mexico Antidrug Strategy held at El Colegio de Mexico, Mexico D.F., on April 28-29, 1988. It considers some aspects of the involution that current antinarcotics strategy has brought about in law enforcement in Mexico and has analyzed this law enforcement involution in the case of Mexico.

31. Mark H. Moore, "Drug Policy and Organized Crime," in President's Commission on Organized Crime, *Report to the President and the Attorney General, America's Habit: Drug Abuse, Drug Trafficking, and Organized Crime*, Appendix (Washington: GPO, 1986).

32. Presidential Determination, *Supra note 24*.

33. "Guns, Drugs, and the C.I.A.," *Frontline*, PBS, May 18, 1988.

34. President's Commission of Organized Crime, 5.

35. See Javier Treviño Cantú, "Evaluación de la Estrategía Internacional de Eradicación de Cultivos," submitted to the El Colegio de Mexico-Harvard Conference on a New Approach to the U.S.-Mexico Antidrug Strategy, held at El Colegio de Mexico, Mexico D.F. on April 28-29, 1988.
36. Mark Moore, op. cit.
37. James Mills, *The Underground Empire, Where Crime and Governments Embrace* (Garden City, NY: Doubleday, 1986). This book is a detailed and thorough research of two successful and one failing Centac operations.
38. INM, op. cit., 48-49.

CHAPTER 9:

1. Sigmund Freud, *Cartas de Amor* (Mexico: Premia Editora, 1983), 13-14.
2. Defined in these terms by President Miguel de la Madrid. To quote him: "The fight against narcotrafficking is for Mexico a state problem which includes national security." *Uno Mas Uno*, March 2, 1988, 1.
3. General Edgardo Mercado Jarrín, "Las Doctrinas de Seguridad y Fuerzas Armadas en Latinoamerica," *Seguridad Nacional y Relaciones Internacionales: Peru*, ed. by J. Cintra (Mexico: Centro Latinoamericano de Estudios Estratégicos, 1987), 13.
4. Amos A. Jordan and William J. Taylor, Jr., *American National Security: Policy and Process* (Baltimore: Johns Hopkins University Press, 1981), 3.
5. On April 8, 1986, President Reagan signed a National Security Decision Directive designating the international drug trade as a national security issue. See Raphael Perl, *Narcotics Control and the Use of U.S. Military Personnel: Operations in Bolivia and Issues for Congress* (Washington: Congressional Research Service, 1986), CRS-1.
6. Mafia is used in the Spanish sense as a synonym for gang.
7. The Anti-Drug Act of 1988 promised to shift more effort to the demand side but Congress did not fully fund the bill. Its terms can be found in Omnibus Drug Initiative Act of 1988, HR5120, *Congressional Record-House*, 100th Congress, 2nd Sess.
8. Sergio Aguayo in *La Jornada*, March 17, 1988, 10.
9. General Gabriel Puyana García. "La Seguridad Interior en la Defensa Nacional de Colombia," S. Cintra (ed.). *Seguridad Nacional y Relaciones Internacionales: Colombia*, ed. by S. Cintra (Mexico: Centro Latinoamericano de Estudios Estratégicos, 1987).
10. *Excelsior*, March 4, 1988, 3.
11. *Newsweek*, March 28, 1988, 22-28.
12. *La Jornada*, April 8, 1988, 22.
13. Lorenzo Meyer, "Carta Abierta al Alcalde Koch: Certificar al Certificador," *Excelsior*, March 9, 1988, 7.
14. Mexican Senator Salvador Neme Castillo accepted the assertion that there are Mexican officers involved in narcotrafficking. *La Jornada*, April 11, 1988, 6.
15. *Excelsior*, March 4, 1988, 12-A.
16. *Newsweek*, March 23, 1988, 22.
17. *La Jornada*, February 1, 1988, 11.

18. *Newsweek*, February 8, 1988, 19.
19. *Newsweek*, March 28, 1988, 24.
20. *Excelsior*, April 13, 1988, 2-A.
21. "Colombia: The Drug Economy," *The Economist* (April 2, 1988), 63.
22. *Excelsior*, March 3, 1988, 1-A.
23. *Uno Mas Uno*, March 3, 1988.
24. *New York Times*, April 16, 1988.

CHAPTER 10:

1. "On the Formulation of a U.S. Policy toward Mexico," in *Mexico in Transition*, ed. by Susan Kaufman Purcell (New York: Council on Foreign Relations, 1988), 117.
2. This $100 billion figure is at best a ballpark estimate. One good 1983 estimate put the number at a quarter that, $27 billion. Ken Carlson et al., "Unreported Taxable Income for Selected Illegal Activities," Abt Associates, Cambridge, Mass., 1983.
3. John E. Rielly, ed., *American Public Opinion and U.S. Foreign Policy 1987*, (Chicago: Chicago Council on Foreign Relations, 1987), 9.
4. March 15, 1987.
5. These figures, like all the rest in this chapter, are illustrative estimates only. They are from *The Economist* (April 2, 1988); *New York Times*, October 2, 1988; and GAO, *Controlling Drug Abuse: A Status Report* (Washington: GPO, 1988).
6. See U.S. Narcotics Intelligence Consumers Committee, *The NNICC Report, 1985-86*, (Washington: GPO, 1987).
7. As quoted in the *New York Times*, October 20, 1986.
8. Peter Reuter and Mark Kleiman, "Risks and Prices: An Economic Analysis of Drug Enforcement," *Crime and Justice*, July 1986, 293.
9. U.S. Department of State, *International Narcotics Strategy Report* [hereafter cited as *INSR*] (Washington: GPO, 1988), 108.
10. Health ministry estimate cited in the *Christian Science Monitor*, January 12, 1987.
11. Kevin Healy, "The Cocaine Industry and Bolivian Peasants," *Andean Focus*, 3 (June 1986), 4.
12. As quoted in the *New York Times*, August 5, 1986.
13. *INSR*, 31.
14. The proposal is Samuel del Villar's. He and his colleagues are engaged in a project with a group of Americans organized by Harvard to explore its implications in detail.
15. National Institute for Drug Abuse, *National Household Survey on Drug Abuse*, (Washington: GPO, 1985).
16. April 2, 1988. The most detailed argument for legalization is made by Ethan A. Nadelmann, "U.S. Drug Policy: A Bad Export," *Foreign Policy* 70 (Spring 1988), 83-108.

CHAPTER 11:

1. William Branigan, "The Mexican Connection," *Washington Post National Weekly Edition*, March 14-20, 1988, 7.

2. Christopher Lasch, *The Culture of Narcissism* (New York, W. W. Norton, 1978); Tom Wolfe, "The 'Me' Decade and the Third Great Awakening," *New York* (August 23, 1976), 26-40.

3. On the limited payoff, see Peter Reuter, *Eternal Hope: America's International Narcotics Effort* (Santa Monica, The Rand Corporation, 1987); Peter Reuter, Gordon Crawford, and Jonathan Cave, *The Effects of Increased Military Participation in Drug Interdiction* (Santa Monica, The Rand Corporation, 1988); Gerald Godshaw, Ross Koppel, and Russell Pancoast, *Antidrug Law Enforcement Efforts and Their Impact* (Bala Cynwyd, Penn.: Wharton Econometrics, August, 1987).

4. John Martsh, "The War on Drug Trafficking: Cooperative Efforts Between the United States and Latin America Countries," speech given to the Mississippi State University Center for International Security and Strategic Studies international conference on The Latin American Narcotics Trade and U.S. National Security, June 16-17, 1988.

5. On the terms of certification, see Congressional Research Service, Library of Congress, *International Narcotics Control and Foreign Assistance Certification: Requirements, Procedures, Timetables, and Guidelines*, Report Prepared for the Use of the Committee on Foreign Relations, U.S. Senate. Washington: GPO, 1988.

6. His analysis of Operation Blast Furnace can be found in Congressional Research Service, *Narcotics Interdiction and the Use of the Military: Issues for Congress* (Washington: GPO, 1988), 6-7.

7. David M. Potter, *People of Plenty: Economic Abundance and the American Character* (Chicago: Phoenix Books, 1958).

8. H. Wayne Morgan, *Drugs in America: A Social History, 1800-1980* (Syracuse: Syracuse University Press, 1981; David Musto, *The American Disease: Origins of Narcotic Control*, expanded ed. (New York: Oxford University Press, 1987).

Bibliography

"A Self-Styled Robin Hood," *Time* (February 25, 1985), 23.

Abrams, Eliot. February 10, 1986 speech to Council on Foreign Relations, *Current Policy* 792, U.S. Department of State, Bureau of Public Affairs.

Andrews, George and David Solomon, eds. *The Coca Leaf and Cocaine Papers*. New York: Harcourt, Brace, Jovanovich, 1975.

Anslinger, Harry J. and William F. Tompkins. *The Traffic in Narcotics*. New York: Funk and Wagnalls, 1953.

Arango Jaramillo, Mario. *Impacto del Narcotráfico en Antioquía*. Medellín: Editorial J. M. Arango, 1988.

Arango Jaramillo, Mario, and Jorge Child Yelez. *Los Condenados de la Coca*. Medellín, Editorial J. M. Arango, 1985.

Asencio, Diego, and Nancy Asencio. *Our Man Is Inside*. Boston: Little, Brown, 1983.

Ayatollah, "Guerrillas y Narcos, Cuentas Pendientes," *El Tiempo*, November 15, 1987, 5A.

Bagley, Bruce. "Colombia and the War on Drugs," *Foreign Affairs* 67:1 (Fall 1988), 70-92.

_____. "The Colombian Connection: The Impact of Drug Traffic on Colombia," in *Coca and Cocaine: Effects on People and Policy in Latin America*. edited by Deborah Pacini and Christine Franquemont. Peterborough, N.H.: Cultural Survival and Cornell University, 1986.

Barnes, Deborah. "The Biological Tangle of Drug Addiction," *Science* 241 (July 22, 1988), 415-17.

"Belisario No Entregará a Ningún Colombianos," *Quindio Libre*, October 1, 1983, 8B.

Boaz, David. "Let's Quit the Drug War," *New York Times*, March 17, 1988, 25y.

Boffey, Philip. "Drug Users Not Suppliers Hold Key to Problem," *The New York Times*, April 12, 1988, A1, A10.

"Bolivia Asks U.S. for Big Loan to Make Up Lost Cocaine Income," *New York Times*, July 31, 1986, A4.

Bonnie, Richard J. and Charles H. Whitehead. *The Marihuana Conviction: A History of Marihuana Prohibition in the United States*. Charlottesville, University Press of Virginia, 1974.

Boyce, Daniel. "Narco-Terrorism," *FBI Law Enforcement Bulletin*, October 1987.

Brading, David A. *Miners and Merchants in Bourbon Mexico, 1763-1810*. New York, Cambridge University Press, 1971.

Branigan, William. "The Mexican Connection," *Washington Post National Weekly Edition*, March 14-20, 1988, 7.

Bridges, Tyler. "Resurgence of Bolivia's Drug Trade Sparks New Prevention Push with US," *Christian Science Monitor*, (July 1, 1987), 6-7.

Brinkley, Joel. "Bolivia Asks U.S. for Big Loan to Make Up Lost Cocaine Income," *New York Times*, July 31, 1986, A4.

Bullington, Bruce. *Heroin Use in the Barrio*. Lexington, Mass.: Lexington Books, 1977.

Carlson, Ken, et al. *Unreported Taxable Income for Selected Illegal Activities*. Cambridge, MA, Apt Associates, 1983.

"Carta Abierta de Roberto Suárez," *El Diario* [La Paz], October 19, 1988.

Castillo, Fabio. *Los Jinetes de la Cocaina*. Bogotá: Editorial Documentos Periodistas, 1987.

Chase, Stuart, and F. J. Schlink. "Consumers in Wonderland: What We Get For Our Money When We Buy From Quacks and Vendors for Cure-Alls," *New Republic* 49 (February 16, 1927), 348-51.

"Civismo en Marcha," *Medellín Cívico*, March 1984, 2.

Clark, Norman H. *Deliver Us from Evil: An Interpretation of American Prohibition*. New York: W. W. Norton, 1976.

Cockburn, Leslie. *Out of Control*. New York, 1987.

Collett, Merrill. "Colombia's Drug Lords Waging War on Leftists," *Washington Post*, November 14, 1987, 14A, 22A.

_____. "The Myth of the Narcoguerrillas," *The Nation* (August 13-20, 1988), 132.

"Colombia: The Drug Economy," *The Economist* (April 2, 1988), 63.

Congressional Research Service, Library of Congress. *Narcotics-Related Foreign Aid Sanctions: An Effective Foreign Policy?* report for the Caucus on International Narcotics Control, U.S. Senate. 1987.

_____. *Combatting International Drug Cartels: Issues for U.S. Policy*. Report for the Caucus on International Narcotics Control, U.S. Senate. 1987.

Cooper, Nancy. "Drugs, Money and Death," *Newsweek* (February 15, 1988), 32-36, 38-39.

Courtwright, David T. *Dark Paradise: Opiate Addiction in America before 1940*. Cambridge, Harvard University Press, 1982.

_____. "Opiate Addiction as a Consequence of the Civil War," *Civil War History* 25 (June 1978), 101-11.

"Crack Secret Police Outfit to Combat Shining Path's New Offensive," *The Andean Report* (March 1987).

Craig, Richard B. "*La Campaña Permanente*: Mexico's Antidrug Campaign," *Journal of Interamerican Studies and World Affairs*, 20 (1978), 107-31.

_____. "Colombian Narcotics and United States-Colombian Relations," *Journal of Interamerican Studies and World Affairs* 36 (1981), 243-70.

_____. "Domestic Implications of Illicit Drug Cultivation, Processing, and Trafficking in Colombia," *Journal of Interamerican Studies and World Affairs*, 25 (1983), 325-50.

_____. "Human Rights and Mexico's Antidrug Campaign," *Social Science Quarterly*, 60 (1980), 691-701.

_____. "Illegal Drug Traffic," in *Borderlands Sourcebook: A Guide to the Literature of Northern Mexico and the American Southwest*. Edited by E.R. Stoddard, R. L. Nostrand, and J.P. West. Norman, University of Oklahoma Press, 1983, 209-13.

_____. "Illicit Drug Traffic Implications for South American Source Countries," *Journal of Interamerican Studies and World Affairs* 29:2 (Summer, 1987), 1-34.

_____. "Illicit Drug Trafficking and U.S.-Latin American Relations," *Washington Quarterly* 8 (1985), 105-24.

_____. "Operación Intercepción: una política de presión internacional," *Foro Internacional* 22 (1981), 203-30.

_____. "Operation Condor: Mexico's Antidrug Campaign Enters a New Era," *Journal of Interamerican Studies and World Affairs* 22 (1980), 345-63.

Craig, Richard B., and Michael A. Turner. "International Control of Narcotics and Dangerous Drugs," *Indian Political Science Review* 11 (1977), 33-47.

"Creating Customers for Dangerous Drugs," *Outlook* 82 (April 7, 1906), 778-79.

Cristian, Shirley. "Drug Trafficking and Output Rising Sharply in Argentina," *New York Times*, April 28, 1988.

Crowell, Lorenzo. "U.S. Domestic Terrorism: An Historical Perspective," *Quarterly Journal of Ideology* 11:3 (1987), 45-56.

Cumberland, Charles. *Mexico: The Struggle for Modernity*. New York: Oxford University Press, 1968.

De Olloqui, José Juan. "On the Formulation of a U.S. Policy toward Mexico," in *Mexico in Transition*. edited by Susan Kaufman Purcell. New York: Council on Foreign Relations, 1988.

del Villar, Samuel I. "Drogas: el Nudo Gordiano," *Nexos* 126 (junio, 1988).

_____. "The Illicit Drug Market between Mexico and the United States: Failure and Alternative." (Mexico, D.F., 1988), scheduled to appear in a book on U.S.-Mexican relations of the School of Advanced Social Studies, Johns Hopkins University).

Dionne, E. J. "Drugs as 1988 Issue: Filling a Vacuum," *New York Times*, May 24, 1988, 14y.

Douglass, Joseph D., Jr., and Jan Sejna. "International Narcotics Trafficking: The Soviet Connection," *Nightwatch Special Report*, Washington, 1987.

"The Drug Bill's 2.3 Billion Promise," *New York Times*, October 25, 1988, 26y.

Duster, Troy. *The Legislation of Morality: Law, Drugs, and Moral Judgement*. New York: The Free Press, 1970.

"The Drug Flames Rise Higher," *New York Times*, March 3, 1988, 30.

Eddy, Paul, with Hugo Sabogal and Sara Walden. *The Cocaine Wars*. New York: W. W. Norton, 1988.

EFE News Agency. "Colombia Might Repudiate Extradition Treaty with U.S.," *Miami Herald*, May 17, 1988, 11a.

Ehrenfeld, R. "Narco-Terrorism: The Kremlin Connection," The Heritage Foundation, February, 1987.

_____. "The United States and the Drug Problem," *The World and I* (October 1986).

Ehrenfeld, R. and M. Kahan. "The 'Doping of America': The Ambivalence of the Narco-terrorist Connection and a Search for Solutions," in *Contemporary Research on Terrorism*, edited by Paul Wilkinson and A. M. Stewart. Aberdeen: Aberdeen University Press, 1987.

_____. "The Narcotic-Terrorism Connection," *Wall Street Journal*, February 10, 1986.

"El Dossier de Medellín," *Semana*, January 27, 1987, 25.

"El Dinero Caliente Pretende Entrar en Política," *Guión*, July 15-21, 1983, 21.

"El tráfico de drogas es mecanismo de autodefensa," *El Espectador*, July 3, 1984.

"Estupor por Subornos de la Mafia," *El Tiempo*, January 10, 1988, 9A.

"Existen Mas de Dos Millones de Desempleados," *Medellín Cívico*, May 1987, 6.

Fagg, John Edwin. *Latin America: A General History*. New York: Macmillan Publishing Company, 1977.

Falco, Mathea. "The Historical Record: U.S. Narcotics Control Collaboration with Turkey, Mexico and Colombia" (Bilateral Commission on the Future of United States-Mexico Relations, Working Documents, Mexico D.F., August 1987).

Fox, J. Edward. Department of State Memorandum accompanying "Report to Congress, Section 2013, P.L. 99-570, Reports and Restrictions Concerning Certain Countries, May 1, 1988.

Freud, Sigmund. *Cartas de Amor*. Mexico: Premia Editora, 1983.

Gaviria Berrio, Hernan. Letter to Fabio Castillo, *Medellín Cívico*, April, 1987.

Godshaw, Gerald, Ross Koppel, and Russell Pancoast. *Antidrug Law Enforcement Efforts and Their Impact*. Bala Cynwyd, PA: Wharton Econometrics, August, 1987.

González, Raul. "Trafficking, Subversion in Upper Huallaga," *Quehacer*, September-October 1987, 55-72.

"Governments' Sweetheart Deals and Subsidies Attempt to Stop Widening the Gaps in the Financial Circuit." *The Andean Report*, October 1986, 141-142.

Graham, Bradley. "Bolivia Runs Risk in Drug Drive," *Washington Post*, July 16, 1986, A1.

_____. "Drug Killings Cow Colombians," *Washington Post*, February 6, 1987, A14.

_____. "Impact of Colombian Drug Traffickers Spreads," *Washington Post*, February 24, 1988, 41.

_____. "The International Cocaine Conspiracy," *Washington Post National Weekly Edition* (March 14-20, 1988), 6-7.

Graham-Mulhall, Sara. "The Evil of Drug Addiction," *New Republic*, 26 (May 18, 1921), 357.

"Guns, Drugs, and the C.I.A.," *Frontline*, PBS, May 18, 1988, 34.

Halloran, Richard. "In War against Drugs, Military is Found Wanting," *New York Times*, May 30, 1988, 20y.

Haub, Carl. *1981 World Population Data Sheet*. Washington: Population Reference Bureau, Inc., 1981.

"Hay Que Hablar con los Narcos Dicen 2 Obispos," *El Tiempo*, February 13, 1988, 1A.

Healy, Kevin. "Bolivia and Cocaine: A Developing Country's Dilemma," *British Journal of Addiction*, 1988.

_____. "The Boom Within the Crisis: Some Recent Effects of Foreign Cocaine Markets on Bolivian Rural Society and Economy," *Coca and Cocaine*, edited by Deborah Pacini and Christine Franquemont. Peterborough, NH: Transcript Publishing Company, 1986.

_____. "The Cocaine Industry and Bolivian Peasants," *Andean Focus*, 3, June 1986, 4.

Helmer, John. *Drugs and Minority Oppression*. New York: Seabury Press, 1975.

Henry, David. "How to Make 7 Million in 7 Years," *Forbes*, October 5, 1987.

Hersh, Seymour M.. "Why Democrats Can't Make an Issue of Noriega," *New York Times*, May 4, 1988, 31y.

Hilton, Robert E. "Recent Developments Relating to the Posse Comitatus Act," *Army Lawyer* 121 (January 1983), 1-8.

"Hitting Kingpins in Their Assets," *US News and World Report*, December 8, 1988.

Hogan, Harry, et al. "Drug Control: Highlights of P.L. 99-570, Antidrug Abuse Act of 1986." Washington: Congressional Research Service. Library of Congress, 86-968 GOV, October 31, 1986.

Hoge, Warren. "Bolivians Find A Patron in Reputed Drug Chief," *New York Times*, August 15, 1982, 1.

Hunt, Michael H. *Ideology and U.S. Foreign Policy*. New Haven: Yale University Press, 1987.

"Is Prohibition Making Drug Fiends?" *Literary Digest* 69 (April 16, 1921), 19-20.

"Jacobo Arenas Discusses Lehder," *Semana*, March 10, 1987, 22-25.

Kamstra, Jerry. *Weed: Adventures of a Dope Smuggler*. New York: Bantam Books, 1974.

Keen, Benjamin, ed.. *Latin American Civilization: The Colonial Origins*. Boston: Houghton Mifflin, 1974.

Kerr, Peter. "The Unspeakable is Debated: Should Drugs be Legalized?", *New York Times*, May 15, 1988, 1.

_____. "U.S. Drug Crusade Is Seen Undermining Itself," *New York Times*, October 26,1987, 13y.

Kinder, Douglas Clark. "Bureaucratic Cold Warrior: Harry J. Anslinger and Illicit Narcotics Traffic," *Pacific Historical Review*, 50 (May 1981), 169-191.

_____, and William O. Walker III. "Stable Force in a Storm: Harry J. Anslinger and United States Narcotic Policy, 1930-1962," *The Journal of American History*, 72:4 (March 1986), 908-927.

King, Rufus. *The Drug Hang-Up: America's Fifty Year Folly*. New York: W. W. Norton, 1972.

Kleiman, Mark A. and Christopher E. Putala. "State and Local Drug Enforcement: Issues and Practice," Program in Criminal Justice Policy and Management, John F. Kennedy School of Government, Harvard University, Cambridge, Mass., March 1987.

Kolb, Lawrence and A. G. DuMez. "The Prevalence and Trend of Drug Addiction in the United States and the Factors Influencing It," *Public Health Reports* 23 (May 1924), 1198.

Kraar, Louis. "The Drug Trade," *Fortune*, June 20, 1988, 27.

"La Conexión," *Caretas*, September 7, 1987, 36.

"La Mafia Asesino a Pardo Leal," *El Tiempo*, November 13, 1987, 3A.

"La Patria Acorralada," *Quindio Libre*, October 1, 1983, 2A.

"La Paz es la Justicia Social," *Medellín Cívico*, November 1986, 3.

Lasch, Christopher. *The Culture of Narcissism*. New York: W. W. Norton, 1978.

League of Nations, Advisory Committee on Traffic in Opium and Other Dangerous Drugs. *Report on the Work of the Committee During its Second Session*, held at Geneva from April 19-29, 1922 C. 233 (1).1922.XI (Geneva, 1922), 1-3.

League of Nations, Opium Advisory Committee. Report to the Council on the *Work of the Fifth Session* (May 24 to June 7, 1923) A.13.1923.XI. 12.

Lee, Rensselaer W., III. "The Drug Trade and Developing Countries," *Policy Focus* 4, (June 1987).

Lee, Rensselaer W., III. "Drugs," in *The U.S. Economy and Developing Countries: Campaign 88 Briefing Papers for Candidates*, edited by Richard Feinberg and Gress Goldstein. Washington: Overseas Development Council, 1988.

Lee, Rensselaer W., III. "Drugs and the Third World," *Policy Focus*, 4 (June 1987).

Lee, Rensselaer W., III. "Economic Impact of the Drug Trade," *Economic Impact* (Spring 1988).

Lee, Rensselaer W., III. "The Latin American Drug Connection," *Foreign Policy* (Winter-Spring 1985), 142-159.

Lee, Rensselaer W., III. *The White Labyrinth: Cocaine Trafficking and Political Power in the Andean Countries*. New Brunswick: Transaction Publishers, 1989.

Lee, Rensselaer W., III. "Why The U.S. Cannot Stop South American Cocaine," *Orbis* 32:4 (Fall 1988), 499-519.

"Libre Capo de la Mafia porque Ningún Juez Quiso Procesarlo," *El Tiempo*, February 9, 1988, 24.

Lindau, J. D.. "Percepciones mexicanas de la política exterior de Estados Unidos: el caso Camarena Salazar," *Foro Internacional*, 27 (1987), 562-575.

Lindesmith, Alfred R. *The Addict and the Law*. Bloomington: Indiana University Press, 1965.

_____."Traffic in Dope": Medical Problem," *Nation*, 182 (April 21, 1956), 337-338.

"Lo Unico que Hacemos Es el Oso," *El Tiempo*, February 22, 1988.

Long, William. "Powerful Medellín Cartel Safe in its Colombian Base," *Los Angeles Times*, February 21, 1988, 18.

"Los barrios Pobres y la Eradicación de la Pobreza," *Medellín Cívico*, October 1986, 3.

Mabry, Donald J. "The Latin American Narcotics Trade and Hemispheric Security," *International Third World Studies Journal and Review* 1 (1988), 1-7.

_____. "The U.S. Military and the War on Drugs in Latin America," *Journal of Interamerican Studies and World Affairs* 30:2 (Summer-Fall 1988).

Malcomson, Scott L. "Cocaine Republic," *Village Voice*, August 26, 1986.

Marshall, Eliot. "A War on Drugs With Real Troops?" *Science* 241 (July 1, 1988), 13-15.

May, Herbert L. "The International Control of Narcotic Drugs," *International Conciliation* 441 (May 1948), 301-371.

McAlister, Lyle N. "Social Structure and Social Change in New Spain," in *Readings in Latin American History*, edited by Lewis Hanke. New York: Thomas Y. Crowell, 1966, 154-171.

McCoy, Alfred W., with Cathleen B. Reed and Leonard P. Adams II. *The Politics of Heroin in Southeast Asia*. New York: Harper and Row, 1972.

McFadden, Peter. "New Eradication Program Winning Over Coca Farmers," *Business News*, December 31, 1987, 8.

Mercado Jarrín, General Edgardo. "Las Doctrinas de Seguridad y Fuerzas Armadas en Latinoamericana," in *Seguridad Nacional y Relaciones Internacionales: Peru*, edited by J. Cintra. Mexico: Centro Latinoamericano de Estudios Estratégicos, 1987.

Mexico, Office of the President, Bureau of Social Communication. "The Mexican Army and the Fight Against Drugs," *Mexico Today* (April, 1987), 6-7.

Meyer, Lorenzo. "Carta Abierta al Alcalde Koch: Certificar al Certificador," *Excelsior*, March 9, 1988, 7.

"Mientras el Pueblo Padece Hambre, Varias Industrias Se Enriquen," *Medellín Cívico*, April 1987, 4.

"Military-Drug Trafficking Link Alleged," Radio Patria Libre (Clandestine) to Colombia, November 15, 1988.

Mills, James. *The Underground Empire, Where Crime and Governments Embrace*. Garden City, New York: Doubleday, 1986.

Mills, Reid G. "Panama Future Clouded," Associated Press Dispatch, February 15, 1988.

Mohr, C. "Drug Bill Passes, Finishing Business of 100th Congress," *New York Times*, October 23, 1988, 1y, 16y.

Molano, Alfredo. *Selva Adentro*. Bogotá, 1987.

Moore, Mark H. "Drug Policy and Organized Crime" in President's Commission on Organized Crime, *Report to the President and the Attorney General, America's Habit: Drug Abuse, Drug Trafficking, and Organized Crime*, Appendix. (Washington: GPO, 1986).

Moore, W. John. "No Quick Fix," *National Journal*, November 21, 1987, 2954.

Morgan, H. Wayne. *Drugs in America: A Social History, 1800-1980*. Syracuse: Syracuse University Press, 1981.

Morganthau, Tom. "Anatomy of a Fiasco," *Newsweek* (June 6, 1988), 36-37, 39.

"Multinacional de la Droga: Quién Esta Detrás?" *El Tiempo*, February 17, 1986, 10.

Musto, David F. *The American Disease: Origins of Narcotic Control*. New Haven: Yale University Press, 1973. Expanded ed. New York: Oxford University Press, 1987.

Nadelmann, Ethan A. "Cops Across Borders: Transnational Crime and International Law Enforcement," Unpublished Ph.D. dissertation in political science, Harvard University, 1987.

_____. "U.S. Drug Policy: A Bad Export," *Foreign Policy* 70, Spring 1988, 97-108.

National Institute for Drug Abuse. *National Household Survey on Drug Abuse*, Washington, GPO, 1988.

National Narcotics Intelligence Consumer's Committee. *The NNICC Report, 1985-1986*. Washington, 1987.

"National Menace of the Dope Traffic," *Literary Digest* 76 (February 24, 1923), 34-35.

Nicholl, Charles. *Fruit Palace: An Odyssey Through Colombia's Cocaine Underworld*. New York: St. Martin's Press, 1985.

"No a la Extradición," *Medellín Cívico*, March 1984, 7.

Orozco, Jorge Eliecer. *Lehder: El Hombre*. Bogotá, 1987.

Owens, Gerald. "Costs of Production: Coca." unsolicited report to AID, December 31, 1986.

Pacini, Deborah, and Christine Franquemont. *Coca and Cocaine: Effects on People and Policy in Latin America*. Peterborough, NH: Cultural Survival and Cornell University, 1986.

Parkes, Henry Bamford. *A History of Mexico*. Boston: Houghton Mifflin, 1969.

"Paro armado de 72 horas," *Bases Huallaga*, August 1988, 1.

"Patent Medicine Crusade," *Nation* 81 (November 9, 1905), 376.

"Patent Medicines and Poverty," *Outlook* 83 (June 2, 1906), 253-254.

Pérez Escamilla Costas, Juan Ricardo. "La Estructura Administrativa de la Administración de Justicia en México" (submitted to the El Colegio de Mexico-Harvard Conference on a New Approach to the U.S.-Mexico Antidrug Strategy held at El Colegio de Mexico, Mexico D.F., on April 28-29, 1988).

Pellens, Mildred. *The Opium Problem*. New York: The Bureau of Social Hygiene, 1928.

Perl, Raphael F. "Congress, International Narcotics Policy, and the Antidrug Abuse Act of 1988," *Journal of Interamerican Studies and World Affairs* 30:2 (Summer-Fall 1988).

_____. *International Narcotics Control and Foreign Assistance Certification: Requirements, Procedures, Timetables, and Guidelines*. Report prepared for the Committee on Foreign Relations, U.S. Senate. Washington: GPO, 1988.

_____. *International Narcotics Control: The President's March 1, 1988 Certification for Foreign Assistance Eligibility and Options for Congressional Action*. Washington: Congressional Research Service, 1988.

Perry, Stuart H. "The Unarmed Invasion," *Atlantic Monthly* 135 (January 1925), 70-77.

Pinto Flores, Aquiles. *Yo fuí rehén del M-19 (61 días en la Embajada de la República Dominicana*. Bogotá: Canal Ramírez-Antares, 1980).

The President's Commission on Organized Crime. *America's Habit: Drug Abuse, Drug Trafficking and Organized Crime*. Report to the President and the Attorney General, March 1986.

Puyana, Alicia. "El Narcotráfico y la Sociedad Colombiana, Notas para el Estudio del Fenómeno," (paper presented in the "El Colegio de Mexico-Harvard on a New Approach to the U.S.-Mexico Antidrug Strategy, held at El Colegio de Mexico, Mexico, D.F. April 28-29, 1988).

Puyana García, Gabriel. "La Seguridad Interior en la Defensa Nacional de Colombia," in *Seguridad Nacional y Relaciones Internacionales: Colombia*, edited by S. Cintra. Mexico: Centro Latinoamericano de Estudios Estratégicos, 1987.

"Quien Esta Matando a la mafia," *Semana*, April 1, 1986, 32.

"Quien Fue," *Semana*, January 25, 1986.

Rangel, Charles B. "Legalize drugs? Not on Your Life," op. ed., *New York Times*, May 17, 1988, A25.

"Reactivación Económica por Dinero Caliente," *El Espectador*, October 3, 1987, 1A, 7A.

Reuter, Peter. *Eternal Hope: America's International Narcotics Effort*. Santa Monica: The Rand Corporation, 1987.

_____. "Eternal Hope: America's Quest for Narcotics Control," *The Public Interest* 79 (Spring 1985).

Reuter, Peter, Gordon Crawford, and Jonathan Crane. *Sealing the Borders: The Effects of Military Participation in Drug Interdiction*, Santa Monica, Rand Corporation, 1988.

Reuter, Peter, and Mark Kleinman. "Risks and Prices: An Economic Analysis of Drug Enforcement," *Crime and Justice* (July 1986), 293.

"'Rey de la Cocaina,' Roberto Suárez. Dice que se entrego para solucionar problemas de narcotráfico boliviano," *Los Tiempos*, September 25, 1988, 10.

Ricks, Thomas. "The Cocaine Business: Big Risks and Profits, High Labor Turnover," *Wall Street Journal*, June 30, 1986, 16.

Riding, Alan. "Colombia Says U.S. Reprisals Weakens Support for Drug Fight," *New York Times*, January 13, 1988, A13.

_____. "Colombians Grow Weary of Waging War on Drugs," *New York Times*, February 1, 1988, 8y.

Rielly, John E., ed. *American Public Opinion and U.S. Foreign Policy 1987*. Chicago: Chicago Council on Foreign Relations, 1987.

Schmeckebier, Lawrence F. and Francis X. A. Eble. *The Bureau of Internal Revenue: Its History, Activities, and Organization*. Baltimore: The Johns Hopkins University Press, 1923.

Schmoke, Kurt L. "Decriminalizing Drugs, It Just Might Work--and Nothing Else Does," *Washington Post*, May 15, 1988, B1.

Sciolino, Elaine, with Stephen Engelberg. "Narcotics Efforts Foiled by U.S. Security Goals," *New York Times*, April 10, 1988, 1y, 10.

Segal, Nicholas, and Lillian Segal. "The Drug Evil," *New Republic*, 34 (March 7, 1923), 41-43.

"Seized Honduran Drug Baron or Robin Hood," *New York Times*, April 16, 1988, 4.

Shafer, Robert J. and Donald J. Mabry. *Neighbors--Mexico and the United States*. Chicago: Nelson-Hall, 1981.

Shannon, Elaine. *Desperados: Latin Drug Lords, U.S. Lawmen, and the War America Can't Win*. New York: Viking Press, 1988.

Siegel, Loren. "Zero Tolerance and Calls for the Military Spark Debate about Decriminalization," *Civil Liberties* (Spring/Summer, 1988), 4-5.

Simpson, Eyler N. *The Ejido: Mexico's Way Out*. Chapel Hill: University of North Carolina Press, 1937.

"6 de Cada Mil Colombianos Son Consumidores de Basuco," *El Occidente*, February 11, 1988.

"The Superstition of Dope," *Literary Digest* 54 (June 30, 1917), 1990.

Taylor, Arnold H. *American Diplomacy and the Narcotics Traffic, 1900-1939: A Study in International Humanitarian Reform*. Durham: Duke University Press, 1969.

"Text of Drug Traffickers's Terms for Ending Activities," *El Tiempo*, July 7, 1984, 1A,11C.

"Thinking the Unthinkable," *Time*, May 30, 1988, 14.

Thomas, Jon. *Mexico and Narcotics: A Must-Win Situation*. Tempe, AZ: INCAMEX, 1987.

Thompson, Mark. "Senate Oks Bill Pitting Military Against Drugs," *Miami Herald*, May 28, 1988, 8a.

Timberlake, James H. *Prohibition and the Progressive Movement, 1900-1920*. Cambridge: Harvard University Press, 1966.

"Tocache: Some Things Go Better With...," *The Andean Report*, December 1985.

Toro, Maria Celia. "Acuerdos de Cooperación Fallidos: México y Estados Unidos frente al Narcotráfico," submitted to the El Colegio de Mexico-Harvard Conference on a New Approach to the U.S.-Mexico Antidrug Strategy, held at El Colegio de Mexico, Mexico D.F. on April 28-29, 1988. 24.

Torry, Saundra. "Call to Debate Legalization of Drugs Becomes Louder," *New York Times*, May 15, 1988, 1.

Treverton, Gregory F. "U.S. Interests in Mexico Beyond Drugs," paper prepared for the "El Colegio de Mexico-Harvard Conference on a New Approach to U.S.-Mexico Antidrug Strategy," held at El Colegio de México, Mexico D.F. on April 28-29, 1988.

Treviño Cantú, Javier. "Evaluación de la Estrategía Internacional de Erradicación de Cultivos," submitted to the El Colegio de México-Harvard Conference on a New Approach to the U.S.-Mexico Antidrug Strategy, held at El Colegio de México, Mexico D.F. on April 28-29, 1988.

"Turf War Over Coca-Growing Territory Leaves 34 Dead, 11 Wounded in Peru," *Miami Herald*, October 14, 1987, 3A.

United States, Department of the Treasury. "Bolivia," *Latin American Reports* (March 3, 1988), 8.

_____. *Traffic in Narcotic Drugs: Report of the Special Committee of Investigation Appointed March 25, 1918, by the Secretary of the Treasury* (Washington: GPO, 1919).

United States Department of State, Bureau of International Narcotics Matters. *International Narcotics Control Strategy Report*. Washington: 1987.

_____. *International Narcotics Control Strategy Report*. Washington: GPO, 1988.

United States General Accounting Office. *Drug Control: U.S.-Supported Efforts in Colombia and Bolivia*. Washington: GPO, November 1988), 54.

United States House of Representatives. *Report No. 852 of the Ways and Means Committee: Importation and Exportation of Narcotic Drugs*, 67th Congress, 2nd sess., March 27, 1922.

United States Narcotics Intelligence Consumers Committee. *The NNICC Report, 1985-86*, (Washington: 1987). As quoted in the *New York Times*, October 20, 1986.

United States Senate. *Hearings Before the Subcommittee on Improvements in the Federal Criminal Code of the Committee of the Judiciary Pursuant to S. Res. 67*, 84th Congress, 1st sess., June 2 to December 15, 1955.

_____. Joint Hearing of the Subcommittee on Security and Terrorism, Committee on Judiciary, the Subcommittee on Western Hemisphere Affairs of the Foreign Relations Committee, and the Senate Drug Enforcement Caucus. *The Cuban Government's Involvement in Facilitating International Drug Traffic*, April 30, 1983, p 45-46.

Van Wert, J. W. "Government of Mexico Herbicidal Opium Poppy Eradication Program: A Summative Evaluation," Unpublished Ph.D. dissertation in political science, University of Southern California, 1985.

Walker, William O. III. "Control Across the Border: The United States, Mexico, and Narcotics Policy, 1936-1940," *Pacific Historical Review* 47 (1978), 91-106.

_____. "Drug Control and National Security," *Diplomatic History* 12:2 (Spring, 1988).

_____. *Drug Control in the Americas*. Albuquerque: University of New Mexico Press, 1981.

Warner, Roger. *Invisible Hand: The Marijuana Business*. New York: Beech Tree Books, 1986.

Weinberger, Caspar. "Our Troops Shouldn't be Drug Cops," *Washington Post*, May 22, 1987, c2.

Weppner, Robert S., ed. *Street Ethnography: Selected Studies of Crime and Drug Use in Natural Settings*. Beverly Hills: Sage Publications, 1977.

Whitaker, Arthur P. *The United States and the Southern Cone: Argentina, Chile, and Uruguay*. Cambridge: Harvard University Press, 1976.

Wiley, Harvey W. "Another Soothing Syrup Victim," *Good Housekeeping* 60 (June 1915), 709-10.

Wilkie, James W. *The Mexican Revolution: Federal Expenditure and Social Change Since 1910*. Berkeley: University of California Press, 1967.

Wolfe, Tom. "The 'Me' Decade and the Third Great Awakening," *New York* (August 23, 1976), 26-40.

Wrobleski, Ann B. "Presidential Certification of Narcotics Source Countries," U.S. Department of State Bureau of Public Affairs, *Current Policy* 1061, Washington, D.C., 1988.

Yang, J. "Congress Passes Anti-drug Bill Including a Death Penalty," *Wall Street Journal*, October 24, 1988.

Young, James Harvey. *The Medical Messiahs: A Social History of Health Quackery in Twentieth Century America*. Princeton: Princeton University Press, 1967.

_____. *The Toadstool Millionaires: A Social History of Patent Medicines in America Before Federal Regulation*. Princeton: Princeton University Press, 1961.

Index

About the Contributors

Bruce M. Bagley, Associate Professor of International Studies, University of Miami, received his Ph.D. in political science from the University of California, Los Angeles. He is the author of numerous studies on Colombia and on the narcotics trade.

Richard Craig, Professor of Political Science, Kent State University, earned his Ph.D. in political science from the University of Missouri. He has published extensively on U.S.-Mexican narcotics diplomacy.

Samuel del Villar, Doctor of Juridical Science from Harvard University, is a research professor at El Colegio de Mexico and a former legal adviser to President Miguel de la Madrid. He is the foremost auhtority on Mexican-U.S. narcotics diplomacy.

Douglas Clark Kinder, historian from Ohio University writes on the career of Harry J. Anslinger, former head of the Federal Bureau of Narcotics.

Rensselaer W. Lee III, President, Global Advisory Services, earned his Ph.D. in political science and history at Stanford. A consultant on narcotics policy for the U.S. government, he has published numerous scholarly articles on the drug trade.

Donald J. Mabry, Professor of History, Mississippi State University, earned his Ph.D. in history from Syracuse University. A senior fellow of the Center for International Security and Strategic Studies at Mississippi State, he has published extensively on contemporary Mexican politics and on the narcotics trade.

Raphael Perl, specialist in international narcotics policy for the Congressional Research Service of the Library of Congress, received his law degree from Georgetown University. His published works include both reports to Congress and scholarly articles.

José Luis Reyna, professor in El Colegio de Mexico, earned his Ph.D. in sociology from Cornell. His many published works focus on Mexican politics.

Gregory F. Treverton, Senior Fellow, Council on Foreign Relations, received his Ph.D. in political science from Harvard. His published works have focused on international politics and U.S. public policy.